American Bedrock:

Exploring the

Declaration of Independence

and the U. S. Constitution

By

Steven A. Carlson

GUARDIAN
PUBLISHING, LLC

This edition published in February 2024 in association with

Guardian Publishing, LLC
Holt, Michigan

guardianpublishingllc.com

Table of Contents

SECTION 2: THE CONSTITUTION: THE PREAMBLE AND ARTICLES

TITLE	PAGE

SECTION 3: THE CONSTITUTION: THE AMENDMENTS

Preface

Setting the Stage

This work is offered to provide those who are interested with a layman's perspective of the documents upon which the United States was founded – specifically, the Declaration of Independence and the U. S. Constitution. The objective is to guide the reader to a deeper appreciation of these documents by exploring the impressive steps taken by the founders to secure the birth of a nation.

As a matter of supporting information, the Federalist Papers will be cited on occasion to provide a better understanding of the reasoning behind certain aspects of the Constitution. The Federalist Papers constitute a collection of 85 articles and essays penned by Alexander Hamilton, John Jay, and James Madison in 1787 and 1788 to encourage ratification of the Constitution. They offer valuable insight into the thought processes behind the words of the Constitution.

Full disclosure – this work is not coming from an attorney or legal professional, but from a retired accountant. While the Constitution was constructed by legal minds, it was intended for the people. Hopefully, the reasoned logic that the accounting profession demands will assist in providing a helpful explanation of some of the most important documents ever known.

Republic v. Democracy

The United States consists of various political factions, but the two most notable parties are known as Republicans and Democrats. Republicanism is generally seen as a somewhat conservative brand while Democrats tend to be more liberal. There are, of course, varying degrees of conservatism and liberalism, but these two views tend to dominate the political landscape.

One of the political contentions offered up by each party involves warnings about the dangers posed by the opposition. Republicans often contend that selecting Democrats to elected office will *destroy democracy*. Similarly, Democrats insist that *democracy is at risk* if Republicans are in charge. The same volatile rhetoric is heard from political pundits on both sides of the ideological aisle.

Such political rants are not uncommon and are to be expected since the two sides seem to hold disparate views about the very meaning of democracy. Still, it is necessary here to correct their statements. In truth, the United States is not a democracy. The government was designed as a representative republic. The word *democracy* does not appear in the Constitution. It can be found in the Federalist Papers, but there the case is made that this should *not* be a democracy as the weaknesses of a democratic system are juxtaposed against the strengths of a republic.

Admittedly, those who so casually utter the word *democracy* in heated political debate likely intend it in a generic sense to depict a government *of the people*. However, when seriously considering the words and meaning of the Constitution, it is important to draw clear

2

lines of distinction. A pure democracy is a form of government that is really no government at all. It is a design of rule where every individual has an equal voice in all decision-making. In other words, the majority *always* rules. For this reason, a democracy is only effective in a limited setting with very few members. However, in a republic, the members choose delegates whose role is to represent their constituents' interests where government decisions are concerned. Perhaps the plainest explanation of this distinction is that penned by James Madison in 1787. Writing in Federalist No. 14, he noted:

> …in a democracy, the people meet and exercise the government in person; in a republic, they assemble and administer it by their representatives and agents. A democracy, consequently, will be confined to a small spot. A republic may be extended over a large region.[1]

The founding of the United States was not the first attempt at establishing a government *of the people*. For instance, Greece, early in the fifth century BC (Before Christ), developed what is considered one of the closest forms of a pure democracy. At that time, the city-state of Athens formed a system whereby every male citizen had equal political rights and actively participated in the political arena.

In Athens, citizens were deeply engaged in the democratic system, actively joining the process of establishing the rules by which they lived. They also personally served in the institutions that governed them, directly controlling all parts of the political process. Other Greek

---

[1] Madison, James, Federalist No. 14.

city-states like Argos, Syracuse, and Rhodes had governmental systems similar in design to that of Athens.

Rome developed its own republican system of government in 509 BC, replacing the Roman monarchy that was in place prior. The monarchs were removed from their positions of power and citizen-elected magistrates served as the peoples' representatives in Rome. The Roman Republic survived nearly five hundred years but was overtaken by what came to be known as the Roman Empire in 27 BC. Republics also developed in other countries over the centuries including Iceland, Phoenicia, Mesopotamia, India, and others, with varying degrees of success.

Constitutional Relevance

Certain modern voices in the United States insist that the U. S. Constitution, written in the eighteenth century, is no longer relevant in today's society. Thus, it should be discarded. However, the Founding Fathers intended the Constitution to be timeless. It contains principles that have been recognized across the history of humanity – principles that should always be applicable where human relations are concerned. It also expresses individual rights that should never be done away (e.g., freedom of speech, religion, etc.).

Unlike the Constitution, laws can, over time, lose relevance. For instance, there are times when changes in technology can impact the usefulness of certain laws, and there are other factors. Still, it can be a challenge to determine why certain laws were even passed. Consider the following.

- Chicago forbids fishing while sitting on a giraffe's neck. (Evidently this law is taken seriously in Illinois. No offense is intended).
- In Alabama, it is illegal to wear a funny fake mustache to church if it disrupts the assembly. (Such disruption is considered disorderly conduct).
- Iowa ministers must obtain a permit to transport liquor across the state line. (It might be entertaining to know the background for this statute).

Most people will likely view these laws as outlandish and even laughable. Yet, there was undoubtedly some logic behind the passing of these statutes. On the other hand, certain other laws have, since their inception, truly become irrelevant. For instance:

- In certain locations in Texas, it is illegal to be barefoot in public without a permit.
- It is evidently illegal to dance in a bar in Maine unless the bar has a "special amusement" license.

While outdated laws like these remain on the books in most states, it should be obvious they have, over the course of time, become irrelevant. However, the same is not true of constitutional principles. The rights to freedom of expression (First Amendment) and protection from unreasonable search and seizure (Fourth Amendment), are intended to continue perpetually. In fact, the Bill of Rights explicitly prevents government from infringing on certain personal freedoms. Those amendments are as much about government limitations as they are about personal rights. Limiting government was, and is, understood as the means for protecting individual rights – a distinguishing characteristic for a government *of the people*.

The enduring character of the Constitution does not mean that the Founding Fathers did not understand changing times. For this reason, they provided the means for states to add amendments to the document as circumstances dictate. As an example, the Eighteenth Amendment established prohibition of alcohol and the Twenty-first Amendment vacated the Eighteenth Amendment. Of course, amending the Constitution is an onerous exercise, as it should be, but it is still possible when necessary to keep it relevant in changing society.

Individual Rights

Three categories of individual rights exist in the United States. There are unalienable, constitutional, and statutory rights. The rights to *life, liberty, and the pursuit of happiness* are delineated in the Declaration of Independence where they are deemed to be unalienable (natural) rights granted by the Creator. In other words, they are not rights that apply strictly to citizens of the United States. In the eyes of the founders, every human being equally shares these God-given rights. Given their unalienable, universal status, there was no need to specifically name these rights in the Constitution, though the Fifth Amendment forbids the government from depriving an individual of life, liberty, or property, without due process of law.

Unalienable rights seem self-explanatory; however, there is much confusion when it comes to understanding the difference between *constitutional* rights and *statutory* rights. Constitutional rights are those directly protected by the U. S. Constitution. Statutory rights are those for which laws are written as a complement to the Constitution, for various kinds of individual protections.

Early on, there was serious debate about the advantages and disadvantages of enumerating specific rights in the Constitution. Those in favor ultimately won the day as Congress acquiesced. It was decided that certain rights could be awarded constitutional status by using the amendment process. This resulted in the addition of the first ten amendments to the Constitution (commonly known as the Bill of Rights) in 1791. These include the rights to free expression, religious liberty, and peaceful assembly (First Amendment), the right to bear arms (Second Amendment), and more.

This list was not intended to be comprehensive. The founders understood that there were certainly other privileges that may later be deemed to be rights, and their absence from the Bill of Rights was not meant to prohibit inclusion of those rights (Ninth Amendment). However, adding constitutional rights requires following the designated process for amending the Constitution. In fact, this has been done on occasion. An example of this is found in the Nineteenth Amendment, which affords women the right to vote. Consequently, this is deemed to be a *constitutional* right.

Statutory rights are those legislated by either the state or federal government and generally involve matters like interactive commerce, employment, safety, and other areas of personal concern. For instance, the right to receive a minimum wage is a statutory right. In this case, while the federal government has established a nationwide minimum wage, certain states have set their own minimum wage that exceeds that established by the federal government. Similarly, many statutes (both federal and state) address a person's right to engage in commerce (buying and selling) and protections against those who fail to participate in good faith commerce. However, laws concerning minimum wages and commerce are not constitutional rights. They are statutory rights.

There is common understanding in jurisprudence, implicitly addressed in the Fourteenth Amendment, that there are occasions when a person's rights may be legitimately limited through due process. Laws are designed to provide for the peaceful existence of the citizenry. However, when someone infringes on the rights of another, generally through the breaking of one or more laws, part of the consequence for such action may well involve that person's loss of his/her opportunity to exercise those rights (e.g., a prison sentence limits a person's right to liberty).

Finally, not every right is intended to be established at the federal level. Some rights, particularly those dealing with certain ethical/moral issues, are generally trusted to the governance of individual states. In keeping with the principle of federalism, where authority is vested with the states in matters not designated to the federal government, states may establish certain rights based on what is deemed best for the state's citizenry.

A more detailed look into individual rights will be undertaken during an examination of the Bill of Rights and other constitutional amendments. The insights offered above are intended to help establish a foundation for that discussion.

Legal vs Constitutional

This heading may invite some raised eyebrows, but it is a legitimate topic for consideration. Contrary to what many people may think, the Constitution of the United States is not intended to be the law of the land, at least, not in a statutory sense. This is made clear within the Constitution itself when, in Article III, Section 2, while discussing judicial authority, a clear distinction is drawn between "…this Constitution, the Laws of the United States, and Treaties made." Article VI, Clause 2, casually combines the Constitution with laws and treaties, calling them "the supreme Law of the Land," but that language was used as the founders weighed the supremacy of the U. S. Constitution and federal laws against the authority of state constitutions and state laws.

The Constitution is the founding document that establishes the *form* of the United States government, but it does not create laws. Amendments generally address individual rights or issues pertaining to the operation of the government. The single constitutional amendment that appeared to take statutory form was the Eighteenth Amendment, which initiated Prohibition. This amendment was later repealed when Congress passed, and the states ratified, the Twenty-first Amendment.

Rather than establishing laws, the U. S. Constitution lays out the principles upon which laws are to be constructed. On the federal level, when a statute is passed by the legislature and signed by the president, it becomes law. However, any law that is passed should not conflict with those constitutional principles. This is mentioned briefly in Federalist No. 81 where is stated:

> …the Constitution ought to be the standard of construction for the laws, and that wherever there is an evident opposition, the laws ought to give place to the Constitution.[2]

While the Constitution does not establish laws, it is important where written laws are concerned since it contains the principles by which laws are evaluated. It is authoritative since it was adopted by the people, having been unanimously ratified by the thirteen states that were part of the Union at the time. Other states who later joined the Union understood that they, too, would be governed by the provisions of this document.

From time to time, legislatures pass laws that do not survive constitutional scrutiny. While a bill passed by Congress may become law that does not mean that every statute passed is in keeping with the Constitution. Still, as long as no one challenges the constitutionality of the statute, it may well remain law. A prime example is a New York statute concerning concealed carry (of guns). This law was actively enforced by New York authorities for more than one hundred years. When it was finally challenged in 2022, the Supreme Court determined that it conflicted with the right to bear arms that is delineated in the Second Amendment and, as a result, deemed it to be unconstitutional.

---

[2] Hamilton, Alexander, Federalist No. 81.

Some may wonder why selected representatives would be willing to pass laws that conflict with the Constitution, particularly when each member must take an oath to uphold the Constitution in executing his/her representative role. The reasons are numerous, including self-interest or personal conviction in a certain matter. It could even involve altruism, believing it is best for the country. Still, it is good to be aware that legality does not equal constitutionality

Another illustration of the clash between legality and constitutionality is seen in the Supreme Court's 2022 reversal of an earlier Court decision concerning abortion in *Roe v. Wade*, (1973). The difference here is that the legality of abortion was not a result of congressional statute nor of constitutional amendment, but of a ruling by the earlier Court. In the original case the Supreme Court, in a finding that purported to offer balance between a woman's right to privacy concerning her body and the state's interest in protecting life, proclaimed by fiat that to a certain point in a pregnancy, abortion must be deemed a woman's constitutional right. Yet this decision, on its face, appears to directly conflict with the previously recognized unalienable right to life (for the child).

What might the 1973 Supreme Court have done constitutionally in the case of *Roe*? It seems the most reasonable argument is that the Court would be obliged to apply greater weight to one's unalienable (inherent) right which, in this case, was the right to life. The justices would then have to acknowledge that neither the Court, nor mankind generally, can determine the precise moment a child's life begins.

It is a responsibility of the government, including the courts, to protect the rights of the U. S. citizenry – particularly the right to life. If it is not possible for men to know the exact moment life begins, as a matter of cautious jurisprudence it seems the Court's wisest approach would have been to presume that life begins at conception and rule in favor of protecting that life.

There has been some debate about which has primacy – unalienable rights or constitutional rights – when those rights appear to conflict. The founders seemed to recognize that unalienable rights are rights of the highest order in that they exist with or without the U.S. Constitution or the law. It is difficult to make the case that the Constitution supersedes natural rights when it was the very goal of the framers to fortify individual rights rather than weaken them. James Madison wrote in Federalist No. 51:

> In the compound republic of America, the power surrendered by the people is first divided between two distinct governments, and then the portion allotted to each subdivided among distinct and separate departments. Hence a double security arises to the rights of the people.[3]

The primacy of unalienable rights is reinforced by the Fifth Amendment and the Fourteenth Amendment. The Fifth Amendment states that an individual may not be deprived of certain enumerated rights, including the right to life, without due process and the Fourteenth Amendment equally applies that restriction to the states. That portion of the Fifth Amendment reads as follows:

---

[3] Madison, James, Federalist No. 51.

...nor shall any person...be deprived of life, liberty, or property, without due process of law.

In keeping with the premise that unalienable rights are primacy rights, the right to life should have been given primary consideration in *Roe v. Wade*. The unalienable right would have then outweighed a woman's constitutional right to privacy (Fourteenth Amendment) that was used to elevate the right to an abortion to constitutional status. This would have precluded the Court from crafting and declaring a constitutional right via Court edict. The ruling fell outside the boundaries of the limited authority assigned to the Supreme Court as the constitutionally authorized devices of legislative statute or amending the Constitution were circumvented.

The second decision the Court might have made would have been to recognize that powers not delegated to the federal government must be left to the states (Tenth Amendment). This is a less persuasive position constitutionally, since the Court would have been leaving it up to individual states to determine when life begins, potentially violating the right to life. Still, it would have been a stronger constitutional decision. This is the reasoning the Court employed in overturning *Roe* in 2022. Nonetheless, in terms of legality, for forty-nine years abortion was deemed to be legal nationwide until the Supreme Court determined that the 1973 ruling lacked constitutional support.

While the above analysis will undoubtedly ruffle the feathers of many in the pro-choice crowd, these observations about *Roe v Wade* are not intended to be political. On the contrary, they are expressly apolitical, as was the Court's overturning of *Roe*. This can be seen in the fact that the pro-life community, many of whom are in favor of an unqualified abortion ban, is not thrilled about the Court's most recent ruling.

In the 2022 decision, the Court did not remove a constitutional right, as many claim, since that right was not constitutionally based. In this case, the Court simply recognized that it is not the role of the Supreme Court to manufacture a constitutional right, as had been done in 1973. Neither did the Court criminalize abortion with this decision. They merely returned decisions about abortion to the individual states.

The late Ruth Bader-Ginsburg (1933-2020) was recognized even by her adversaries as a brilliant jurist. She served on the Supreme Court from 1993 until her death. Ms. Bader-Ginsburg was also a staunch pro-choice defender throughout her career. However, she recognized the inherent weakness of the Court's 1973 decision and believed it might well be overturned if future justices were positioned to review the case. She understood that the reasoning employed by the Court made the decision vulnerable. In a 1984 speech given at the University of North Carolina she stated that, in *Roe v Wade*, the Court "…ventured too far in the change it ordered and presented an incomplete justification for its actions."[4]

---

[4] Blake, Aaron, citing Ruth Bader-Ginsburg, *What Ruth Bader Ginsburg really said about Roe v. Wade* - The Washington Post, https://www.washingtonpost.com, accessed August 17, 2022

Articles of Confederation

Lest some readers wonder about a seeming omission, here is a brief statement concerning the first Constitution of the United States, known as the Articles of Confederation. During the Revolutionary War, the members of Congress spent much of their time dealing with and strategizing over wartime matters. There was little time for much else. When the Congress of the Confederation took over in 1781, they were aware that it was incumbent upon them to formalize a centralized government to manage the many challenges the colonies faced.

After the Declaration of Independence was signed, the members of Congress drafted a provisional constitution through which they could do the nation's work. Written in 1776–77 and adopted by the Congress on November 15, 1777, the Articles of Confederation provided for a much weaker central government than is found in the current Constitution, but it served its purpose at the time. The document was not fully ratified by the states until March 1, 1781. This book does not review the Articles since they hold no sway over the lives of twenty-first century Americans. Still, for those interested in a deeper look at the founding of The United States, that is a document worth reading.

The Title of "America"

Some may wonder about the origin of the name "America." The title was given to the new land in honor of the Italian explorer, Amerigo Vespucci. He traveled to the new world twice in the post-Columbus era. His first expedition took place in 1499 and the second in 1502.

When Christopher Columbus arrived in the new world in 1492, he believed (and hoped) that he had landed in an unknown region of the Indies in Eastern Asia. He thought that he had simply discovered a new route to that distant land. Anxious confidence in Columbus's claim blinded most people to the truth that this was not Asia, but an altogether separate and unknown continent.

It was Amerigo Vespucci who realized the truth concerning this land – that it was not Asia – and he spent his time documenting his findings. The accounts of his journeys were published in the early years of the sixteenth century (between 1502 and 1504) and were widely read throughout the European continent.

How and when was the name "America" applied to this land? It happened not long after the publishing of Vespucci's journals. A German cartographer by the name of Martin Waldseemüller set out to draw a world map in 1507. The map was to be constructed of twelve wood panels and the final product would be roughly 96" wide and 54" tall (8 ft. x 4½ ft.).

While some were not yet completely sold on the idea of a new continent, Waldseemüller was fully convinced that Vespucci was correct in his assessment and set out to incorporate that belief in his world map. Historically, in his mapmaking, Waldseemüller assigned feminine names to the various lands, and America was no exception. As he drew his map of the new continent, he honored the explorer's work by naming it America, which is the feminine counterpart to

Vespucci's first name – Amerigo. Consequently, without pomp and circumstance…without fanfare or celebration…America was born.

Section 1

The Declaration

of

Independence

Chapter 1
A Declaration of Autonomy

The Early Days of the Revolution

Among the American colonies in the early to mid-1700's there was little talk about total separation from Great Britain. It was not until the 1760's that the idea of an independent nation came into greater view. The prospect of independence was embraced by men like John Adams, who was part of a resistance movement as Britain began to assert itself, through taxation and political pressure, upon the colonies.

The resistance questioned Parliament's standing to remotely tax the citizens of the colonies when those citizens were allowed no voice in the political process. In 1765, John Adams wrote *A Dissertation on the Canon and Feudal Law*, which was a brutal indictment of the kind of tyrannical governments that had so mistreated citizenry throughout history. In it, he boldly accused Great Britain of wearing the very autocratic garb condemned in his words.

At the time, men like Adams were considered radicals. However, as Great Britain became more oppressive, the people in the colonies took heed. In the years following Adam's dissertation, Britain levied heavy taxes on the colonies through The Stamp Act (1765), The Townshend Act (1767), and The Tea Act (1773). This caused many in the colonies to begin to embrace the idea of independence.

Most Americans have likely heard of the term *Continental Congress*. This Congress consisted of representatives from the American colonies. It was formed by the colonies to coordinate their efforts in dealing with what most considered unfair treatment they were receiving from Great Britain. The First Continental Congress, which consisted of representatives from every colony except Georgia, met in Philadelphia in September 1774. The goal was not separation from England. The members simply hoped to receive reasonable treatment from the mother country. This Congress reached out to Britain to hopefully resolve differences.

Attempts at finding common ground proved futile. In November of 1774, in a speech to Parliament, King George III made it clear that he had no intention of bowing to colonial demands and Parliament should disregard those demands. Britain then began asserting itself militarily to squash resistance in the colonies resulting in the Battle of Lexington and Concord (April 19, 1775). This response led to the formation of the Second Continental Congress, which first met in Philadelphia in May of 1775. At that time, the Congress did what governments do. They raised an army. On June 17, 1775, the Battle of Bunker Hill at what was then known as Charlestown, Massachusetts, demonstrated that the war for independence from Britain was in full swing.

In early 1776, Thomas Paine, in his publication titled *Common Sense*, made strong points about the role of government, describing it as a "necessary evil.*"[5]* He argued that the colonists' Revolution

---

[5] Paine, Thomas, *Common Sense*, Fall River Press, 1995, p. 1.

against Britain was not just about that specific separation but served as a statement about citizens' relationship with government generally. In other words, they were not merely fighting for their own independence from England; they were fighting for the general state of mankind and how the citizenry is treated by those in power.

British aggression escalated over the months following the publication of *Common Sense* and it soon became clear that it was incumbent upon the colonists to formally declare independence from Great Britain. On June 11, 1776, a five-man team consisting of John Adams (Massachusetts), Roger Sherman (Connecticut), Benjamin Franklin (Pennsylvania), Robert Livingston (New York), and Thomas Jefferson (Virginia), was appointed to develop that formal declaration, though it was Jefferson who was the primary author. In his own words:

> ...the other members of the committee "unanimously pressed on myself alone to undertake the draught [sic]. I consented; I drew it; but before I reported it to the committee I communicated it separately to Dr. Franklin and Mr. Adams requesting their corrections...I then wrote a fair copy, reported it to the committee, and from them, unaltered to the Congress."[6]

Introduction

The completed Declaration of Independence was presented to Congress on July 2, 1776, and a few revisions were made over the course of the next two days. Finally, on July 4, 1776, it was approved by the representatives of the colonies. Delegates from all thirteen colonies (a total of 56 men) signed the document on August 2, 1776,

---

[6] Mullen, Matt, Onion, Amanda, Sullivan, Missy, Zapatra, Christian, editors, *Writing of Declaration of Independence*, www.history.com, accessed Jun 23, 2022

declaring independence from England. The Declaration begins with the following introduction, explaining the reasoned necessity of the colonists' separation from England.

When, in the course of human events, it becomes necessary for one people to dissolve the political bands which have connected them with another, and to assume, among the powers of the earth, the separate and equal station to which the laws of nature and of nature's God entitle them, a decent respect to the opinions of mankind requires that they should declare the causes which impel them to the separation.

This document served as a formal declaration of the colonies' break from England. Given the tyrannical actions of King George III and Parliament, the colonists decided that it was time "…to dissolve the political bands which have connected them."

While the eloquence of the document is impressive, it is the substance that is most compelling. The foundational basis for the declaration is "…the laws of nature and of nature's God." This statement demonstrates plainly that the establishment of U. S. independence was initially grounded in the Judeo-Christian belief in the existence and supremacy of God. According to this statement, without God and the natural laws he has established, the colonies would not be entitled to a "…separate and equal station."

Statements recognizing the role of "…the laws of nature and nature's God" in the establishment of the United States are seen as problematic for many who do not believe in God. These individuals tend to balk at the notion that their rights are derived from a Supreme Being. However, this should not be a divisive issue, even among steadfast atheists. What is important is that the Founding Fathers fully believed the decisions they made were righteous in God's eyes. Those who do not believe in God should still appreciate the fact that they may never have known the freedoms they now enjoy had those men in 1776 failed in their convictions.

Government and Unalienable Rights

The reasoning having been established in the introduction (above), the founders continued. The balance of the document not only provides deeper insights into the separation but, in keeping with the reasoning Thomas Paine employed in *Common Sense*, offers greater insights into what they understood should be the right and natural relationship between government and the governed.

> *We hold these truths to be self-evident, that all men are created equal, that they are endowed by their Creator with certain unalienable rights, that among these are life, liberty, and the pursuit of happiness. That, to secure these rights, governments are instituted among men, deriving their just powers from the consent of the governed. That, whenever any form of government becomes destructive of these ends, it is the right of the people to alter or to abolish it, and to institute new government, laying its foundation on such principles, and organizing its powers in such form, as to them shall seem most likely to affect their safety and happiness.*

The members of Congress made no attempt to *establish* rights for the colonial citizenry in this document. Rather than establishing rights in the Declaration of Independence, they simply *recognized* those rights to which people are naturally entitled. This wording was undoubtedly intended to distinguish between natural human rights and the rights artificially *permitted* by a human government. It is not the role of governments to permit rights that naturally belong to everyone. Additionally, not only are those rights recognized as a natural entitlement, but it is deemed self-evident (to any reasonable person) that people have these rights and that they apply to everyone equally.

To what rights are people naturally entitled? Congress did not seek to identify *every* right to which individuals are entitled, but stated that *among* those natural rights are life, liberty, and the pursuit of happiness. These are not intended to depict rights for the colonists, but rights for humanity. The goal was to present a big picture of human dignity. Rights specific to the citizenry of America are documented later in the U. S. Constitution.

Severing Ties

Having recognized the natural rights of human beings, the authors of the Declaration continued, explaining that, when those in power begin to infringe upon unalienable rights, it can only be reasoned that the citizens' relationship with that government must be addressed in a manner satisfactory to the governed.

Prudence, indeed, will dictate that governments long established should not be changed for light and transient causes; and, accordingly, all experience has shown, that mankind are more disposed to suffer, while evils are sufferable, than to right themselves by abolishing the forms to which they are accustomed.

But, when a long train of abuses and usurpations, pursuing invariably the same object, evinces a design to reduce them under absolute despotism, it is their right, it is their duty, to throw off such government, and to provide new guards for their future security. Such has been the patient sufferance of these colonies; and such is now the necessity which constrains them to alter their former systems of government. The history of the present King of Great

Britain is a history of repeated injuries and usurpations, all having in direct object the establishment of an absolute tyranny over these states. To prove this, let facts be submitted to a candid world.

The groundwork was thus laid. England had overreached. Despite the colonists' patience, there was no reasoning with King George III or Parliament. As such, the founders recognized an additional right which derived from the rights of liberty and the pursuit of happiness. It was their right, and indeed, it was "…their duty to throw off such government" that refused to respect the natural rights to which they were entitled.

A Seeming Inconsistency

This section of the Declaration begs the question: **How could slave owners write so eloquently and persuasively about the equality of all men and the unalienable right of liberty?** Were men like Washington, Franklin, and Jefferson oblivious to the glaring disconnect between the unalienable right of liberty for all and those slaves who were denied that right? In fact, history shows that a majority of those who signed the Declaration of Independence were slave owners.

Slavery was commonplace in the eighteenth-century society into which these men were born, and Benjamin Franklin owned some slaves in his early life. However, one of his slaves escaped in Europe while accompanying Franklin in 1762. It is not fully clear if this is the incident that opened his eyes to the wrongs of slavery, but for the balance of his life, Benjamin Franklin worked toward the abolition of this unseemly practice. In partnership with a man by the name of

Benjamin Rush, Franklin helped to found the *Pennsylvania Society for Promoting the Abolition of Slavery* in 1774. He also wrote persuasive essays encouraging abolition including, *A Plan for Improving the Condition of the Free Blacks, An Address to the Public*, which was the written form of a speech he offered in Philadelphia (1789). Additionally, it has been reported that in his will, Franklin stipulated that his children could only receive their inheritance if they freed their slaves.

There is some ambiguity in deriving Alexander Hamilton's relationship with slavery. In a paper published in 2020, based on newly discovered evidence, Jessie Serfilippi of the Schuyler Mansion State Historic Site in Albany, New York, wrote, "Not only did Alexander Hamilton enslave people, but his involvement in the institution of slavery was essential to his identity, both personally and professionally."[7] Some historians, like Christopher Klein, concur with those findings while others like Michael Newton and Douglas Hamilton (a descendant) do not.

Slave ownership seems contrary to Hamilton's public persona and his biographers generally depict him as an unapologetic abolitionist. In fact, it is said that he abhorred slavery and dreamed of the day it might be done away in America. If Hamilton owned slaves, it means his political and personal views must have been engaged in a fierce tug-of-war battle. However, where politics was concerned, there is little

---

[7] Schuessler, Jennifer, citing Jessie Serfilippi, New York Times, *Alexander Hamilton, Enslaver? New Research Says Yes* | https://www.nytimes.com, Accessed October 31, 2023

doubt that he hoped and believed America would one day be slave-free.

Thomas Jefferson, who was the primary author of the Declaration of Independence, owned more than two hundred slaves. Yet, Jefferson seemed to determine early in his life, contrary to his upbringing, that slavery undercut his view of equality that he so eloquently expressed in the Declaration. He longed for the eventual emancipation of slaves, and surely wished it would happen in his lifetime. The issue for Jefferson, who was an undeniably brilliant man, was that he did not know how to make it happen. He wrote "…there is nothing I would not sacrifice to a practicable plan of abolishing every vestige of this moral and political depravity."[8] He did not release his own slaves because he could not derive a means, given the times in which he lived, to integrate them into the norms of civil life. They would have nowhere to go.

It was Jefferson's goal to establish a colony in Africa where those who lived there could be provided with a decent education, allowing them to develop in a manner that was respectful. He also wanted to free all slaves and establish them as an independent people. In 1824 he wrote the following in a letter to his friend Jared Sparks, an American educator who later became President of Harvard College:

> In the disposition of these unfortunate people, there are two rational objects to be distinctly kept in view. 1. the establishment of a colony on the coast of Africa, which may introduce among the Aborigines the arts of cultivated life, and the blessings of civilisation

---

[8] Jefferson, Thomas, *Thomas Jefferson on Slavery* https://studyboss.com/essays/thomas-jefferson-on-slavery.html, , accessed June 26, 2022

and science. by doing this, we may make to them some retribution for the long course of injuries we have been committing on their population. and considering that these blessings will descend to the 'nati natorum, et qui nascentur ab illis,' (meaning: the children of our children and those who will be born of them), we shall, in the long run, have rendered them perhaps more good than evil. to fulfil this object the colony of Sierra leone promises well, and that of Mesurado adds to our prospect of success. under this view the colonization society is to be considered as a Missionary society, having in view however objects more humane, more justifiable, and less aggressive on the peace of other nations than the others of that appellation.

The 2^d object, and the most interesting to us, as coming home to our physical and moral characters, to our happiness and safety, is to provide an Asylum to which we can, by degrees, send the whole of that population from among us, and establish them under our patronage and protection, as a separate, free and independant people, in some country and climate friendly to human life and happiness.[9]

The letter was lengthy as Jefferson detailed his plans to accomplish his proposals. It can be viewed online at various websites. Unfortunately, Thomas Jefferson passed from this life roughly two years after authoring these words. It might be fair to say that those who have judged Thomas Jefferson harshly may wish to rethink their opinion of the man. It is safe to say that, but for the work of men like Thomas Jefferson, who died four decades before the emancipation, slaves may not have known freedom until a much later time.

Without delving into the many individual stories, the same may well be said of others who signed the Declaration of Independence. At the time of that signing, it is reasonable to believe that many, if not most of those men understood the consequences of the document.

---

[9] Jefferson, Thomas, Founders Online, *From Thomas Jefferson to Jared Sparks, 4 February 1824,*, https://founders.archives.gov/documents/Jefferson/98-01-02-4020, accessed August 8, 2023

Where these men were concerned, they saw the end of slavery couched within the words they endorsed.

Chapter 2
Grievances and Separation

The Grievances

With the lay of the land before them, it was time for the founders to get specific about those actions on the part of the motherland that brought them to this point. The colonists catalogued twenty-seven specific actions of King George III and his allies in Parliament against the colonies in America. In the Declaration of Independence, these appear simply as a list of grievances that led the colonists to choose to cast off the bondage forced upon them and establish their own identity as the United States of America.

It should be noted that many historians denounce the charges of abuse that follow below, insisting that the King was not the intolerable tyrant portrayed in these words. It is also fair to say that, while the grievances seem to be directed toward the King, they were also aimed, surreptitiously, at Parliament. Nonetheless, these are the grievances claimed by the founders.

> **Grievance No. 1:** *He has refused his assent to laws the most wholesome and necessary for the public good.*

The early colonies were evidently obliged to receive England's approval for any internal laws they wished to implement locally. Yet Britain, it is said, tended to be uncooperative, even when the colonists deemed those laws to be "…wholesome and necessary for the public good."

An example of this was King George III's refusal to comply with the colonies' attempts to abolish the importing of slaves in America. The King, purportedly seeking to protect this profitable British trade, thwarted attempts by the colonies to curtail it. This specific issue was presented in detail in Jefferson's original draft of the document where he accused the King of waging "…cruel war against human nature itself, violating its most sacred rights of life and liberty in the persons of a distant people who never offended him, captivating and carrying them into slavery in another hemisphere or to ineur miserable death in their transportation thither."[10] (see Grievance No. 27).

> **Grievance No. 2:** *He has forbidden his governors to pass laws of immediate and pressing importance, unless suspended in their operation till his assent should be obtained; and when so suspended, he has utterly neglected to attend to them.*

The document accused the King of stalling the execution of laws the colonists deemed critical to their well-being. When laws were passed in the various colonies and signed by their governors, the King, who refused to allow implementation without his consent, would simply ignore their appeals for approval. Often these requests lay dormant for years. In 1774, in a work titled *Summary View of the Rights of British America*, Jefferson wrote, "With equal inattention to the necessities of his people here has his majesty permitted our laws to

---

[10] Jefferson, Thomas, *Why Thomas Jefferson's Anti-Slavery Passage Was Removed from the Declaration of Independence*, history.com, Accessed November, 2023.

lie neglected in England for years, neither confirming them by his assent, nor annulling them by his negative."[11]

> **Grievance No. 3:** *He has refused to pass other laws for the accommodation of large districts of people, unless those people would relinquish the right of representation in the legislature; a right inestimable to them and formidable to tyrants only.*

In the years prior to the Revolution, the colonists insisted on political representation/participation. This led to the selection of representatives in the colonies whose role was to interact with Britain. As the colonies grew and new communities were added, more and more representatives were selected. Colonies like New Hampshire, South Carolina, New York, and Virginia passed laws allowing for the establishment of new communities with the right to select their own representatives.

The British government feared that the representative assemblies of the colonies were growing too large and too powerful for comfort, so the King refused to recognize them. The colonists insisted that a legitimate government must have the consent of the governed while Britain maintained that representation was a privilege that could be granted by the King alone. In other words, the people were expected to "…relinquish the right of representation." Surrender of their right to representation was not only unacceptable where the colonists were concerned, but it was considered an unreasonable demand. According

---

[11] Jefferson, Thomas, *Summary View of the Rights of British America*, Avalon Project - Summary View of the Rights of British America, https://avalon.law.yale.edu. Accessed March 8, 2023.

to Jefferson's words, this kind of demand could only come from a tyrannical government.

> **Grievance No. 4:** *He has called together legislative bodies at places unusual, uncomfortable, and distant from the depository of their public records, for the sole purpose of fatiguing them into compliance with his measures.*

With the bitter taste of the 1773 Boston Tea Party lingering, Parliament passed The Massachusetts Government Act in 1774. With this act, the royal governors, (particularly in Massachusetts and Virginia where the colonists were seen as agitators) were allowed, and even encouraged, to move the meeting sites of the representative assemblies to places more favorable to those regions that were seen as loyal to England.

While the claim was made that the changes in venue were a matter of safety, these actions were taken to inconvenience the colonists. They were required to travel to remote locations, and it put distance between the representatives and the records they would require for issuing requests or making their case when disagreements arose. They could, of course, take the necessary records with them, but that would only burden them with volumes of additional documents on a journey that was already arduous. The colonists were fully aware of the duplicity, knowing that it was England's "…sole purpose of fatiguing them into compliance."

> **Grievance No. 5:** *He has dissolved representative houses repeatedly, for opposing, with manly firmness, his invasions on the rights of the people.*

Britain's relationship with the colonial assemblies steadily deteriorated. For instance, in 1768, the assembly of Massachusetts issued a letter, to be circulated among the colonies, accusing the King and Parliament of violating the rights of Americans. When the British government learned of the letter, they demanded that it be withdrawn and renounced. Governor Bernard of Massachusetts was ordered to dissolve the assembly if they refused. Not surprisingly, the colonists rejected Britain's request and the Governor ordered their dissolution. When the assembly sought to meet again in May 1769, they were met by a weaponized military guard, which included the presence of a canon.

An issue also arose in New York when that assembly refused to execute Parliamentary edicts. Specifically, they declined to carry out a Parliamentary provision known as The Quartering Act that required them to house British troops within the colonies. For this, the New York legislature was disbanded twice. It first occurred in 1767. However, the defiant assembly met again in 1769 and, still refusing to acquiesce, was disbanded once more. It was England's mischievous manipulation of the assemblies that led to the inclusion of this grievance in the Declaration of Independence.

> **Grievance No. 6:** *He has refused for a long time, after such dissolutions, to cause others to be elected; whereby the legislative powers, incapable of annihilation, have returned to the people at large for their exercise; the state remaining in the meantime exposed to all the dangers of invasion from without, and convulsions within.*

This builds on the previous grievance concerning the disbanding of representative assemblies. Upon the dissolution of assemblies, the King would often refuse to allow the selection of replacements. Having no assemblies to manage the affairs of this new world left the colonies vulnerable to "…the dangers of invasion from without, and convulsions within."

With the King refusing to see to proper representation from America, the colonists held that the right of self-governance naturally reverted to the people. The only solution was for the colonists to take matters into their own hands and establish assemblies without England's consent as a matter of self-preservation. On those occasions when their assemblies were disbanded by Britain, the people would hold special conventions for the selection of representatives and the passing of necessary local legislation.

Grievance No. 7: *He has endeavored to prevent the population of these states; for that purpose obstructing the laws for naturalization of foreigners; refusing to pass others to encourage their migrations hither, and raising the conditions of new appropriations of lands.*

The colonies passed laws to encourage immigration to America, given the abundance of land and opportunities available. However, the King opposed these laws for numerous reasons. For instance, he feared it would prove tempting to those in the homeland, potentially reducing England's population, luring away workers who were needed to maintain that economy.

Another issue was the great influx of Germans in America. The Germans had strong views of political and personal freedoms and the

King was concerned about their influence on the colonies. Additionally, like the Germans, people from numerous other countries, people who had no allegiance to England, sought to avail themselves of the evident opportunities in this new land. This was problematic for the King and Parliament and led to Parliament, in 1773, revoking The Plantation Act of 1740, which had given each colony the right to enact laws of naturalization. Yet, immigration was not the only issue where this grievance was concerned.

At the conclusion of the lengthy French and Indian War (1754-1763), England sought to tighten its grip on the colonies. In 1763, Parliament passed The Proclamation of 1763, seeking to appease the Indian nations by limiting European encroachment deep into America. The proclamation established a boundary, known as the *proclamation line*, along the Appalachians, to prevent the settlers from moving west. The colonists were to remain in the lands east of that line. These boundaries were revised in the 1768 Boundary Line Treaty, but this did not resolve issues concerning what the colonists saw as unused land with much potential. The colonists believed these treaties were far too limiting.

Another key component of this grievance was recognition of land ownership in America. The colonists believed the government should make all unused land in America available, either through homesteading or auction, to those who would put it to use. The King, on the other hand, claimed ownership of all land in America and believed it was his right to grant this land to whomever he chose and to deny it to those he deemed unworthy or unhelpful. These actions by England simply added to dissatisfaction among the colonists.

Grievance No. 8: *He has obstructed the administration of justice, by refusing his assent to laws for establishing judiciary powers.*

Several of the colonies, including Pennsylvania, North Carolina, and South Carolina, attempted to set up court systems and passed laws to regulate court proceedings. Britain would have none of this, insisting that the establishment of a justice system was reserved to the sovereign power of the King. As a result, the colonies were deprived of an adequate system of justice. England's actions once again smacked of intolerance and defied the colonial insistence that a legitimate government must receive its authority from the consent of the governed.

Grievance No. 9: *He has made judges dependent on his will alone, for the tenure of their offices, and the amount and payment of their salaries.*

This charge serves as a follow-up to the previous one and addresses the need for government separation of powers – specifically, separation between the executive and judicial branches. In 1761, Britain declared that judges in colonial courts would serve at the King's pleasure. In other words, they could be dismissed anytime with, or without reason.

Later that year, in New York, certain judges refused to carry out their duties unless it was agreed that continuance in office be based on good behavior rather than the King's discretion. New York agreed and passed a law to that effect. However, when the King and Parliament heard of this, instructions were sent to the colonial governors denying the colonies the right to pass laws pertaining to the tenure of judges.

A separate but related situation arose when, in 1773, Parliament passed an act stating that judges' salaries would come directly from England rather than from the local assemblies. Rather than allowing the local colonies to pay the judges, the King (highly) taxed the colonies through duties for these judicial services. In 1774, the Massachusetts Assembly inquired whether Chief Justice Peter Oliver intended to receive his salary from the King or the people. Oliver, a British loyalist who referred to the Revolutionary War as a rebellion, answered that he would be paid by the King. The Assembly led by John Adams responded with an unsuccessful attempt at impeachment.

The judges receiving compensation from England naturally led to a situation where they were beholden to the entity who signed their checks – England. As a result, many colonists, contrary to English law, were denied trial by jury or equal treatment under the law. These activities led to this charge of the King making judges, "…dependent on his will alone."

Grievance No. 10: *He has erected a multitude of new offices, and sent hither swarms of officers to harass our people, and eat out their substance.*

The English sought to maintain tighter control over the colonies, particularly after the French and Indian War. This led to the placement of more and more English officials among the colonies – officials not approved by the colonists. The role of these officials was to enforce

Parliamentary regulation in America. One of the best-known examples involved the many officials assigned to implement and enforce The Stamp Act (1765), a tax the colonists insisted was unfair. It was a duty imposed on newspapers and legal documents as a means of raising money for England. The colonial opposition was so intense that the act was rescinded in 1766.

Rescinding The Stamp Act did not alter British attitudes toward those in America. The influx of English officials continued – officials deemed illegitimate by the colonists who believed it was their right to select their own officials. Nor did vacating The Stamp Act deter England from continuing to seek to raise tax dollars from the colonies while forbidding colonial political representation.

The colonists believed England had overstepped in its attempt to regulate and control American trade, an intervention that eventually led to violence. Interference with trade reached its apex when Britain assigned the naval vessel *HMS Gaspee* to patrol Narragansett Bay in Rhode Island with the task of preventing the import of items the colonists sought to smuggle (trade without England's approval) into America. It has been said that the captain of *The Gaspee*, Lt. William Duddingston,[12] often exceeded his authority by stopping ships without cause and even looting when the opportunity presented itself.

The people of Rhode Island quickly tired of the interruption of trade. On June 9, 1772, a local by the name of Captain Benjamin Lindsey, who had his own small ship known as *The Hannah*, as an act

---

[12] Three different spellings can be found including Dudingston, Duddington, and Duddingston.

of defiance, refused to lower his flag as he passed *The Gaspee*. Duddingston considered this to be an act of disrespect and chased *The Hannah* deep into the bay. Lindsey, who was intimately familiar with those waters, lured Duddingston into the shallows where *The Gaspee* came aground on a sandbar.

With *The Gaspee* stranded, Lindsey quickly went ashore and explained the situation to the people. It did not take long for a number of men to devise a plan to bring an end to *The Gaspee's* interference. Under the cover of darkness, a large group of men rowed toward *The Gaspee*, intent on arresting Duddingston. However, when the English saw them coming, a battle of verbal assaults began and, in the heat of the argument, a colonist shot and killed Duddingston. The colonists then boarded the ship, captured the crew, and burned *The Gaspee*.

The King offered a reward for anyone who would hand over the perpetrators, seeking to take them to England for trial. However, his attempt to secure those involved proved futile. The colonists refused to cooperate. This prewar encounter served as a prime example of English meddling in the lives of Americans, adding to the tensions between the colonist and Great Britain. Incidents like these were well-remembered by both sides and highly influenced the grievances charged against England.[13]

Grievance No. 11: *He has kept among us, in times of peace, standing armies, without the consent of our legislatures.*

---

[13] Details of this episode derive from a Brown University article titled *The Story of the 1772 Gaspee Affair.* https://blogs.brown.edu/gaspee/history/, accessed March 13, 2023, and an article on the ushistory.org website title *The Gaspee Affair*, https://www.ushistory.org/declaration/related/gaspee.html, accessed March 13, 2023.

With the end of the French and Indian War in 1763, the colonists expected the King and Parliament to withdraw British soldiers, returning them to England. That, however, did not happen. Many of the troops remained in America. Adding insult to injury, in 1765, Parliament passed The Quartering Act, which placed responsibility for the housing and support of British troops on the colonies (see Grievance No. 5).

Even in the homeland, British citizens had a long-standing, inherent mistrust of full-time armies, particularly in times of peace. A professional army was always seen as an apparatus that could potentially be weaponized against the citizenry. When ratification of the U.S. Constitution was being debated, the idea of a standing army in times of peace was a huge sticking point for many. The presence of British troops in America in the 1760's, whose role was to maintain British control over the people, served as a prime example for those who spoke against standing armies in times of peace.

Grievance No. 12: *He has affected to render the military independent of and superior to the civil power.*

Tensions grew between America and Great Britain over the use of British troops. While the presence of British troops in America was itself a matter of outrage among the colonists, the King made things worse when he insisted that the civilian government in America should be subject to the rule of the British military. This was contrary to the British practice where the military reported to civilian Parliament. The

British military commander in America at the time was General Thomas Gage.

During the French and Indian War, General Gage and George Washington fought on the same side as British soldiers, these two arguably preventing the total annihilation of the British army during what has come to be known as Braddock's Campaign in the Battle of Monongahela (July 9, 1755). In the years following, it is said that General Gage and George Washington had a relatively close friendship. However, over time, the two began to look at America and the people of the colonies through two different lenses. Washington soon returned to civilian life while Gage continued to seek higher military office. In his eyes, he saw the mindset of independence among the colonists as problematic.

Eventually achieving the position of Commander of British troops in America, Gage began heavily positioning soldiers inside some of the larger cities like New York and Boston. This naturally caused friction between the colonists and the troops and was largely responsible for what has come to be known as the Boston Massacre (March 5, 1770) where five colonists were killed by British soldiers. These actions on the part of the British military were fresh on the minds of those who approved and signed the Declaration of Independence.

Grievance No. 13: *He has combined with others to subject us to a jurisdiction foreign to our constitution, and unacknowledged by our laws; giving his assent to their acts of pretended legislation:*

The people of America, at least those with a British heritage, generally believed in the King's legitimacy viewing him in the role of a chief executive. However, his interference in their activities was wearing thin by the mid 1700's. While their relationship with the King was deteriorating, it is safe to say that there was virtually no respect for Parliament among the colonies. This explains why, in the Declaration of Independence, that body is deliberately referred to as *others* rather than honoring the name of Parliament.

In this grievance, the King is accused of conspiring with Parliament against the colonies. This was inconsistent with the constitution – not the U.S. Constitution, which was not yet written, but England's constitution. The Americans believed that in a foreign land, England's constitution granted them the right to self-governance. Thus, they believed they should not be subject to the pretentious legislation passed by Parliament. The colonists were disappointed that King George III had refused to veto much of the legislation passed by this body of pretenders and began to view him as Parliament's accomplice.

This grievance is possibly a jab at a committee known as the Board of Trade instituted by King George III and Parliament in 1767, which was designed to enforce colonial revenue laws. However, this is only one of many Parliamentary actions that could be in view with this statement.

Grievance No. 14: *For quartering large bodies of armed troops among us;*

It should be evident by now, given the number of grievances that touch on this subject, that the presence of British troops in America was a matter of concern. This objection was partly in response to The Quartering Act, passed by Parliament in 1765, authorizing the British-appointed colonial governors to lodge British troops in privately owned establishments in American cities.

The reference to "large bodies of armed troops" may have been more pointed than a general complaint about a ten-year-old law passed by Parliament. It is likely that this phrase points to specific actions in early 1775. At that time, the King and Parliament sent roughly 10,000 soldiers who were to be stationed in some of the largest cities like New York, Boston, and Philadelphia.

In Massachusetts, anti-England sentiment had been growing steadily since the Boston Tea Party (1773). With this new influx of troops, General Thomas Gage, who now served as Royal Governor of Massachusetts, was ordered by Britain to move against those rebels in his state who were pushing for independence. Under these orders, Gage moved to confiscate the colonists' militia supplies in Concord, Massachusetts.

Gage's actions infuriated the colonists and triggered the battle that sparked the Revolutionary War. On April 19, 1775, the sizeable and well-armed Massachusetts militia met Gage's troops at Lexington and Concord, pushing them back to Boston. While other actions undoubtedly contributed, this incident would have heavily influenced the charge of the excessive presence of British troops in America.

Grievance No. 15: *For protecting them, by a mock trial, from punishment for any murders which they should commit on the inhabitants of these states;*

In the years prior to the Declaration of Independence, a couple of skirmishes between colonists and British troops left death in their wake. In Annapolis, Maryland in 1768, several citizens were killed by troops. Later, on March 5, 1770, the Boston Massacre left five colonists dead as soldiers shot into an unruly crowd.

This grievance charged England with protecting these soldiers by engineering mock trials to circumvent justice. In the case of the Annapolis incident, the soldiers involved were fully acquitted. Where the Boston Massacre was concerned, eight soldiers were charged. Six were acquitted of all charges as they were deemed to have acted in self-defense. Two were found guilty of the lesser charge of manslaughter.

The charge of "…protecting them, by a mock trial" may be a bit frivolous. In the case of the Boston Massacre, it was John Adams, who was hardly a British sympathizer, who assumed the role of defense counsel. He took that role, insisting that American principles demanded that everyone, even English soldiers, should be afforded an equal opportunity where legal defense was concerned.

Grievance No. 16: *For cutting off our trade with all parts of the world;*

More than one-hundred years prior to the Declaration of Independence, Parliament passed a law seeking to limit trading options for the colonies. The Navigation Act (passed in 1651 and expanded in

46

1660) was not designed to thwart colonial trade, but to boost wealth in England. The reasoning was that, if the colonists only traded with England, it could provide England with an economy unmatched among the nations. It would also help assure that England could track and receive all available tax revenue due from American trade.

This law was not enforced until the 1760's as England saw her grip on the colonies beginning to loosen. Parliament and the King decided failure to enforce The Navigation Act was not only costing England considerable tax revenue, but it was bolstering the notion in America that the colonists did not need England. They could build their own serious wealth without British oversight.

The colonists saw unfettered economic movement as vital to the health and wealth of the citizenry. Thomas Paine wrote powerfully about the importance of free trade in an article penned in 1777, writing:

> The freedom of trade, likewise, is, to a trading country, an article of such importance, that the principal source of wealth depends upon it; and it is impossible that any country can flourish, as it otherwise might do, whose commerce is engrossed, cramped and fettered by the laws and mandates of another - yet these evils, and more than I can here enumerate, the continent has suffered by being under the government of England.[14]

Beginning in 1764, England took steps to enforce The Navigation Act by limiting America's trade with Spain and France. This new enforcement stretched so far as to attempt to limit English colonies'

---

[14] Paine, Thomas, *The Crisis*, https://www.ushistory.org/Paine/crisis/c-03.htm, Accessed March 21, 2023.

trade with French, Spanish, and Dutch colonies in America. Enforcement was attempted through Parliament's passage of several pieces of legislation. The first was the Sugar Act, which increased duties on non-British good shipped to America. The second piece of legislation was The Currency Act as England sought to prohibit the colonists from issuing their own currency. The third act passed by Parliament in 1764 was The Stamp Act. With this act, England hoped to be able to closely track legal documents in America in order to prevent smuggling and assure that England received her fair share of revenue from economic trade.

Colonial revolt against The Stamp Act was exacted through intimidation (threats, etc.) of England's collection agents – those individuals sent to retrieve Stamp Act revenue. This was accomplished primarily through a clandestine organization known as the Sons of Liberty. The intimidation was so effective that before the act went into effect all collection agents had resigned their positions.

Grievance No. 17: *For imposing taxes on us without our consent;*

In the eyes of the colonists, England's appetite for tax revenue was boundless. This craving reached a high point in 1767 with Parliament's passage of The Declaratory Act. This legislation placed taxes on everything from glass and paper to paint and tea. The colonial response was overwhelmingly negative, and the British were forced to retract the imposition of these taxes. They later sought to restore the tax on tea through passage of The Tea Act, which was not only designed to enforce a tax on tea, but to provide the struggling British

East India Tea Company with a market advantage over American tea distributors. This led to rebellion in the form of the Boston Tea Party (1773).

The colonists had issues with these various taxes for a couple of reasons. First, these many taxes were being imposed while England sought to limit American representation in England (taxation without representation). The colonists were being forced to pay taxes without the consent of the governed. The second issue for the colonists was that they were being singled out. These same taxes were not being imposed on the citizenry in the homeland. This only served to infuriate the colonists, leading to even greater friction with England. It was concerns such as these that led men like John Adams to begin encouraging permanent separation from Great Britain.

It seems England should have been aware of the problems that would result from the passage of The Declaratory Act. Two years prior, in response to England's attempts at enforcing the Navigation Act, representatives from the colonies gathered and wrote a Declaration of Rights and Grievances (1765). In that document, they insisted that England had no right to impose taxes unless those being taxed were provided with adequate governmental representation. Passage of The Declaratory Act sent a message to the colonists that Parliament was not concerned with their grievances.

Grievance No. 18: *For depriving us, in many cases, of the benefits of trial by jury;*

Admiralty Courts were a sticking point for the colonists. The British formed these courts, which were designed to hear cases involving maritime crimes and matters of overseas trade and contracts. Since maritime law is complex and deals with issues with which the common citizen is often unfamiliar, Admiralty Courts did not have juries. Rather each case was heard and decided by a single judge.

The British expanded the use of Admiralty Courts to take on pretty much any case the crown decided. This was especially true in cases involving differences with Britain. Parliament occasionally brought charges against Americans for failing to adhere to English laws. The Admiralty Courts often heard cases where colonists had purportedly violated the provisions of The Stamp Act. Since the judges were appointed and paid by Britain, their rulings generally favored Parliament.

The relationship between the judges and England was unacceptable where the colonists were concerned. To them, Admiralty Courts served as puppets with England pulling the strings. The colonists naturally believed they would fare much better if these cases were heard in the colonial court system.

Grievance No. 19: *For transporting us beyond seas to be tried for pretended offenses;*

In April 1774, a bill was introduced into Parliament aimed at disciplining colonists who interfered with, or committed crimes against, British soldiers, diplomats, or others working on behalf of the mother country within the borders of America.

To achieve justice on British terms, the bill declared that any colonists charged with such crimes must be transported to another colony or (preferably) to England for trial. King George III and Parliament believed these crimes would go unpunished if trials were heard by the sympathetic ears of juries consisting of neighbors of the accused. Conversely, the founders saw this as a matter of injustice. It was believed that no accused colonist would receive a fair hearing in a British court, particularly in England where witnesses for the defense would likely be unavailable.

While the bill was purportedly written in direct response to the Boston Tea Party of 1773 (Massachusetts was evidently named in the bill), other acts, such as the 1772 burning of *The Gaspee* in Narragansett Bay in Rhode Island, undoubtedly influenced Parliament's actions.

It has been reported that at about this time, and partially in response to the introduction of this bill, certain members of Parliament began to question England's treatment of the colonists. This grievance sent the message to England that usurping the authority vested in the colonial court system was considered an intolerable act.

> **Grievance No. 20:** *For abolishing the free system of English laws in a neighboring province, establishing therein an arbitrary government, and enlarging its boundaries, so as to render it at once an example and fit instrument for introducing the same absolute rule into these colonies;*

This grievance took aim at England's relationship with, and manipulation of, the Canadian colony of Quebec. Through The

Quebec Act of 1774, Parliament provided strong support to French Catholics in Quebec, expanding the colony's borders to include land desired by other colonies. While the people of Quebec viewed this as British encouragement, it was hardly a selfless act where England was concerned. Given growing tensions between Britain and the colonists, the English sought to establish a safe place to gather their troops in case of open rebellion. Ingratiating themselves with the neighboring Canadian colonies seemed to be a reasonable approach.

The Royal Proclamation of 1763 sought to impose an English-styled culture on the French-Canadian population of Quebec. The plan was to lure the English colonial population to Canada as a means of developing a rising tide of English support in the region. However, the attempt failed miserably, and the French-Canadian culture and population prevailed.

The Quebec Act was politically advantageous for the colonists of Quebec. It provided very favorable treatment to the Catholic Church and allowed the church to heavily influence Canadian civil government in both form and practice, which pleased the citizenry. Given this support of the church and the expansion of their territory, the colonists tended to be more tolerant of and more loyal to the crown than their southern neighbors.

The people of New England, and particularly those who had come to America to freely practice their Protestant faith, recognized the devious nature of Britain's actions. Prior to The Quebec Act, Parliament and the King had been less than friendly with the Catholic

Church, working to stamp out Catholicism and its influence at every opportunity. Giving the Catholic Church such a strong foothold in Quebec could lead to strong Catholic influence in their own colonies while the crown heavily influenced those in the Catholic Church.

Perhaps the greater issue where the colonists were concerned was the expansion of Quebec's territory. The Boundary Line Treaty of 1768 severely limited westward movement. When England expanded Quebec's territory, it made westward colonization even more difficult as they now had to deal with the French-Canadian population who believed much of that territory, particularly in the Ohio Valley, belonged to them.

> **Grievance No. 21:** *For taking away our charters, abolishing our most valuable laws, and altering fundamentally the forms of our governments;*

Here the Declaration addresses another intolerable act by Parliament. Colonial charters, or constitutions, generally addressed the rights of the colonists, but those rights were always perceived as their rights as English citizens. In other words, English colonists were deemed to enjoy the same rights as all other English citizens. As such, Britain recognized the colonists' right to a considerable portion of self-governance. These rights were so indelibly grounded in British history that it is difficult to pinpoint their origin. However, this perception slowly began to change in the late 1600's as England became more and more anxious about losing its grip on the people of America.

With The Boston Port Bill of March 1774, Parliament decided, without consent of the governed, to alter the Constitution of

Massachusetts, giving the King the authority, through his personally selected governor, to appoint the members of the Massachusetts Council. This act eliminated the practice of town meetings and gave the King complete control over the selection and removal of all judges. It also granted him the power to appoint attorney generals, justices of the peace, and sheriffs.

The act so overstepped the long-recognized British right of self-governance that it was even described by certain members of Parliament as usurpation of the rights of Massachusetts citizens. Because these colonial charters addressed the rights of the colonists as English citizens – rights Parliament had seemingly trampled underfoot – they served to provide a convincing argument against parliamentary intrusion in the 1760's by men like John Adams who favored complete separation from England.

Grievance No. 22: *For suspending our own legislatures, and declaring themselves invested with power to legislate for us in all cases whatsoever.*

This serves as an additional complaint about the <u>Boston Port Bill</u> (see Grievance No. 21), although from a slightly different perspective. This grievance refers to the power conferred on royal governors by the King and Parliament to adjourn colonial legislatures and, through royal decrees, enact new laws. Prime examples can be found during those times when Parliament stepped in and dissolved those colonial legislatures who refused to observe <u>The Quartering Act</u> (see Grievance Nos. 6, 11, and 14).

Grievance No. 23: *He has abdicated government here, by declaring us out of his protection, and waging war against us.*

At this point, the focus of the grievances turns from England's not so subtle violation of the rights of the English citizens living in America to the mother country's physical (military) attacks. King George III addressed Parliament concerning the colonies in October of 1775. In his address he asserted that the thirteen colonies were in open rebellion against the government and that he, as King, was committing British military forces to put down the rebellion. With these words he was in essence declaring war on the colonies. This meant he no longer recognized them as being under British protection but considered them a threat that must be overcome. The King's address to Parliament resulted in a series of actions taken by George III in preparation for his attacks on America. On December 22, 1775, and again on February 27, 1776, the King approved acts passed by Parliament declaring that the colonies were no longer under the King's protection.

By the time the Declaration of Independence was penned, England had invaded America militarily to quell what was seen as full rebellion. While the colonies had not yet declared their independence at the time of the King's parliamentary address, it could be said that with his words the King formally disavowed the colonies, and that the ensuing Declaration of Independence, which was approved by Congress nine months later, was simply the colonists' recognition and acceptance of the King's proclamation. At least, this is how certain men among the colonies read the King's words. John Adams reflected upon the irony of the King's declaration in a letter to Horatio Gate in

March 1776, stating: "It throws thirteen colonies out of the royal protection, levels all distinctions, and makes us independent in spite of our supplications and entreaties...It may be fortunate that the act of independency should come from the British Parliament rather than the American Congress."[15]

> **Grievance No. 24:** *He has plundered our seas, ravaged our coasts, burnt our towns, and destroyed the lives of our people.*

John Murray, commonly referred to as Lord Dunmore, was the Fourth Earl of Dunmore and served as Virginia's last royally appointed governor. He was a member of the House of Lords and, in 1771, reluctantly vacated his New York governorship to assume the office of governor of Virginia. In November 1775 he issued a proclamation declaring martial law. The proclamation also offered freedom to those slaves who agreed to fight for the British against the colonies. For these reasons he was loathed by slave owners. However, he gained respect, at least to a certain extent, from those who sought to abolish slavery in America.

In the fall of 1775 through early 1776, Lord Dunmore put together a small army along with a naval force and attacked several towns on the Virginia coast and along the colony's inland rivers. He and his troops burned several Virginia towns where the citizens had demonstrated loyalty to the colonies rather than to the crown.

These actions by Lord Dunmore occurred during the same period (September 1775 - February 1776) that King George III was

---

[15] Founders Online, Adams, John, *From John Adams to Horatio Gates, 23 March 1776,* https://founders.archives.gov, Accessed October 25, 2023

developing his own plans to attack the colonies. All of this was done under the pretext that the colonists were rebelling against their lawful rulers. However, the Americans saw things a bit differently in that it was their right as English subjects to develop their own form of self-governance.

Over the course of several months, from the fall of 1775 to the spring of 1776, more and more colonists began to see themselves not as Englishmen, but simply as Americans. Britain's attacks were not reflective of a legitimate government quelling an insurrection, but a foreign government assaulting a free people. This grievance underscored the principle that a legitimate government does not wage war against its own citizens.

> **Grievance No. 25:** *He is at this time transporting large armies of foreign mercenaries to complete the works of death, desolation, and tyranny, already begun with circumstances of cruelty and perfidy scarcely paralleled in the most barbarous ages, and totally unworthy the head of a civilized nation.*

This grievance addresses what proved to be the tipping point where many colonists were concerned. Prior to 1776, the squabbles over taxes, self-governance, and other issues between the colonists and Britain were treated as internal matters between America and the mother country. However, in 1776 as England began military attacks on American cities, King George III went a step further. He rented forces from the government of Germany to fight on England's behalf. They were called Hessians by the colonists. The term was an American synecdoche encompassing all Germans who fought for

Britain in America as most of those roughly 30,000 troops derived from the lands of Hesse-Kassel and Hesse-Hanau.

It was not uncommon at the time to supplement one's own military with foreign troops in times of war, but the colonists were outraged by England's treacherous tactics. For the colonists, this move escalated the conflict to an entirely new level and explains why many in America no longer viewed England as a mother country, but as a foreign invader. Sending a foreign army to kill what were supposedly English citizens helped unite the colonies and solidify the call for independence from England.

> **Grievance No. 26:** *He has constrained our fellow citizens, taken captive on the high seas, to bear arms against their country, to become the executioners of their friends and brethren, or to fall themselves by their hands.*

In December 1775, Parliament passed The Prohibitory Act, which was designed to wage economic warfare against the colonies. The goal was not to merely limit international trade between the colonists and other nations, but to eliminate it completely. England's strategy was to scour the shipping lanes and intercept all cargo ships sailing to and from America.

While it may seem that choking off international trade for the colonies would be stifling, The Prohibitory Act went much further. When a colonial or foreign trade ship was discovered on the high seas, this act allowed England to confiscate the ship and cargo. Once a ship was captured, the crew could be taken to England and forced to fight in the Royal Navy against their American homeland or face execution.

In other words, those Americans who were captured were forced "to become the executioners of their friends and brethren."

Congress was furious over what they considered dishonorable British tactics. In fact, the scheme was deemed to be so egregious that there was considerable resistance even within the walls of Parliament. However, the opposition was not powerful enough to overcome England's anger over the rebels in America. In retaliation, Congress immediately issued Letters of Marque to non-military American ship owners allowing them to capture any English ships they encountered on the open seas and confiscate the cargo as a reward for their efforts.

Grievance No. 27: *He has excited domestic insurrections amongst us, and has endeavored to bring on the inhabitants of our frontiers, the merciless Indian savages, whose known rule of warfare is an undistinguished destruction of all ages, sexes, and conditions.*

The charge of exciting "domestic insurrection" was aimed primarily at Lord Dunmore's promise of freedom to those slaves who would join him. The colonists' concern was not merely about the hundreds of slaves who did accept Dunmore's offer, but the fear of an even larger slave revolt in response to the governor's proposal.

Congress also accused the King of seeking to entice the Indians in America to join the fight against the colonies. Britain evidently thought this would be an easy sell believing that many Indians hated these European intruders who had occupied so much of the land and interrupted their way of life. However, from Congress's perspective, this was an unscrupulous act given their belief that Indians were brutal warriors, slaughtering men, women, and children without distinction. Indeed, many Indians sided with Britain and took up the fight.

Much could be written, and has been written, concerning the dual grievances mentioned here. Generally, those who reflect on Grievance No. 27 address it from their own ideological perspective. In fact, at the time, Jefferson's originally proposed language (see discussion on Grievance No. 1), which was seen as self-incriminating by many of the Founding Fathers, was modified prior to congressional approval mostly as a matter of diplomacy. The challenge for Congress was that the practice of slavery in America clashed with the equality of men and the inalienable right of liberty proclaimed in the document.

England, and even the colonists themselves, recognized the insincerity in these words. The watered-down language that eventually received congressional approval was an attempt to veil what could be viewed as blatant hypocrisy on the part of the colonists. On the other hand, many American slaves were purportedly transported to America and sold via the British slave trade system. It seems it was equally disingenuous for someone like Lord Dunmore to offer freedom to slaves in exchange for military service on behalf of a country who had equally contributed to, and profited from, their slavery.

Where the complaint about Britain's recruitment of American Indians is concerned, it can be said that Congress was being a bit underhanded. While many Indians hated these intruders, this was not true of every tribe. In fact, certain tribes like the Oneida, Catawba, and Stockbridge-Mohicans supported the colonists during their struggle for independence. This suggests that the colonists were accusing Britain of applying the same strategy they themselves were using.

In truth, Indians served on both sides in the Revolutionary War. It must also be admitted that broadly applying the term "merciless Indian savages" to all Native Americans at the time was disingenuous at best. Still, the grievance provided a meaty morsel for those colonists hungry for independence.

The Separation

The list of grievances was long, and the offenses were egregious. It stands to reason that the King treated the colonies severely partly because of the distance between them. He may have believed that a tight grip was his only means to maintain control. Ironically, the actions by which he hoped to sustain his authority were the very actions that led the colonists to sever their connection with England.

> *In every stage of these oppressions, we have petitioned for redress, in the most humble terms. Our repeated petitions have been answered only by repeated injury. A prince, whose character is thus marked by every act which may define a tyrant, is unfit to be the ruler of a free people.*

> *Nor have we been wanting in attentions to our British brethren. We have warned them from time to time of attempts by their legislature to extend an unwarrantable jurisdiction over us. We have reminded them of the circumstances of our emigration and settlement here. We have appealed to their native justice and magnanimity, and we have conjured them by the ties of our common kindred, to disavow these usurpations, which would inevitably interrupt our connections and correspondence. They too have been deaf to the voice of justice and of consanguinity. We must, therefore, acquiesce in the necessity, which denounces our separation, and hold them, as we hold the rest of mankind, enemies in war, in peace friends.*

Separation from England must have been difficult and emotional. No doubt, many of the colonists were British at heart, having close ties to England and the friends and relatives who remained there. For these reasons, the colonists had done everything they could reasonably do to avoid this move. However, every attempt at resolution was answered with "repeated injury."

Attempts to reach a reasonable agreement had come to an end. King George III and Parliament had failed to act in good faith. They were warned continuously that their aggression would not be tolerated, but they had "...been deaf to the voice of justice and consanguinity." Their attempts to dominate the colonies through force would certainly be met with equal force. From this moment, England would be treated as "...enemies in war, in peace friends."

We, therefore, the representatives of the United States of America, in General Congress assembled, appealing to the Supreme Judge of the world for the rectitude of our intentions, do, in the name, and by authority of the good people of these colonies, solemnly publish and declare, that these United Colonies are, and of right ought to be free and independent states; that they are absolved from all allegiance to the British Crown, and that all political connection between them and the state of Great Britain is and ought to be totally dissolved; and that, as free and independent states, they have full power to levy war, conclude peace, contract alliances, establish commerce, and to do all other acts and things which independent states may of right do. And for the support of this declaration, with a firm reliance on the protection of Divine Providence, we mutually pledge to each other our lives, our fortunes, and our sacred honor.

This last section constitutes the final, unequivocal proclamation of the colonists' independence. They declared themselves "...free and independent states," absolving themselves of any "...allegiance to the

British Crown." No doubt the self-proclaimed "...power to levy war" was as much a subtle warning as a pronouncement of autonomy, but it was complemented with the powers to "...conclude peace, contract alliances," etc.; the same powers enjoyed by all other independent nations. Relying firmly "...on the protection of Divine Providence," they then mutually pledged "...to each other our lives, our fortunes, and our sacred honor," sealing their proclamation of independence.

Riots in the Streets

On July 9, 1776, a mere five days after The Second Continental Congress approved the Declaration of Independence George Washington stood on the steps of city hall in New York City and read the document to the crowds. The response was swift. There was jubilation in the streets as word spread and, it is safe to say, the participants got a bit carried away, tearing down a statue of King George III that had been erected in the city. Whether a matter of sweet revenge or providence, it is interesting to note that the statue was later melted down, providing the material to produce 42,000 musket balls that were used by the colonists in their fight against Britain.

Section 2

The Constitution: The Preamble and Articles

Chapter 3
Introduction to the Constitution

Constitutional Theme

Two complementary themes run through the pages of the U. S. Constitution. First, the document provides for the establishment and maintenance of a Republican form of government with representatives selected, directly or indirectly, by the people. The design of the government, including the processes by which representatives are chosen, is spelled out in seven constitutional Articles, although certain adjustments to those processes are provided in some of the amendments that follow.

The second theme is the recognition of the individual rights, or freedoms, of the people of the United States. These rights are delineated primarily in the various amendments the have been added to the Constitution. Yet, what is most significant is how those rights are preserved. A few rights are named explicitly, such as the right to free speech (First Amendment). However, the primary method employed in protecting individual rights is not through proclamation or hierarchal mandates. The Founding Fathers sought to protect individual rights by placing restrictions on the actions of elected representatives, thus limiting government's intrusion into the lives of the citizenry.

The objectives of the U. S. Constitution are explained in the Preamble (below). These words set the stage for the balance of the document. While neither the form of government nor the rights of the people are detailed here, the goals of establishing limited government protecting a free people are certainly couched within the words.

Preamble

We the People of the United States, in Order to form a more perfect Union, establish Justice, insure domestic Tranquility, provide for the common defence, promote the general Welfare, and secure the Blessings of Liberty to ourselves and our Posterity, do ordain and establish this Constitution for the United States of America.

We the People

Arguably the most significant words in the U.S. Constitution, "We the People" speaks to ownership. Unlike the multitude of tyrannies and oligarchies scattered across history, the nation was to be owned and governed according to the will of the people. Rather than a top-down regime, this nation would be ruled from the bottom-up.

This experiment of bottom-up governance was fully evident in 1787 and 1788. There were multiple debates in various states including some strong opposition to the adoption of the Constitution. The Federalist Papers were published in public newspapers over the course of a year to appeal to the people, making the case in favor of support. After all, absent the consent of the people, there would be no Constitution. "We the People" finally spoke, with all thirteen states ratifying the Constitution of the United States.

A More Perfect Union

In 1781, the thirteen states ratified the Articles of Confederation, formally establishing the Union of the states. Thus, the Union existed prior to the development of the Constitution. However, given the challenges the Revolution presented, the Articles of Confederation served only as a provisional document. The government outlined in the Articles was not intended to be permanent. It was understood that, if the colonies succeeded in their effort to break from England, it would be necessary to design a stronger form of government than that provided by the Articles.

Certain weaknesses in the Articles of Confederation needed to be rectified. For instance, under the Articles, Congress had no power to tax. Other than assorted taxes collected by the states and remitted to the federal government, Congress had no means to raise the money necessary to pay national expenses (armies, etc.). Also, while the government coined money, the value of coinage was often disputed since the Articles provided no firm standard to determine the worth of that money. Furthermore, there was no provision for the federal government to effectively deal with international trade or treaties. These issues and more needed to be addressed for the Union to succeed.

With the words "a more perfect Union," the founders seemed to have two things in mind. First, their aim was to provide, through the Constitution, a better Union than that developed under the Articles. However, they also wanted to send a message that it was their goal to form a Union better than could be seen in the pages of history. This

Union would be better than the Roman Republic or the democracy of Athens. They hoped to "form a more perfect Union" – one that would be admired by the nations.

Establish Justice

With their attention focused on the war with Britain, the Founding Fathers had not completed the task before them. For instance, there was no federal court system and very few laws. This establishment of a justice system would be accomplished with the ratification of the Constitution.

Yet, the words go far deeper than merely setting up a justice system. In keeping with the Declaration of Independence, where it is stated that "…all men are created equal," part of the goal was to establish a system that treated everyone equally in keeping with that principle. Of course, with the presence of slavery and the second-class citizenship of women at the time, it would be a while before this goal would be met. In fact, many believe the country still falls well short of the goal of *justice for all*. Still, it was the goal of the founders that equitable justice would one day be achieved.

Justice, where the founders were concerned, meant 1) providing for the protection of individual rights, 2) where possible, realizing fairness for every citizen in every situation, and 3) holding government accountable for its actions, thus preventing the abuse or discriminatory treatment of the citizenry by their leaders.

Ensure Domestic Tranquility

On the heels of a brutal war with Great Britain, the word *tranquility* must have seemed most attractive to the people of the United States. Years of war had taken its toll in lives, wealth, and a peaceful existence. The founders saw the Constitution as an opportunity to provide for the kind of peace the people sought.

Throughout history, it has ostensibly been a fundamental objective of government to provide for the peaceful coexistence of the citizenry. While not all governments have done this well, particularly where oligarchies and tyrannies are concerned, this seems to be a natural role of those in positions of authority. After all, what government performs well, or in the best interest of its constituency, if the people are in revolt against the government or fighting among each other?

The founders were establishing a government *of the people*, but it was also a Union of the states. The idea behind domestic tranquility was that the federal government, as formed in the Constitution, could assist not only in peace between individuals, but especially peace between the various states who would each have their own government and their own interests.

In the early stages, many individuals, rather than forming a Union of states, believed it would be better for each state to become its own individual country, thus avoiding the establishment of a central government. Much time is spent in the Federalist Papers explaining the advantages of the Union as opposed to the formation of nations. Those arguments included recognizing that, as individual nations, the states would inevitably become competitors – perhaps even hostile competitors – leading to weakened individual nations. This would ultimately lead them to be "enemies in war, in peace friends." The Union, on the other hand, could provide a brotherhood by which peace among the states could be achieved. Alexander Hamilton explained this, writing in Federalist No. 8:

> Assuming it therefore as an established truth that the several States, in case of disunion, or such combinations of them as might happen to be formed out of the wreck of the general Confederacy, would be subject to those vicissitudes of peace and war, of friendship and enmity, with each other, which have fallen to the lot of all neighboring nations not united under one government...[16]

Tranquility among the citizenry is certainly important. However, most individual issues would and should be handled at the state and local levels. It would not be necessary or wise for a national government to become involved at that level. Tranquility, where the federal government is concerned, would be focused on peaceful coexistence of the states, which could only serve to strengthen the Union.

Provide for the Common Defense

The "common defense" of the United States of America speaks primarily to the federal government's constitutional charge to develop a military branch of the government for protection from foreign adversaries. During the days of the writing of the Constitution, some raised numerous concerns about the establishment of a federal military, particularly in times of peace, and its potential use against the

---

[16] Hamilton, Alexander, Federalist No. 8.

very citizens it was meant to protect. The argument was that an armed citizenry would be less likely to turn on neighbors while a formal military could be considered an internal threat.

The argument opposing a federal military in times of peace waned in the end as it was realized that an armed citizenry would be no match for the trained military and weaponry they would face if invaded by a well-prepared and well-armed adversary. An unprepared nation would too easily be overcome. Hamilton addressed this truth in Federalist No. 19, writing:

> Military preparations must be preceded by so many tedious discussions, arising from the jealousies, pride, separate views, and clashing pretensions of sovereign bodies, that before the diet can settle the arrangements, the enemy are in the field; and before the federal troops are ready to take it, are retiring into winter quarters.[17]

> ...cases are likely to occur under our government, as well as under those of other nations, which will sometimes render a military force in time of peace essential to the security of the society...[18]

Promote the General Welfare

The term *welfare* carries with it certain connotations that do not particularly apply to the expression "general welfare." When many people hear the term *welfare*, what comes to mind is feeding, housing, and clothing the poor, especially when that work is done through government programs. However, that is not necessarily what is in view where the general welfare of the country is concerned.

The general welfare of a country (in this case, the United States) speaks more deliberately to the *well-being* of the nation socially,

---

[17] Hamilton, Alexander, Federalist 19
[18] ibid

politically, financially, etc. While caring for the poor in some fashion may be considered a matter of a nation's well-being, it is but a small part.

Generally, it is a natural role of government to oversee the well-being of the citizenry. Of course, that role is seen differently depending, to a large degree, on the form of the government. In a monarchy, the leader of the country will make broad decisions concerning what is best for the country – decisions that are often based primarily on what is best for the monarch and his immediate underlings. Similarly, in an oligarchy, where the nation is ruled by a few in an elite class, decisions made may primarily benefit those in a position to make those decisions while the cost is most often borne by the citizenry.

In a republic, decisions about the nation's well-being are made by representatives chosen by the citizens. When those decisions begin to drift from the will of their constituents, those representatives may be replaced by the people by whom they were selected. In that respect, decisions about the well-being of a republic ultimately rest on the shoulders of the people who choose their representatives.

There can be considerable differences of opinion when it comes to determining the precise role of the federal government with respect to promoting the general welfare of the Union. Those differences generally focus on how federal funds are spent and/or the intrusiveness of the federal government in the lives and businesses of the constituency. Quite often, those arguments seek to distinguish between the respective roles of the state and federal governments.

Secure the Blessings of Liberty

Among the reasons for the Constitution that are listed in this section, "secure the blessings of liberty" is an idea that is rather unique to the United States. Prior to the establishment of the United States republic, there had been but a few attempts to establish a government *of the people* (republic or democracy) where protection of individual liberty was primary. Earlier republican forms of government tended to focus on protecting the state (and the people) from outside forces rather than safeguarding individual rights.

What does it mean to secure the blessings of liberty? This phrase points primarily to the preservation, or protection, of the rights and freedoms shared by the citizens of the United States. In fact, it might be said that ensuring the rights and freedoms of the people should be considered the foremost role of the government of the United States. It is couched in all the reasons given for the writing and ratification of the Constitution including *establishing justice, ensuring domestic tranquility, providing for the common defense,* and *promoting the general welfare* of the nation. These governmental responsibilities demonstrate *how* the government would go about protecting the rights and freedoms enjoyed by the people of the United States.

Chapter 4
The Structure of the Legislative Branch

Design of the Articles

Each of the seven articles found in the Constitution serves a distinct purpose and it was these seven articles, along with the Preamble, that were submitted to the states for ratification. In other words, when the Constitution was ratified by the original colonies, the Preamble and these seven articles represented the Constitution in its entirety.

The first three articles establish the branches of the government of the republic. The three branches of The U.S. government are legislative, executive, and judicial. The Constitution was so well written, and these branches so well defined, that the basic form of the government has not changed in the nearly 240 years since these articles were penned. It is true that the number of representatives in the House of Representatives and the Senate has grown, but this is due to the addition of dozens of states and the natural increase in the population,

Article IV primarily deals with intra-union relationships. It addresses communication and collaboration between state and federal governments as well as the interaction between the governments of the individual states. It even goes so far as to consider certain matters that may involve dealings between the individual citizens of one state and the government of another state.

It would have been absurd to think that the Constitution, in its original form, could satisfy every unforeseen circumstance that would eventually be faced by the Union. Realizing this, the founders included Article V where they established the method by which the Constitution might be amended. Indeed, many amendments have been added to the Constitution, beginning with the Bill of Rights, which were added in 1791.

Article VI contains some general statements about the viability of the federal government. This includes issues like national debts that may result from the government borrowing money and the effect of treaties with other governments. It also addresses the need for the people's representatives, both federal and state, to be allegiant to the Constitution and the republican principles contained therein. Finally, Article VII simply states that acceptance of the Constitution would require ratification by a minimum of nine of the thirteen states of the Union.

Article I
Section 1

Clause 1: *All legislative Powers herein granted shall be vested in a Congress of the United States, which shall consist of a Senate and House of Representatives.*

The legislative branch of the federal government is arguably the strongest of the three branches, partly because this body was given the responsibility of writing laws and partly because it has the largest number of elected officials who serve as representatives of the people. At the time the Constitution was written, the Union consisted of thirteen states. Each state would be represented by two senators and each state would also be represented by a certain number of members in the House of Representatives based on population.

Section 2

Clause 1: *The House of Representatives shall be composed of Members chosen every second Year by the People of the several States, and the Electors in each State shall have the Qualifications requisite for Electors of the most numerous Branch of the State Legislature.*

With the power to write laws, the framers worked to develop a counterbalance within the framework of the legislative branch. Additionally, they sought a means to distinguish between representatives of the individual citizens vs. representatives of the individual states. After all, if Congress was designed to solely represent the population, this would certainly disadvantage smaller states. On the other hand, if equal representation was given to each state, the individuals in states with larger populations, it could be argued, would be underrepresented. James Madison recognized these arguments in Federalist No. 38, writing:

An objector in a large State exclaims loudly against the unreasonable equality of representation in the Senate. An objector in a small State is equally loud against the dangerous inequality in the House of Representatives.[19]

Each side voiced a legitimate concern, and the Founding Fathers sought to consider both viewpoints fairly. It was determined that the best way to provide equitable representation was to develop a legislature comprised of two chambers. One chamber, the House of Representatives, would be designed to proportionately represent the citizens of the states based on the population of each state. This resulted in the House of Representatives providing a natural legislative advantage to states with larger populations.

The second chamber, known as the Senate, would represent the states equally by providing two representatives from each state regardless of the population size. Each Senator, or state, would have an equal vote when it came to the passing of laws. This chamber, then, provided an advantage to states with smaller populations, giving them equal influence in the passing of legislation. If a proposed statute passed both chambers with a majority vote, it could be said that it had been approved by *both* the peoples' representatives and the states' representatives.

Clause 2: *No Person shall be a Representative who shall not have attained to the Age of twenty five Years, and been seven Years a Citizen of the United States, and who shall not, when elected, be an Inhabitant of that State in which he shall be chosen.*

Given their distinctive roles, the Senate, as representatives of the various states, would be considered the upper chamber, or the more

---

[19] Madison, James, Federalist No. 38.

prestigious of the two houses of Congress, since each Senator's vote carried greater weight (two Senators per state). The House of Representatives, representing the proportionate population of each state, would be considered the lower chamber.

It was necessary to establish certain qualifications for the members of the House of Representatives, but it was determined that those qualifications should be minimal, making it possible for people of all backgrounds to participate in their own government. This would provide for a government whose members could be chosen from among the constituency.

The first requirement was that a member of the House of Representatives must have attained a minimum age of twenty-five years. It seemed unwise to delegate such authority to someone with too little life experience to be responsible for sweeping national decisions. Additionally, one who chose to run for a seat in the House of Representatives must have been a citizen of the United States for no less than seven years and must also be a resident of the state they sought to represent.

Clause 3: *Representatives and direct Taxes shall be apportioned among the several States which may be included within this Union, according to their respective Numbers, which shall be determined by adding to the whole Number of free Persons, including those bound to Service for a Term of Years, and excluding Indians not taxed, three fifths of all other Persons. The actual Enumeration shall be made within three Years after the first Meeting of the Congress of the United States, and within every subsequent Term of ten Years, in such Manner as they shall by Law direct. The Number of Representatives shall not exceed one for every thirty Thousand, but each State shall have at Least one Representative; and until such* *enumeration shall be made, the State of New Hampshire shall be entitled to chuse three, Massachusetts eight, Rhode Island and Providence Plantations one, Connecticut five, New-York six, New Jersey four, Pennsylvania eight, Delaware one, Maryland six, Virginia ten, North Carolina five, South Carolina five, and Georgia three.*

It was necessary for the Founding Fathers to establish the number of representatives to be selected by the individual states. This was done based on a state's population and it stands to reason that each state would seek as much representation as possible. Initially, given the population of each state, the resulting House of Representatives consisted of sixty-five members.

The long-term feature, approved in this section, provided for a census every ten years to adjust representation based on the population of each state. However, while the Declaration of Independence declared that all men are created equal, this was not originally the case where representation was concerned. For instance, Native Americans, who did not pay taxes at the time, were excluded from the census when determining a state's population.

A conundrum arose where slaves were concerned when it came to determining a state's representation. Slave owners sought to have the best of both worlds. First, they did not wish to count slaves as equals, legally speaking, since this would add to lingering questions concerning the practice of slavery itself. In other words, if slaves were equals, how could they be *owned* by other *equals* and treated as property? On the other hand, including slaves in the count of a state's population would provide that state with greater representation where the federal government was concerned.

A compromise was finally reached as each slave would be counted as three-fifths of a person. However, after the Civil War, slavery was abolished in 1865 with the addition of the Thirteenth Amendment. Later, Section 2 of the Fourteenth Amendment, which was finally ratified by the states in 1868, repealed the three-fifths rule and previous slaves were counted as equals.

Prior to the American Revolution, the colonies were subject to taxation from England. These generally consisted of tariffs and excise taxes (fees charged on goods and services) and evidently amounted to somewhere around 5%-7% of an individual's income depending on their purchases. While the text of Section 2 mentions American taxation of states "...according to their respective Numbers," these taxes were not based on population directly. At the time, as with taxation from England, taxation was primarily realized through tariffs and excise taxes that were grounded in economic activity (sales of certain products and services). The individual states were simply responsible for collecting these taxes and remitting that money to the federal government. Things like payroll taxes, income taxes, and corporate taxes did not exist at the time.

Clause 4: *When vacancies happen in the Representation from any State, the Executive Authority thereof shall issue Writs of Election to fill such Vacancies.*

The authors of the Constitution reasoned that, whether through illness, death, resignation, expulsion, or other circumstances, certain individuals may be unable to fulfill the commitment to their term in the House of Representatives. This would result in underrepresentation for any state whose member no longer filled that seat in Congress. In such a case, it is, according to Section 2, the privilege/responsibility of the chief executive (governor) of that representative's state to select a temporary replacement until the next general election, or until a special election might take place, depending on the amount of time left for that representative's term.

Clause 5: *The House of Representatives shall chuse their Speaker and other Officers; and shall have the sole Power of Impeachment.*

It is up to the members of the House of Representatives to select the leadership for that chamber. The totality of the membership selects that person (Speaker), who would oversee the management of the chamber as a whole as well as any other management positions deemed necessary. The role of Speaker is of great significance since the Speaker of the House is third in line, right behind the vice president, when it comes to succession to the presidency. This would occur if/when both the president and vice president simultaneously cannot fulfill their obligation to carry out the duties of the presidency.

It is interesting that this article does not specify that the Speaker must be selected from within the ranks of the chamber. Though it has never happened historically, nothing would prevent the members of the House from selecting an outsider to preside as Speaker and accept the responsibility as third in line where succession is concerned. However, if the members were to select a non-elected individual to this position, that person could have no vote where legislation is concerned.

Each party within the House of Representatives is also expected to select leaders to represent them among the leadership in this chamber. Thus, Republicans select members from their own ranks and Democrats select members from among their own ranks to represent their party in the management of the House.

The word *impeach* generally means *to accuse* or *to call to account*. Impeachment is the legislative instrument by which government officials are held accountable for their actions while in office. Generally, the purpose of impeachment, first mentioned in this section, is to remove someone from a government office due to some kind of misconduct.

The founders placed responsibility for the impeachment of government officials in the hands of the House of Representatives. Interestingly, that is all this section has to say on the topic. In fact, there is actually very little discussion in the Constitution on this subject, which is perhaps why it is so misunderstood. More detailed insight into impeachment will be offered where it is addressed briefly over the next couple of sections.

Section 3

Clause 1: *The Senate of the United States shall be composed of two Senators from each State, chosen by the Legislature thereof, for six Years; and each Senator shall have one Vote.*

While the members of the House of Representatives would be numbered based on population, each state would be represented by just two Senators. Given the thirteen states involved, the original House of Representatives had sixty-five representatives while the corresponding Senate had twenty-six members. Consequently, the vote of a member of the Senate (1 of 26) carried more weight than a vote of a House member (1 of 65).

Unlike the members of the House of Representatives, who were to be selected directly by the citizenry through the general election process, members of the Senate would be appointed by the members of the legislature of each state. Additionally, while the length of term for a member of the House of Representatives would span two years, each Senator would be selected for a six-year term.

Clause 2: *Immediately after they shall be assembled in Consequence of the first Election, they shall be divided as equally as may be into three Classes. The Seats of the Senators of the first Class shall be vacated at the Expiration of the second Year, of the second Class at the Expiration of the fourth Year, and of the third Class at the Expiration of the sixth Year, so that one third may be chosen every second Year; and if Vacancies happen by Resignation, or otherwise, during the Recess of the Legislature of any State, the Executive thereof may make temporary Appointments until the next Meeting of the Legislature, which shall then fill such Vacancies.*

The prestige of the Senate begged for a longer term of office than the two-year term assigned to the House of Representatives. However, the Founding Fathers also sought to maintain some consistency in the Senate. In the House of Representatives, where elections would be held every two years, it could be possible, although highly unlikely, that the entire membership might be overturned in one fell swoop if all members were voted out in one election.

To establish more consistency, it was decided that, while each Senator would be appointed for six years, one third of those members would be appointed for an initial two-year period. Therefore, among the first class of Senators, one third of the members were chosen to be replaced or re-appointed at the end of the first two years of the Senate normal six-year term. Another third would be replaced or reappointed after the fourth year. The final third would go through this process at the end of their sixth year in office. Beyond that initial six-year chapter, members would be replaced or reappointed as their terms expired so that, every second year, one third of the Senate would be either reinstated or replaced.

As with a member of the House who might not be able to fulfill his commitment to serve a two-year term, in the case of a Senator who was incapable of completing a full six-year term, the governor of that Senator's state could appoint a temporary alternate until such time when the state legislature could meet to select a new appointee for the balance of the term.

Clause 3: *No Person shall be a Senator who shall not have attained to the Age of thirty Years, and been nine Years a Citizen of the United States, and who shall not, when elected, be an Inhabitant of that State for which he shall be chosen.*

As with members of the House of Representatives, the authors of the Constitution decided to keep the qualifications for the office of Senator quite simple, though the requirements are slightly more stringent than those for the House. First, it was determined that a member of the Senate must have been a citizen of the United States for no less than nine years (compared to seven years for the House of Representatives) and, as with the House, a Senator must be a resident of the state he/she would represent.

The framers also determined that there must be a higher level of maturity in that chamber. Hamilton wrote in Federalist No. 62:

> A senator must be thirty years of age at least; as a representative must be twenty-five. And the former must have been a citizen nine years; as seven years are required for the latter. The propriety of these distinctions is explained by the nature of the senatorial trust, which, requiring greater extent of information and stability of character, requires at the same time that the senator should have reached a period of life most likely to supply these advantages; and which, participating immediately in transactions with foreign nations, ought to be exercised by none who are not thoroughly weaned from the prepossessions and habits incident to foreign birth and education.[20]

It was decided by the Founding Fathers that the greater responsibility given to the Senate naturally required a more experienced and more mature membership. This necessitated a minimum age requirement in that chamber that represented that maturity. The chosen minimum age for a member of the Senate was set at thirty years. It was reasoned that this was an age when youthful folly and naivety should have been replaced with sufficient life experience and, hence, sound judgment.

Clause 4: *The Vice President of the United States shall be President of the Senate, but shall have no Vote, unless they be equally divided.*

---

[20] Hamilton, Alexander, Federalist No. 62.

The Constitution called for the House of Representatives to select a person to serve as the primary manager of that chamber (the Speaker). Where the Senate was concerned, the founders designated the Vice President of the United States as the president of that chamber. However, the vice president would not be considered a *member* of the chamber and, as such, would have no vote in matters before the Senate except as a tie breaker in the case of an equally divided vote.

Clause 5: *The Senate shall chuse their other Officers, and also a President pro tempore, in the Absence of the Vice President, or when he shall exercise the Office of President of the United States.*

Given additional responsibilities within the executive branch, it would not always be possible for the vice president to attend every session of the Senate. To address this issue, the members of the chamber were expected to select a President pro tempore. In the absence of the vice president during a senatorial session, this individual would serve as a stand-in for the vice president and guide Senate sessions. Senators would also determine which other management offices were necessary and appoint individuals to those positions.

Clause 6: *The Senate shall have the sole Power to try all Impeachments. When sitting for that Purpose, they shall be on Oath or Affirmation. When the President of the United States is tried, the Chief Justice shall preside: And no Person shall be convicted without the Concurrence of two thirds of the Members present.*

Where the impeachment of a governmental official is concerned, the founders placed that responsibility on the House of Representatives. In other words, the House of Representatives is responsible for gathering evidence and, if warranted, bringing charges against the target of impeachment. This could involve any government official (excluding members of Congress) elected by the people or appointed by the president and approved by the Senate through the process of Advice and Consent (see Article II, Section 2).

If charges against a government official are accepted in the House of Representatives (by a vote of the majority of the members of the chamber), a contingent of the membership of the House is selected to serve as prosecutor and present the charges and evidence to the Senate where the members of that chamber serve as jury. Also, the charged official has the right, as in a court of law, to offer a defense before the members of the jury.

> **Clause 7:** *Judgment in Cases of Impeachment shall not extend further than to removal from Office, and disqualification to hold and enjoy any Office of honor, Trust or Profit under the United States: but the Party convicted shall nevertheless be liable and subject to Indictment, Trial, Judgment and Punishment, according to Law.*

The design of the impeachment process was lifted from the pages of Great Britain's model where the lower chamber of Parliament held the reins of impeachment and the higher chamber served as judge. Hamilton, writing in Federalist No. 65, noted:

> The model from which the idea of this institution has been borrowed, pointed out that course to the convention. In Great Britain it is the province of the House of Commons to prefer the impeachment, and of the House of Lords to decide upon it.[21]

---

[21] Hamilton, Alexander, Federalist No. 65.

If the Senate finds the person who is being impeached guilty of the charges brought by the House, that person is removed from office. A guilty finding also precludes that person from serving in public office in the future. This is the full extent of consequences where impeachment is concerned. Congress does not have the standing to bring legal charges against the individual. However, it does not mean that an impeached individual is immune from legal prosecution. The Justice Department can still seek indictment if the charges rise to that level of legal misconduct.

It is extremely difficult to remove someone from a federal office through the impeachment process for a couple of reasons. First, agreement by two-thirds of the Senate is required to achieve a guilty verdict, which almost never happens. Then there is the underlying reason that it is so difficult to achieve a two-thirds majority in favor of a guilty verdict. While impeachment purportedly arises from Treason, Bribery, or other high Crimes and Misdemeanors (see Article II, Section 4), suggesting that impeachment is a matter of illegal activity, it is most often a matter of politics.

Rarely are charges brought against an individual simply because it is believed the law has been broken. Most impeachment charges stem from differences in political points of view. While some may balk at this notion, it is a most reasonable conclusion. Over the course of history, at no time has a House of Representatives led by a Republican majority sought to impeach a Republican official. Neither has a House led by a Democrat majority sought to impeach a Democrat officer.

This has been proven true even in those cases where the charges involved illegalities (perjury, etc.).

Since the inception of the Constitution, the only individuals removed from office through impeachment were eight federal judges. These generally involved charges like *intoxicated while sitting on the bench, unequal application of the law, income tax evasion*, etc. While President Richard M. Nixon resigned upon threat of impeachment, no other individuals have been removed from office through the impeachment process.

Section 4

Clause 1: *The Times, Places and Manner of holding Elections for Senators and Representatives, shall be prescribed in each State by the Legislature thereof; but the Congress may at any time by Law make or alter such Regulations, except as to the Places of chusing Senators.*

Making decisions concerning election details is a state rather than a federal function. These details include how, where, and by whom, votes are received, tallied, and reported. However, where this section declares that states are responsible for the *time* of election, that does not speak to the day on which the election will be held, which is a responsibility of the United States Congress, but more specifically to the *hours* during which votes may be cast. Still, adjustments have been made by many states that have begun to allow early voting (prior to the official Election Day), mail-in ballots, etc.

While it is a function of state legislatures to design the election process, this means that different states might easily develop a plethora of voting methods. For this reason, the founders thought it wise to provide the opportunity for input from Congress (the federal legislature) if necessary to maintain a certain amount of consistency where elections are concerned. While design of the election process is a function of the state legislatures, there may come a time, for instance, when the current date for holding elections might not serve the nation's best interest. If that occurred, Congress could step in and adjust that date to what might be considered a more workable solution.

Clause 2: *The Congress shall assemble at least once in every Year, and such Meeting shall be on the first Monday in December, unless they shall by Law appoint a different Day.*

Originally, the positions of federal legislators (Representatives and Senators) were not viewed as full-time commitments. These roles were filled by people who simply wished to serve their country for a time and, when finished, return to their previous jobs/lives. In fact, even while in office, these individuals would return home to live their lives and work their regular jobs until the country needed them to assemble. Nevertheless, the authors of the Constitution thought it wise for Congress to assemble on a regular basis if only for the maintenance of the nation. It was determined that assembling annually should be a minimum requirement.

In modern times, a Congress that meets but one day each year seems like a preposterous proposition. In the twenty-first century, federal legislators are full-time employees who are very well-compensated for their service. In fact, it is safe to say that most federal legislators spend far more time in the nation's capital than in the states they represent.

Section 5

Clause 1: *Each House shall be the Judge of the Elections, Returns and Qualifications of its own Members, and a Majority of each shall constitute a Quorum to do Business; but a smaller Number may adjourn from day to day, and may be authorized to compel the Attendance of absent Members, in such Manner, and under such Penalties as each House may provide.*

Here the founders dealt with what is known in political circles as bicameralism, and it addresses the matter through four distinct clauses. The term (bicameralism) speaks to the matter of the independent internal governance of each chamber of the legislature as well as their cooperative interactive character.

The first clause, given above, begins by authorizing each chamber to be self-governing. This self-governance explicitly applies to the judging of elections, returns, and qualifications of its members. In other words, it is up to each chamber to assure that its members are both qualified and dually elected to the offices they hold. This can even occasionally involve the review of a state's election numbers to ensure that the individual holding the office is the one legitimately selected by the people. However, over the course of U.S. political history, there have only been a couple of extremely tight political races where the legislature has been involved at that level.

The clause continues, declaring that, to carry out the business of the nation, a chamber must have a quorum of its members present, where a quorum is equal to a majority of the membership. In theory, this means that no laws are to be voted upon without a quorum present. However, this constitutional rule has not been followed precisely throughout the years, but when it is side-stepped it is generally with the consent of the members. While this clause appears to provide the authority for each chamber to compel members' attendance, it is an authority rarely employed. The Supreme Court has held that, as independent governing units, each chamber is responsible for determining when a quorum is present, and it is not the Court's role to micromanage the activities of an equal branch of government.

Clause 2: *Each House may determine the Rules of its Proceedings, punish its Members for disorderly Behaviour, and, with the Concurrence of two thirds, expel a Member.*

This second clause serves a dual purpose. First, it speaks to the right/responsibility of the chambers of the legislature to establish rules and procedures by which business would be conducted in an orderly fashion. Second, it provides for the disciplining of the members, when necessary, within each chamber.

Members of the legislative branches do not face impeachment as do other government officials. Each chamber of the legislature is expected to hold its members accountable for their work and what might be considered misconduct while in office. How might a member be disciplined? Perhaps the most common discipline is what is known as *censure*. This involves a public expression of disapproval of what the members deem to be injudicious activity on the part of the one being censured.

A more drastic method of discipline involves removing a member from office, which requires approval by two-thirds of the members of the chamber. The bar of two-thirds approval is intentionally high since the individual was selected by the people through the election process and overturning the choice of the people is not to be taken lightly. As a result, it is difficult to successfully expel a member of Congress. For this reason, attempts at expulsion are normally only considered in the event of egregious illegal activity on the part of a legislator.

Clause 3: *Each House shall keep a Journal of its Proceedings, and from time to time publish the same, excepting such Parts as may in their Judgment require Secrecy; and the Yeas and Nays of the Members of either House on any question shall, at the Desire of one fifth of those Present, be entered on the Journal.*

Recognizing the value of accurate records, this is deemed one of the most archaic statements in the Constitution. In the digital age of the twenty-first century, with the availability of the live streaming of congressional sessions and daily digital publishing of congressional activity, the requirement that records of legislative activity must be published seems slightly outdated. Nonetheless, at the time this clause was written, the legislatures met infrequently and the primary vehicle available to record meetings were hand-written notes. This clause was included to stress the importance of government record-keeping.

The clause is more about governmental transparency than anything else. It was never intended that the people's representatives should conduct their business in secret where it could be hidden from their constituents. Naturally, certain topics and decisions require a measure of privacy/discretion. However, when the people's representatives make decisions on behalf of the constituents who elected them, those decisions belong to the people, not the legislators.

Clause 4: *Neither House, during the Session of Congress, shall, without the Consent of the other, adjourn for more than three days, nor to any other Place than that in which the two Houses shall be sitting.*

A cooperative and timely exchange between the legislative chambers is a critical component of bicameralism. Even in the early days of the Republic, it was deemed important that, when the two chambers were in session, the atmosphere should be one of cooperation, not competition. Although the two chambers were independent, each was partially dependent on the other. This is what led to the inclusion of this clause on cooperative adjournment. The Founders were concerned about political shenanigans. They sought to prevent the will of one chamber from being thwarted by the other's mischievous absence when contemplating a significant piece of legislation.

Section 6

Clause 1: *The Senators and Representatives shall receive a Compensation for their Services, to be ascertained by Law, and paid out of the Treasury of the United States. They shall in all Cases, except Treason, Felony and Breach of the Peace, be privileged from Arrest during their Attendance at the Session of their respective Houses, and in going to and returning from the same; and for any Speech or Debate in either House, they shall not be questioned in any other Place.*

The members of the Senate and the House of Representatives were to be chosen by the legislatures and citizenry of the individual states they were selected to represent. However, they would not be considered employees of those states. Instead, they would be employed by, and paid through the treasury of, the federal government. This was done to ensure equitable treatment in the legislature (equal compensation, benefits, etc.), and it was done for a reason. If paid by the various states, it would be possible, and quite likely, that two senators sitting next to each other while in session might face considerable disparity in their compensation packages, causing unnecessary rivalries and jealousies that could very well interfere with the work they were sent to complete.

A unique matter where federal legislators are concerned is found in their exemption from arrest while the legislature is in session. However, this protection is limited. Indeed, a legislator could be arrested while in session if charged with treason, the commitment of a felony, or breaking the peace, which appears to cover a broad range of offenses. The reasoning behind this rule was that the work of the federal government was too important to be disrupted by a person's arrest over a neighborhood dispute. Such issues could be easily handled on those occasions when the legislature was not in session. This exemption from arrest would cover the time a representative was in session as well as the time involved in their travel to and from legislative session.

The wisdom of the following privilege is open to debate, but the legislators have been afforded an additional curious exemption from liability. It was decided by the founders that these representatives could not be held liable for anything said during a floor debate while in session (including intentional falsehoods), nor could they be held legally accountable for any claims/promises made while giving a speech from the floor of their respective chamber.

This has, no doubt, led to a plethora of regrettable outcomes over the course of time. Nevertheless, it is a luxury the representatives enjoy, knowing that a person armed with the weaponry of an effective vocabulary can, and often does, do great harm both to the civility of debate and to relationships that might be helpful in the future. Nonetheless, language/debate (often vicious in nature) is the primary instrument used in politics, and it was decided that the peoples' representatives should be allowed unfettered use of that tool when vying for their constituents.

> **Clause 2:** *No Senator or Representative shall, during the Time for which he was elected, be appointed to any civil Office under the Authority of the United States, which shall have been created, or the Emoluments whereof shall have been encreased during such time; and no Person holding any Office under the United States, shall be a Member of either House during his Continuance in Office.*

Whether personally, professionally, or politically, conflict of interest can distort a person's perspective and affect their actions both directly and indirectly. While not all such conflicts can be prevented, the founders thought it wise to remove a couple of potential hazards.

The second clause of Section 6 contains two provisions prohibiting members of Congress from holding another federal office that could serve as a source of conflict. The first provision, commonly known as the Ineligibility Clause, precludes a legislator from accepting any federal civil office that is created (or had a compensation increase) during their congressional term. With the Ineligibility Clause, the founders sought to avoid a situation where a separate branch of government might attempt a form of congressional bribery. The concern was that the other branch might brazenly create, or markedly increase the compensation for, an office, and then offer that position to a legislator in exchange for a favorable vote on a bill or some other legislative benefit. Having served their legislative purpose, the representative could then resign that congressional office and accept the more lucrative position.

The second provision, known as the Incompatibility Clause, forbids a member from holding a congressional office and another federal position simultaneously. Allowing a legislator to serve in multiple offices concurrently, particularly when those offices represent separate branches of government, would too easily result in a conflict of interest, and impact the separation of powers delineated in the Constitution.

The primary distinction between the Ineligibility and Incompatibility Clauses is a matter of timing. The Incompatibility Clause forbids *concurrent* office holding. Under this clause, a congressman would be in compliance by simply resigning the legislative position and assuming the responsibilities of the other office. The Ineligibility Clause, on the other hand, forbids appointment to another federal office that was created or had its compensation increased during the entire length of that person's term in the legislature. Thus, the Ineligibility Clause may apply even in a case where the member is willing to resign the congressional seat to assume the other office.

The inclusion of these clauses in the Constitution was a matter of great debate and considerable wrangling during the framing of the document. Some wished to expand these clauses to include eligibility for both state and federal offices while others believed the restrictions were too harsh and might prevent good people from serving productively. The result was a seeming compromise between the two positions. In Federalist No. 76, Alexander Hamilton wrote that these provisions would serve as "...important guards against the danger of executive influence upon the legislative body."[22]

---

[22] Hamilton, Alexander, Federalist No. 76.

Chapter 5

The Role and Authority of the Legislative Branch

Article I
Section 7

Clause 1: *All Bills for raising Revenue shall originate in the House of Representatives; but the Senate may propose or concur with Amendments as on other Bills.*

There is a noticeable discrepancy between the values of the votes in each of the two legislative chambers. In the Senate, each state is represented by two voting officials. In the current Senate, which consists of 100 members, each individual represents 1.00% of the entire vote on any particular bill or rule. However, in the House of Representatives, which currently consists of 435 members, each member constitutes roughly .20% of the vote. While this makes sense, given the representative character of each chamber (the House represents the populous and the Senate represents the states), it is quite a discrepancy, and the founders sought to offset this disparity in some meaningful way. Part of their solution is found here.

With the first clause of this section, which is known as the Origination Clause, the founders put the nation's purse strings in the hands of the House of Representatives, and this responsibility begins with that chamber providing for the collection of government revenue (taxes). This would help offset, at least in part, the *power discrepancy* between the chambers. Also, the founders believed that having been elected directly by a vote of the people (Senators were originally appointed by state legislatures), members of the House of Representatives would be in a better position to develop tax solutions that would best serve their constituents.

> **Clause 2:** *Every Bill which shall have passed the House of Representatives and the Senate, shall, before it become a Law, be presented to the President of the United States; If he approve he shall sign it, but if not he shall return it, with his Objections to that House in which it shall have originated, who shall enter the Objections at large on their Journal, and proceed to reconsider it. If after such Reconsideration two thirds of that House shall agree to pass the Bill, it shall be sent, together with the Objections, to the other House, by which it shall likewise be reconsidered, and if approved by two thirds of that House, it shall become a Law. But in all such Cases the Votes of both Houses shall be determined by yeas and Nays, and the Names of the Persons voting for and against the Bill shall be entered on the Journal of each House respectively. If any Bill shall not be returned by the President within ten Days (Sundays excepted) after it shall have been presented to him, the Same shall be a Law, in like Manner as if he had signed it, unless the Congress by their Adjournment prevent its Return, in which Case it shall not be a Law.*

The method by which federal laws are developed and established in the United States is established here. According to the previous clause, revenue and spending laws must begin with the House of Representatives. However, other laws can originate in either chamber of Congress.

Every law begins as a thought...an idea. Brought to fruition, that thought results in a bill that is proposed to the legislature. If written by a member of the House of Representatives, along with his/her staff, it is presented to the members of the House for consideration. If penned by a Senator, with the assistance of his/her staff, it is presented to the Senate. Naturally, this process is slightly more involved than these statements suggest since a bill generally must first be approved by a committee responsible for that specific legislative matter. Whether a bill makes it to the entire legislature for a vote may well depend on whether it is deemed acceptable by the party that holds the majority of seats on that committee. If not, chances are slim that such a bill will be presented to the entire chamber for a vote, but those are side details where the process is concerned.

When a bill is presented to the chamber, whether the House or Senate, it is first debated by the members. This process is slightly different in each chamber. In the House of Representatives, a debate is simply that...a debate on the pros and cons of the proposed legislation. However, Senate rules differ in that the chamber provides for what is known as a filibuster. Under this rule, a Senator may hold the Senate hostage, so to speak, refusing to hand over the debate to another member. He/she can continue speaking as long as possible. The rules require a vote of sixty members to end the filibuster. If sixty members do not vote to end the filibuster, the speaker may continue until the Senate drops the proposed bill from the agenda and moves on. For obvious reasons, this is a method most generally used by the minority party to prevent the majority party from forcing through legislation. It serves as an instrument of protection for the minority party and their constituents.

The history of the filibuster is a bit muddy with a couple different perspectives on its origin and usage over the years. However, it is said that this kind of instrument was employed as early as the time of the Roman Republic and was first used by a Roman Senator named Cato the Younger in 60 BC. In the United States, the Senate filibuster purportedly dates back to roughly 1805/1806, but its use was rather limited prior to the Civil War. Evidently the first truly successful filibuster took place in 1837 as the party of the Whigs sought to censure President Andrew Jackson. The filibuster was used to prevent the President's Democrat Party from expunging that censure.

Many changes have occurred over the past two centuries where the filibuster is concerned, but it seems the most useful change, which is not really a Senate rule, is that filibusters rarely take place, primarily because the mere threat of a filibuster is sufficient. If the majority party knows they lack the votes to end the filibuster, the proposal will be dropped, and attention will be given to other matters.

Assuming a bill reaches the floor of the chamber for a vote, it simply takes a majority of the membership to pass that legislation. The Senate requires a "Yea" vote of 51 of the 100 members and a "Yea" vote of 218 of the 435 is needed in the House of Representatives. If the bill is successful in the chamber where it originated, it is then sent to the other chamber for consideration.

It is not unusual for the two chambers to agree on the basic principles included in a bill but disagree on some of the details. For instance, the Senate may challenge certain provisions in a piece of legislation that had been passed by the House of Representatives. In such a case, Senators might revise portions of the bill and pass their own version. When this happens, the two chambers will seek to compromise on matters of dispute and develop a document that will be approved by both the House of Representatives and the Senate.

Once a bill passes both chambers, it is sent to the White House for the president's signature. At that time, the president has three options. He can add his signature to the bill, making it the law of the land. His second option is to reject (veto) the bill and return it to the chamber from which it came. Finally, he can simply do nothing. If, after ten days, the president has neither signed the bill nor returned it to the legislature, the bill automatically becomes law.

What happens if the president vetoes the bill and returns it to Congress? The Congress can 1) accept the president's rejection and do nothing or 2) both chambers may vote again for passage. If two-thirds of each chamber (67 members of the Senate and 290 members in the House) vote in favor of the bill's passage, that vote overrides the president's veto, and the bill becomes a law.

Clause 3: *Every Order, Resolution, or Vote to which the Concurrence of the Senate and House of Representatives may be necessary (except on a question of Adjournment) shall be presented to the President of the United States; and before the Same shall take Effect, shall be approved by him, or being disapproved by him, shall be repassed by two thirds of the Senate and House of*

Representatives, according to the Rules and Limitations prescribed in the Case of a Bill.

Internal rules developed by and for the House of Representatives need not be approved by the president. The same is true of the Senate. These chambers constitute their own self-governing, distinct branch of the government. However, this section makes clear that those matters that affect the citizenry, which includes any decision that must be approved by both chambers, must also be approved by the president. In such a case, all the processes listed above concerning the passing of legislature would apply.

Section 8

Clause 1: *The Congress shall have Power To lay and collect Taxes, Duties, Imposts and Excises, to pay the Debts and provide for the common Defence and general Welfare of the United States; but all Duties, Imposts and Excises shall be uniform throughout the United States;*

While much of the Constitution focuses on governmental limitations as a matter of protecting the rights of the citizenry, this section specifically spells out some of the responsibilities of the federal government. Beyond the role of proposing and passing laws, mentioned in the previous section, here the founders describe the positive role and responsibilities of Congress. For instance, it is the role of Congress, through the processes described in the Constitution, to collect the revenues designed to provide for the efficient operation of that government. However, it is also the responsibility of Congress to see that taxes are collected uniformly. Congress is not to discriminate in its use of the taxation function based on race, sex, etc. Similarly, taxation must not be weaponized against political enemies as a matter of controlling anyone whose ideas fail to harmonize with those in control of Congress. Taxation methods should always be a matter of provision and not a matter of politics.

Clause 2: *To borrow Money on the credit of the United States;*

From time to time, it may be necessary for the federal government to borrow money in order to pay the costs of governmental operations. Historically, this has especially been true during times of war when costs can dramatically and unexpectedly increase. It has often been the practice to borrow that money directly from the citizenry through the sale of government bonds, etc. However, the instrument described here has also led the federal government to borrow from other nations from time to time. This has occurred more often over recent decades. Nonetheless, any debts owed by the government are guaranteed by the full faith and credit of the United States of America.

Clause 3: *To regulate Commerce with foreign Nations, and among the several States, and with the Indian Tribes;*

Regulation of commerce is a significant responsibility of Congress. While intra-state commerce is to be regulated internally, oversight of interstate commerce is, at least partially, a function of the federal government...specifically, Congress. Still, for the most part, Congress need not be too involved in interstate commerce except where issues arise that require federal input.

Much of Congress's oversight of trade focuses on international commerce. Dealing with other nations is not generally a function of individual states. That is not to say that an individual company cannot have dealings with an equally independent company in another country, but such relationships are subject to federal supervision.

Also, Congress is responsible for commerce where Indian tribes are concerned. This often involves special consideration for the indigenous people where business and taxation are concerned, based on the fact that they were here first. The land currently occupied by the United States of America was the home of the Indians (commonly called Native Americans) prior to the influx of European settlers. For this reason, it is believed that Indians deserve certain benefits and considerations where commerce is concerned.

Clause 4: *To establish an uniform Rule of Naturalization, and uniform Laws on the subject of Bankruptcies throughout the United States;*

It is a natural phenomenon for individuals to migrate to various countries across the globe. People relocate for assorted reasons including family, health, economics, etc. The Founding Fathers placed upon the shoulders of Congress the responsibility for developing an equitable system that would provide the opportunity for people of other nations to relocate in the United States…a process known as naturalization.

The idea behind equitable naturalization is that both the United States and those who migrate to the United States should benefit. The process should encourage the immigration of individuals who can contribute societally to the well-being of the country and discourage/prevent the influx of those who might undermine the country's welfare (criminals, etc.).

It is also the responsibility of Congress to establish rules of bankruptcy that apply universally through the states. This was done in recognition of the fact that many creditors (banks, etc.) would quite often have multi-state locations. That being the case, it made sense for Congress to establish rules overseeing the regulation of bankruptcies.

Clause 5: *To coin Money, regulate the Value thereof, and of foreign Coin, and fix the Standard of Weights and Measures.*

The Articles of Confederation failed to provide for the monetization of the colonial economy. Given those circumstances, the assorted states developed some of their own monetary systems. That worked fine within the boundaries of each state, but it made interstate commerce very difficult. James Madison wrote in Federalist No. 44 of the issues arising from coinage by individual states.

> …a right of coinage in the particular States could have no other effect than to multiply expensive mints and diversify the forms and weights of the circulating pieces. The latter inconveniency defeats one purpose for which the power was originally submitted to the federal head; and as far as the former might prevent an inconvenient remittance of gold and silver to the central mint for recoinage, the end can be as well attained by local mints established under the general authority.[23]

The Constitution placed upon the United States Congress the responsibility to develop a monetary system that could apply equally

---

[23] Madison, James, Federalist No. 44.

through the entire country. Along with a consistent system of coinage, including paper money, Congress needed to develop a method of weights and measures to help people and businesses navigate that system.

Some may wonder why the United States uses the English system of measurement rather than the metric system that is employed by so many other nations. The truth is that the English system is the more established form of measurement. At the time Congress set out to establish a system for use in the United States, the metric system was incomplete. It was developed by the French in the eighteenth and nineteenth centuries.

While the metric system has been accepted by many of the world's nations, the English system has a much deeper history dating back to the ancient cultures of Rome, Greece, Egypt, etc. Attempts have been made to employ the metric system in the United States to make international trade easier, but so far success has been limited.

Clause 6: *To provide for the Punishment of counterfeiting the Securities and current Coin of the United States;*

Complementing the responsibility for providing a consistent monetary system, it naturally fell upon Congress to address the counterfeiting of money that was sure to take place. Just as it fell (and falls) upon Congress to establish federal laws for other crimes, the founders recognized the authority of Congress to develop rules concerning coinage and determine equitable punishment for those who sought to take advantage by copying federal coinage for personal gain.

Only the federal government would be allowed to produce coinage and paper money that could be used for business transactions.

Clause 7: *To establish Post Offices and post Roads;*

Some may wonder why the Founding Fathers thought Congress should be given responsibility for postal delivery services, thinking the public might be better served by leaving this to the private sector. It is an issue that is only briefly mentioned in Federalist No. 42. The reason is that they saw this as a matter heavily weighing on interstate commerce and interstate communications. This logic makes even more sense when weighed against the reasoning behind the *post roads*. In Federalist No. 42, James Madison wrote:

> The power of establishing post roads must, in every view, be a harmless power, and may, perhaps, by judicious management, become productive of great public conveniency. Nothing which tends to facilitate the intercourse between the States can be deemed unworthy of the public care.[24]

What is the meaning of the term *post roads*? This phrase deals specifically with roads used by the postal service for mail delivery. At the time the Constitution was written, mail was not delivered to individual residences, but to post offices (often located in general stores). It was held that it should naturally fall upon the shoulders of Congress to establish and oversee roads used by the mail services to assure safe delivery.

---

[24] Madison, James, Federalist No. 42.

In early colonial times mail was generally sent via private couriers or through family members who happened to be traveling. In the mid 1700's, Benjamin Franklin, who was busy overseeing Britain's colonial mail service at the time, developed a system that would circumvent Britain's oversight and speed deliveries among the colonies – particularly between Philadelphia and New York. This was pivotal where the American Revolution was concerned as it allowed the founders to communicate revolutionary strategies below the British radar.

With the constitutional authority granted them, Congress developed a more sophisticated delivery system in the early 1790's that was intended to benefit the citizenry. Businesses (industry, lawyers, etc.) were charged higher prices to help subsidize less costly delivery services for individuals. The development of railroads and the Pony Express later added to the flexibility and efficiency of the postal service.

Clause 8: *To promote the Progress of Science and useful Arts, by securing for limited Times to Authors and Inventors the exclusive Right to their respective Writings and Discoveries;*

Congress is not to be the purveyor of invention/creativity. The founders determined that the private sector would be much more efficient at such things. Nonetheless, it is the role of Congress to provide a level playing field for those in the private sector who would participate.

Providing a level field of play involved ensuring that individuals and/or companies would be credited and justly compensated for their efforts. It was left to Congress to provide a system that would recognize ownership by authors and inventors, preventing copycats from unjustly benefiting from work done by others.

Clause 9: *To constitute Tribunals inferior to the supreme Court;*

Article III of the Constitution establishes the Supreme Court as a separate but equal branch of the federal government. It is interesting, then, that the Founding Fathers determined that subsidiary federal courts should be developed, not by the Supreme Court, but by Congress.

Perhaps the reason for this seeming disconnect was concern that the Supreme Court must be able to review, with an independent and unbiased perspective, decisions handed down by judges in those lower courts. This is one of three major court-related issues discussed in Federalist No. 22 as Alexander Hamilton wrote:

> We often see not only different courts but the judges of the same court differing from each other. To avoid the confusion which would unavoidably result from the contradictory decisions of a number of independent judicatories, all nations have found it necessary to establish one court paramount to the rest, possessing a general superintendence, and authorized to settle and declare in the last resort a uniform rule of civil justice.[25]

He penned similar thoughts in Federalist No. 81 when discussing "…the partition of the judiciary authority between different courts, and their relations to each other,"[26] stressing the need for a court system structured to provide unbiased judgment.

---

[25] Hamilton, Alexander, Federalist No. 22.
[26] Hamilton, Alexander, Federalist No. 81.

Clause 10: *To define and punish Piracies and Felonies committed on the high Seas, and Offences against the Law of Nations;*

The principle behind these words concerning activity on the water is that it was important to avoid giving the criminal element a sense of *free rein* on the oceans. Crime, in a general sense, is deemed to not only be considered an act against another individual or business, but also an act against government. This was discussed by James Madison when, in Federalist No. 42, he wrote:

> The power to define and punish piracies and felonies committed on the high seas, and offenses against the law of nations, belongs with equal propriety to the general government, and is a still greater improvement on the articles of Confederation.[27]

If a person commits a crime on the water, whether piracy, murder, or some other act deemed criminal by the laws of the U. S., and that person is later found within the boundaries of the United States, it is naturally incumbent on government to hold them to account for such infractions. This governmental responsibility is plainly and deliberately established in this article.

Clause 11: *To declare War, grant Letters of Marque and Reprisal, and make Rules concerning Captures on Land and Water;*

The authority to declare war is placed specifically in congressional hands in this clause. This involves the employment of military force in defense of the United States and her allies, or to address situations that involve the security of the country in some fashion.

---

[27] Madison, James, Federalist No. 42.

What did the founders have in mind with the phrase that authorizes "Letters of Marque and Reprisal (see Declaration of Independence, Grievance No. 26) and to make Rules concerning Captures on Land and Water?" In wartime, it may be efficient, from time to time, to engage the services of private citizens, generally as a matter of interrupting the enemy's free flow of commerce, to affect a desired outcome. This often involves vessels on the high seas interfering with the flow of enemy supplies. It is a practice that was heavily used in the Revolutionary War as well as the War of 1812. Congress and courts have typically allowed the owners of vessels involved in this kind of activity to profit from their efforts by keeping the captured goods.

Clause 12: *To raise and support Armies, but no Appropriation of Money to that Use shall be for a longer Term than two Years;*

One of the hotly disputed issues prior to the Constitution's ratification focused on the Founding Fathers' argument in favor of *standing armies*. This term basically speaks to the maintaining of a federal military force in times of peace rather than limiting the raising of an army to those times when it was deemed necessary as a matter of defense. The citizens of many states were concerned that a standing army could be turned against the citizenry by elected politicians who sought to become more powerful than the Constitution intended and/or other leaders (perhaps military) who did not agree with decisions made by elected officials or the citizens who voted them into office. So great was the concern that, at the time, Pennsylvania's Bill of Rights stated specifically that standing armies *are dangerous to liberty, and ought not to be kept up in time of peace*. After all, they were not far removed from a time when England had declared that civil government in America must submit to the authority of Britain's military arm.

Concern over the potential threat of a standing army was certainly legitimate, especially when the power of a standing army was combined with the government's unlimited capacity for taxation. That complement of powers could be combined to completely obliterate the rights of the citizenry. James Madison stated this plainly in Federalist No. 41, describing it as the potential for being "crushed between standing armies and perpetual taxes."[28] Still, the strong case in favor of a standing army was successfully formulated in several sections of the Federalist Papers. Perhaps the most reasonable position favoring standing armies was given by Alexander Hamilton in Federalist No. 25, where he wrote:

> If, to obviate this consequence, it should be resolved to extend the prohibition to the raising of armies in time of peace, the United States would then exhibit the most extraordinary spectacle which the world has yet seen, that of a nation incapacitated by its Constitution to prepare for defense, before it was actually invaded.[29]

Hamilton's argument, along with many other assertions offered in the Federalist Papers, made sense. Still, the issue of a standing army in complement with the unlimited potential for taxation to support that army needed to be addressed. For this reason, the Constitution limits the appropriation of military funding to a period of two years.

---

[28] Hamilton, Alexander, Federalist No. 41
[29] Hamilton, Alexander, Federalist No. 25.

Hamilton wrote the following to explain the cautionary insertion of this provision:

> Next to the effectual establishment of the Union, the best possible precaution against danger from standing armies is a limitation of the term for which revenue may be appropriated to their support.[30]

Admittedly, this seems to provide for a rather weak defense against a powerful military, since much damage could be done over a period of two years. Nonetheless, it offers what might be seen as a small measure of protection against the potential of a military state.

Clause 13: *To provide and maintain a Navy;*

The same rules and arguments related to the raising and sustaining of land military forces also apply to Congress's ability to establish and maintain naval military forces.

Clause 14: *To make Rules for the Government and Regulation of the land and naval Forces;*

The founders determined that it was important to have joint control over the military forces of the United States. While the president serves as Commander in Chief of the military, which will be discussed in detail in Article II, it is on the shoulders of Congress to establish rules and regulations concerning said military. This oversight includes the role of Congress to determine what financial resources should be available for military activity.

---

[30] ibid

The role of Congress with respect to the military was discussed at length by Alexander Hamilton in Federalist No. 23 where he wrote in summary:

> The authorities essential to the common defense are these: to raise armies; to build and equip fleets; to prescribe the rules for the government of both; to direct their operations; to provide for their support.[31]

The idea of shared authority over military forces was adopted from the English model. While the King held executive authority over the military, Parliament was known to intervene on occasion as a matter of balance. It was determined both in England and by the authors of the United States Constitution that collaborative management could provide that necessary balance. According to The University of Chicago Press:

> The whole power is far more safe in the hands of congress, than of the executive; since otherwise the most summary and severe punishments might be inflicted at the mere will of the executive.[32]

As can be seen here, the president's role as Commander in Chief of the military complex is not unrestricted. Executive employment of the U.S. military is limited by the rules and regulations devised by Congress.

Clause 15: *To provide for calling forth the Militia to execute the Laws of the Union, suppress Insurrections and repel Invasions;*

---

[31] Hamilton, Alexander, Federalist No. 23
[32] The Founders Constitution, *Joseph Story, Commentaries on the Constitution 3:§§ 1192--93*, https://press-pubs.uchicago.edu/founders/documents/a1_8_14s3.html, accessed August 19, 2023.

The meaning of the word *Militia* is often debated. Official description of this term is clarified in the U.S. Code, Title 10, Section 246, Subtitle A where it is defined as follows:

> (a) The militia of the United States consists of all able-bodied males at least 17 years of age and, except as provided in section 313 of title 32, under 45 years of age who are, or who have made a declaration of intention to become, citizens of the United States and of female citizens of the United States who are members of the National Guard. (b) The classes of the militia are— (1) the organized militia, which consists of the National Guard and the Naval Militia; and (2) the unorganized militia, which consists of the members of the militia who are not members of the National Guard or the Naval Militia.[33]

While this official definition of *Militia* includes both "Naval Militia" and "Unorganized Militia," it should be noted that only a handful of states maintain a Naval Militia (many states are surrounded by land). Additionally, Unorganized Militia, consisting of citizen militia who are not members of the National Guard or Naval Militia, is neither directly controlled by nor formally subject to the government of the states where they are located. Neither is the unorganized militia subject to federalization by the federal government.

The term *Militia*, as employed in this clause in Article 1, speaks specifically to the National Guard, which is a state-sponsored organization found in individual states of the United States. This distinction is established in The National Defense Act of 1916. The act states that:

---

[33] Justia Law, U.S. Code, Title 10, Section 246, Subtitle A – *Militia: Composition and Classes,*, https://law.justia.com

The provisions of this title in respect to the militia shall be applicable only to militia organized as a land force.[34]

The National Defense Act of 1916 was repealed with the passage of The Military Selective Service Act of 1956, but the definitions of organized an unorganized militia never changed. As a state-sponsored organization, authority over the National Guard falls upon state officials as designated in the constitutions of the individual states. However, Congress reserves the right to call the National Guard into federal service when the need is warranted.

> **Clause 16:** *To provide for organizing, arming, and disciplining, the Militia, and for governing such Part of them as may be employed in the Service of the United States, reserving to the States respectively, the Appointment of the Officers, and the Authority of training the Militia according to the discipline prescribed by Congress;*

Under normal conditions, authority over the National Guard in a particular state lies with that state. However, when the National Guard is called into national service, authority and oversight falls upon the shoulders of the federal government (specifically Congress). During such deployment, the federal government is responsible for "organizing, arming, and disciplining the Militia."

> **Clause 17:** *To exercise exclusive Legislation in all Cases whatsoever, over such District (not exceeding ten Miles square) as may, by Cession of particular States, and the Acceptance of Congress, become the Seat of Government of the United States, and to exercise like Authority over all Places purchased by the Consent of the Legislature of the State in which the Same shall be, for the*

---

[34] U. S. Government Publishing Office, *Armed Forces*, https://www.govinfo.gov/content/pkg/USCODE-2016-title10/pdf/USCODE-2016-title10-subtitleA-partI-chap13.pdf, Accessed August 19, 2023.

Erection of Forts, Magazines, Arsenals, dock-Yards, and other needful Buildings;–And

On June 21, 1783, in what has come to be known as the Pennsylvania Mutiny, anti-government soldiers of the Continental Army marched on the meeting of Congress being held in Philadelphia, physically threatening and verbally abusing the members. When neither the officials of the city of Philadelphia nor the state of Pennsylvania agreed to provide protection, the men of the Congress were forced to flee the city. This incident led to the inclusion of what is known as the Seat of Government Clause or Enclave Clause.

The founders recognized the need for Congress to formally establish a physical location from which the affairs of the people could be conducted. This location, which was not to exceed ten miles square, was to fall outside the jurisdiction of any of the states. Authority over this territory would fall upon Congress. In other words, the members of Congress would be responsible for providing their own security.

Establishing a seat of government outside state authority would ensure that no individual state might seek to exert undue influence upon Congress or other branches of the federal government. In 1790, the District of Columbia was born through the cession of land from the states of Virginia and Maryland.

The founders also recognized the wisdom in allowing Congress to establish other properties that would be strictly subject to federal oversight including locations necessary for the provision and operation of military activities. These properties were to be purchased from the individual states upon approval by the state legislatures.

Clause 18: *To make all Laws which shall be necessary and proper for carrying into Execution the foregoing Powers, and all other Powers vested by this Constitution in the Government of the United States, or in any Department or Officer thereof.*

The Necessary and Proper Clause resulted from the founders' experience with the weaknesses of the Articles of Confederation that had served as the nation's first Constitution. While the current U.S. Constitution limits the scope of federal authority, the Articles of Confederation was much more restrictive. The founders sought to overcome this shortcoming with this clause.

Some have suggested that Clause 18 serves to supersede federal constitutional limitations and that, when deemed proper the federal government may cross the lines of constitutional constraint. In other words, it is argued that The Necessary and Proper Clause dangerously affords the federal government unlimited authority, but that was not the founders' intent. The purpose here was to recognize the federal authority *within the bounds of constitutional restrictions.*

Federal limitation is assigned in the Tenth Amendment where is stated, "The powers not delegated to the United States by the Constitution, nor prohibited by it to the States, are reserved to the States respectively, or to the people." The fact that the Tenth Amendment was written after the introduction of this clause confutes any argument in favor of unlimited federal power. The stronger line of reasoning is that the Tenth Amendment was introduced to clarify and emphasize federal limitations.

A check on federal overreach is recognized within the Necessary and Proper Clause itself as the authority of the legislature "to make all Laws which shall be necessary and proper" is confined to writing of laws that provide for the execution of "foregoing Powers." In other words, the founders' intent was that the legislative branch is to be limited to passing laws within the framework of authority designated to the federal government as provided in the Constitution.

Section 9

Clause 1: *The Migration or Importation of such Persons as any of the States now existing shall think proper to admit, shall not be prohibited by the Congress prior to the Year one thousand eight hundred and eight, but a Tax or duty may be imposed on such Importation, not exceeding ten dollars for each Person.*

The subject matter of the first clause of Section 9 is not fully evident in a candid reading of the text since it could be understood to address the topic of simple immigration. However, the fact is that this clause, commonly referred to as The Slave Trade Clause, specifically tackles the practice of importing slaves.

Even as the Constitution was being written, the founders knew that they would eventually have to deal with the topic of slavery. However, they were also aware that the document would never be ratified by southern states if slavery was outlawed. Therefore, they chose to *kick the can down the road*, so to speak.

It was decided that the federal government's ability to impede the importation of slaves should be postponed for twenty years (these words were written in the late 1780's), Still, the clause provided for a measure of control over the slave trade in that a tax would be levied by the federal government for each slave brought into the country. While this did not prohibit slavery, the hope was that it would discourage the practice by raising the cost for those who wished to participate in that trade. The clause did not speak to the ownership of slaves. It only addressed the importation of slaves.

It is interesting to note that this is the only clause in the Constitution that included an expiration date. Beyond the year 1807, the clause would lose all relevance since the prohibition of federal intervention into the slave trade business expired on January 1, 1808. President Thomas Jefferson, an opponent of the slave trade business (though he was himself a slave owner), anticipated the expiration of this clause. He stated, in an address to Congress in December 1806:

> I congratulate you, fellow-citizens, on the approach of the period at which you may interpose your authority constitutionally to withdraw the citizens of the United States from all further participation in those violations of human rights which have been so long continued on the unoffending inhabitants of Africa, and which the morality, the reputation, and the best interests of our country have long been eager to proscribe.[35]

In 1807, Congress passed a statute prohibiting the importation of slaves. That statue took effect on January 1, 1808. Interestingly, it was argued by some at the time that the statute was unconstitutional since the Constitution did not designate to Congress control over the slave trade business. The argument was overcome as Congress used its

---

[35] The National Constitution Center, *The Slave Trade Clause*, https://constitutioncenter.org/the-constitution/articles/article-i/clauses/761, Accessed September 7, 2023.

authority over foreign and interstate commerce to make the case. However, it seems that, if congressional authority over slave trading was constitutionally limited to a defined period of time, once that time restraint had been satisfied, the Constitution did indeed provide for federal authority over that specific trade.

Clause 2: *The Privilege of the Writ of Habeas Corpus shall not be suspended, unless when in Cases of Rebellion or Invasion the public Safety may require it.*

A Writ is, in a basic sense, a mandatory written order generally proffered by a judge or other person of authority that demands action. The term Habeas Corpus, translated from its Latin origin, means *you should have the body*, or *show me the body*. The Writ of Habeas Corpus, identified in this clause, is often referred to historically and globally as *The Great Writ.*

This privilege has historically served as a protection for individuals against arbitrary and unequal application of the law by those in power. The clause prohibits imprisonment of any individual without a hearing to determine the legitimacy of that confinement. When an individual is accused of a crime and taken into custody by those in authority, that person must be allowed to appear before an independent judge (show me the body) who can determine the legitimacy of the arrest. If it is determined by the judge that detention is not justified, this clause requires that the accused be released from custody.

The clause does not establish the Privilege of the Writ of Habeas Corpus. Instead, the founders simply recognized the worthy historical application of this privilege and considered it a natural or unalienable privilege much like life, liberty, and the pursuit of happiness were deemed unalienable rights in the Declaration of Independence.

Exceptions were written within the clause for certain cases, such as violent rebellions or hostile invasions, where the safety of the public may be at risk. In such cases, the privilege may be suspended. It should come as no surprise that the suspension of habeas corpus has been used and challenged many times. While a host of court decisions have been secured over the years, legitimate application of this suspension clause is generally determined on a case-by-case basis.

Clause 3: *No Bill of Attainder or ex post facto Law shall be passed.*

The U.S. Constitution establishes three equal branches of the federal government. These are the legislative, executive, and judicial branches. This clause was written to prevent assumption of the role of one branch by another branch. Specifically, the founders sought to prohibit the legislature from attempting to usurp the authority of the executive and judicial branches.

A Bill of Attainder involves a special act of the legislature whereby that body assumes the roles of the executive and judicial branches. With such an act, the legislature serves as the accuser, enforcer, and judge. In such a case, the legislature might act as accuser (executive role) as well as judge and jury (judicial role), determining a person's guilt and punishment without the legitimacy of a day in court.

In a broader sense, the clause prohibits the legislature from writing any law that, in effect, serves as a Bill of Attainder. In other words, Congress cannot write/pass legislation aimed at an individual or specific group with consequences that are specific to the person/group targeted in the bill.

Ex Post Facto laws are also prohibited in this clause, partly because they could serve as a substitute for a Bill of Attainder. The Latin phrase *Ex Post Facto* essentially means *retroactive* or *from what is done afterwards.* It is a law that is written *after the fact.* In other words, it is a law written to make someone's previous act unlawful even though it was not unlawful at the time it was carried out. It may also involve writing a statute that increases the penalty for a previous act exceeding the maximum penalty that was in place when that act was committed. An Ex Post Facto law is written to take effect prior to the date the act occurred.

Ex Post Facto arguments are not always as straightforward as one might expect. For instance, consider the following case concerning a 1993 California law.

> In 1993, California enacted a new criminal statute of limitations permitting prosecution for sex-related child abuse where the prior limitations period has expired if the prosecution is begun within one year of a victim's report to police. In 1998, Marion Stogner was indicted for sex-related child abuse committed between 1955 and 1973. Without the new statute allowing revival of the State's cause of action, California could not have prosecuted Stogner. Stogner moved to dismiss the complaint on the ground that the Ex Post Facto Clause forbids revival of a previously time-barred prosecution. The trial court agreed, but the California Court of Appeal reversed. The trial court denied Stogner's subsequent dismissal motion, in which he argued that his prosecution violated the Ex Post Facto and Due Process Clauses. The Court of Appeal affirmed.[36]

---

[36] Oyez, *Stogner v. California*, www.oyez.org/cases/2002/01-1757. Accessed September 7, 2023.

In this case, different courts expressed varying opinions. Ultimately, the Supreme Court, in a 5-4 decision, concluded that Article I, Section 9, Clause 3, did indeed apply and found in favor of Marion Stogner.

Clause 4: *No Capitation, or other direct, Tax shall be laid, unless in Proportion to the Census or enumeration herein before directed to be taken.*

Prior to the ratification of the Sixteenth Amendment in 1913, most federal revenue was derived from tariffs on imports from other countries and excise taxes that were charged against certain goods and services. This clause specifically prevented Congress from charging a per capita (per individual) tax or fee on the states or the citizens.

Clause 5: *No Tax or Duty shall be laid on Articles exported from any State.*

As a matter of encouraging business across state lines, Congress was prevented from charging taxes on interstate commerce. There was some concern that Congress may unevenly levy taxes on the transactions of various states, favoring certain states while, at the same time, levying burdensome and injurious taxes on other states.

At the time the Constitution was written, southern states depended heavily on the export of cash goods (cotton, tobacco, etc.) to other states to maintain a sound economy. It is unlikely that the Constitution would have received the necessary votes for ratification without the presence of this clause.

Clause 6: *No Preference shall be given by any Regulation of Commerce or Revenue to the Ports of one State over those of* *another: nor shall Vessels bound to, or from, one State, be obliged to enter, clear, or pay Duties in another.*

Congress was here prohibited from levying taxes in a fashion that effectively served to favor certain states over others. For instance, taxing certain forms of transport of goods might impact some states more heavily than others. An example might be a tax on transportation by water vessels that could negatively impact fishing and other industries relying heavily on that sort of transport and, as a result, heavily influence the economies of those states with a dependence on water industries. Additionally, charging taxes or fees for vehicles transporting goods between states was forbidden.

Clause 7: *No Money shall be drawn from the Treasury, but in Consequence of Appropriations made by Law; and a regular Statement and Account of the Receipts and Expenditures of all public Money shall be published from time to time.*

Where federal spending is concerned, the power of the purse is vested specifically in the House of Representatives. The reasons for this were explained in the earlier discussion concerning Article I, Section 7, Clause 1. This clause in Section 9, commonly known as The Appropriations Clause, does not grant power, since the House of Representatives was made the holder of the purse in the earlier article. The Appropriations Clause creates a legislative duty for Congress to exercise responsible control over federal funds and enjoins the president and federal agencies to limit spending to funding appropriated by Congress. Here it is made clear that other branches of government and federal agencies must follow proper procedures to be able to access the funds necessary to operate those organizations.

The withdrawal of funds from the federal coffers requires the passage of laws by the House and the Senate and signed by the president. However, all spending bills are to originate in the House of Representatives. This means that if the Senate or Executive Branch seeks access to federal funds, they must persuade the members of the House of Representatives concerning the merit of the request. Once the process has been completed, funds can be transferred from the treasury to the appropriate branch.

What is unstated here, but is implicit within the framework of the Constitution, is that, while the House of Representatives serves as the gatekeeper where spending is concerned, the legislature is constitutionally obligated to provide funding for the basic functions of other branches that are specifically delineated in the document.

Clause 8: *No Title of Nobility shall be granted by the United States: And no Person holding any Office of Profit or Trust under them, shall, without the Consent of the Congress, accept of any present, Emolument, Office, or Title, of any kind whatever, from any King, Prince, or foreign State.*

Prior to the eighteenth century, it was not uncommon for a country's foreign ambassadors, emissaries, and diplomats to receive expensive gifts from those nations where they were stationed, particularly as they left those assignments to return home. No doubt, their efforts and negotiations in foreign matters were often unduly influenced in anticipation of the gifts they hoped to receive.

It seems it was the Netherlands who first addressed this practice and the potential corruption that accompanied it. In the seventeenth century, the Dutch prohibited such gifts or any special recognition or privileges by royal families or foreign governments. In the eighteenth century, other nations took note of the prohibition established by the Dutch and began to follow suit.

In this, The Foreign Emoluments Clause, the founders sought to address the frailty inherent in a Republican form of government. Corruption by those in authority could easily undo all that the founders sought to establish. If ambassadors or others in the federal government were allowed to become improperly entwined with foreign states through clandestine gifts or direct payments of compensation from other nations, the results could be catastrophic.

Understanding that this clause could cause issues with countries who faithfully gifted departing diplomats, the founders offered an exception to the rule. A governmental representative would be allowed to keep what he/she received from a foreign entity by receiving congressional approval. As an example, in 1785, Benjamin Franklin was to return to America, having served several years as America's ambassador to France. Upon his departure, Louis XVI, the King of France, gifted Mr. Franklin with a very expensive diamond-encrusted snuff box (decorated with 408 diamonds). Upon congressional approval, Mr. Franklin was allowed to keep the gift.

This clause also prohibits the granting of titles of nobility by the federal government of the United States. The reason should be obvious in that the establishment of nobility in the United States would be contrary to the very idea of a republic. Establishing a distinct class of nobility would eventually return the colonists to the very kind of government suppression they had fought a Revolution to escape.

Section 10

Clause 1: *No State shall enter into any Treaty, Alliance, or Confederation; grant Letters of Marque and Reprisal; coin Money; emit Bills of Credit; make any Thing but gold and silver Coin a Tender in Payment of Debts; pass any Bill of Attainder, ex post facto Law, or Law impairing the Obligation of Contracts, or grant any Title of Nobility.*

The founders put considerable thought into declaring and defining the limitations placed upon the federal government. Still, certain duties and responsibilities are most effectively addressed at the federal level. It was important to recognize the federal government's authority in those matters. To a certain degree, this was accomplished by restricting states' authority where those matters were concerned. Section 10 delineates some of those responsibilities by prohibiting states from intervening in those duties that must be considered federal obligations.

The first clause in Section 10 addresses certain state restrictions that are also prohibited at the federal level in Section 9. For instance, this clause forbids individual states from granting titles of nobility or establishing a class of noblemen or women. This is a restriction that applies at both the federal and state levels since it would not serve the republic to establish such a class of people. Additionally, the states are not allowed to pass a Bill of Attainder or Ex Post Facto laws.

The states are prohibited from entering into treaties, alliances, or confederations with foreign governments or entities. The reason for this is that it could be difficult to manage foreign relations if individual states wrote agreements that conflicted with agreements written by other states. Additionally, a state's treaty with a foreign government may negatively impact other states, even if that impact was unintentional. States are also barred from granting Letters of Marque and Reprisal. Such documents are generally limited to wartime activities and defense of the nation falls on the federal government, not the states.

States are prohibited from coining money. This is a role assigned to the federal government. Also, states were prohibited from issuing Bills of Credit. This was intended to limit borrowing by the states. These last two restrictions – the coining of money and the restriction on borrowing – stemmed from weaknesses in the Articles of Confederation. Under that document, individual states could coin money. While the federal government reserved the right to declare the value of currency coined by the states, it was a challenging system that reeked economic havoc. Also, some states were known to borrow money while lacking the ability, through taxation, to repay the debt. This, too, caused economic turmoil.

Clause 2: *No State shall, without the Consent of the Congress, lay any Imposts or Duties on Imports or Exports, except what may be absolutely necessary for executing it's inspection Laws: and the net*

Produce of all Duties and Imposts, laid by any State on Imports or Exports, shall be for the Use of the Treasury of the United States; and all such Laws shall be subject to the Revision and Controul of the Congress.

The states are limited, but not fully prohibited from imposing duties (fees) on imports and exports. The founders recognized the costs involved in transporting goods and left the door open for states to recoup those costs. However, the imposition of duties was subject to congressional oversight and approval. Additionally, any tariffs collected in excess of cost must be submitted to the U.S. Treasury.

In the mid-1800's the argument was raised that this clause applied not only to tariffs and fees collected from foreign countries, but also fees charged for imports and exports from other states within the Union. In 1869, the Supreme Court ruled that the founders' clear intent was to prevent individual states from collecting duties from foreign countries, determining that they did not intend this clause to apply to interstate commerce.

Clause 3: *No State shall, without the Consent of Congress, lay any Duty of Tonnage, keep Troops, or Ships of War in time of Peace, enter into any Agreement or Compact with another State, or with a foreign Power, or engage in War, unless actually invaded, or in such imminent Danger as will not admit of delay.*

The Compact Clause required very little debate among the founders. The clause blocks any state from maintaining a military force in times of peace. Additionally, no state may form military alliances with any foreign nation; nor could an individual state engage in war unless invaded. The framers of the Constitution were fully aware that military alliances between states or between the states and foreign powers would seriously threaten the Union. However, the clause does not apply to the National Guard.

The Articles of Confederation contained comparable prohibitions, but this language is much stronger than the original. The framers of the Constitution believed it was critical to communicate this in robust terms through clearly defined verbiage to ensure federal control over foreign affairs.

Chapter 6
The Executive Branch

Article II
Section 1

Clause 1: *The executive Power shall be vested in a President of the United States of America. He shall hold his Office during the Term of four Years, and, together with the Vice President, chosen for the same Term, be elected, as follows…*

The authority of the legislative branch of the federal government is vested in the numerous senators and representatives elected in the various states. There are currently 435 members in the House of Representatives and 100 members in the Senate. The Judicial branch currently holds nine Supreme Court justices in whom authority is vested. It is true that there are numerous lower courts, but ultimate federal judicial authority lies with those nine justices.

When it comes to executive authority, that power is vested in one individual, and that is the President of the United States (often referred to as P.O.T.U.S.). Authority is not vested in the president's Cabinet or in the various agencies under the umbrella of the executive branch. It is the role of the Cabinet to advise the president and to oversee the various agencies within the framework of the executive branch, but authority is vested in the president.

The president was to be elected for a four-year term but could run for additional terms. At the time, the terms of the office were not limited, so a president could continue in office if elected by the people every four years. However, Franklin D. Roosevelt is the only president who was elected beyond his second term. He was elected as president four times, but died on April 12, 1945, shortly after the start of his fourth term in office.

Generally, when campaigning for the presidency, the presidential candidate will choose an individual to run for the office of vice president. That individual serves as the back-up when the president is unable, for any reason, to fulfill the duties of the presidency. The vice president serves the president as second in command and is often given responsibility for key projects within the executive branch. This individual also serves as the President of the Senate (see Article I, Section 3, Clause 4).

Clause 2: *Each State shall appoint, in such Manner as the Legislature thereof may direct, a Number of Electors, equal to the whole Number of Senators and Representatives to which the State may be entitled in the Congress: but no Senator or Representative, or Person holding an Office of Trust or Profit under the United States, shall be appointed an Elector.*

It was incumbent on the founders to develop a system for the election of a president that, like the configuration of the legislature, considered not only the votes of the people, but the votes of the states. To meet this challenge, they formed what is known as the Electoral College consisting of what the founders called Electors. The idea behind the Electoral College was that the president should be selected by the states with the people of each state deciding, through the election process, who should receive those votes.

To accomplish this goal, it was decided that the Electoral College would consist of one vote for each of a state's members of the House of Representatives and one vote for each member of the Senate. This was intended to offer a balance between the selection of the president directly by the people and selection of a president by the states. The Electoral College currently consists of 538 votes representing 435 members of the House of Representatives and 100 Senators. In 1931, with the passage of the Twenty-third Amendment, 3 votes were added to the Electoral map to represent the District of Columbia in presidential elections.

Elected officials were forbidden from taking the role of an Elector, given the potential conflict of interest they would face in choosing the president. Most elected officials would want to choose the candidate from their own party. In fact, there has been an ongoing debate about what are known as Faithless Electors who decide to set aside the popular vote in their state and vote as they choose since no federal statute addresses the issue.

Certain states have passed laws requiring their Electors to vote according to the popular vote of the people. Other states have chosen to award electoral votes proportionally based on the percentage of popular votes received by each candidate. Still, many states have seemingly left the door open for their Electors to cast their vote for president without considering the vote of the people. Historically, however, this practice is relatively rare.

> **Clause 3:** *The Electors shall meet in their respective States, and vote by Ballot for two Persons, of whom one at least shall not be an Inhabitant of the same State with themselves. And they shall make a List of all the Persons voted for, and of the Number of Votes for each; which List they shall sign and certify, and transmit sealed to the Seat of the Government of the United States, directed to the President of the Senate. The President of the Senate shall, in the Presence of the Senate and House of Representatives, open all the Certificates, and the Votes shall then be counted. The Person having the greatest Number of Votes shall be the President, if such Number be a Majority of the whole Number of Electors appointed; and if there be more than one who have such Majority, and have an equal Number of Votes, then the House of Representatives shall immediately chuse by Ballot one of them for President; and if no Person have a Majority, then from the five highest on the List the said House shall in like Manner chuse the President. But in chusing the President, the Votes shall be taken by States, the Representation from each State having one Vote; A quorum for this Purpose shall consist of a Member or Members from two thirds of the States, and a Majority of all the States shall be necessary to a Choice. In every Case, after the Choice of the President, the Person having the greatest Number of Votes of the Electors shall be the Vice President. But if there should remain two or more who have equal Votes, the Senate shall chuse from them by Ballot the Vice President.*

Early in the history of the Union, the individual who received the most electoral votes was awarded the presidency and the person with the second highest number of electoral votes was named vice president. This caused predictable issues in that the president and vice president were opponents with differing political perspectives. For example, John Adams was elected president in 1796 and his political opponent, Thomas Jefferson, was chosen to serve as vice president. This approach was changed in 1804 with the adoption of the Twelfth

Amendment providing for the election of the *team* of president and vice president.

The process for choosing a president and vice president is intended to be simple. The people of each state vote for their favored candidate (although technically they are voting for the Elector for that candidate). After the popular votes from each state have been cast and certified, the Electors meet the following month to cast their votes. The electoral votes are then sent to the Senate for counting. The theory is that the candidate with a majority of electoral votes (currently at least 270) then takes the office in January of the following year. However, the process can become a bit messy if no candidate attains the 270 votes necessary for appointment to the office.

It is possible, particularly if an election involves more than two presidential candidates, that a single individual may not reach the 270 electoral votes necessary for appointment to the office of president. It is also possible that, with only two candidates, each candidate could receive 269 votes, resulting in a tie. If this happens, the responsibility falls upon the House of Representatives to choose who will be president.

If the decision concerning the appointment of the president goes to the House of Representatives, it is not a simple majority vote of the members of the House as one might expect. Instead, each state is allotted a single vote and the individual receiving the most votes is appointed to the office. It stands to reason, then, that the candidate whose party has a larger state representation within the House will have a significant advantage if the process goes that far. For instance, if one party holds the majority of seats in twenty-seven states and the other party holds the majority of seats in only twenty-three states, the party with the advantage in twenty-seven states will likely select their party's candidate as president.

Clause 4: *The Congress may determine the Time of chusing the Electors, and the Day on which they shall give their Votes; which Day shall be the same throughout the United States.*

All elections, whether local, state, or federal, are administered by the individual states. Thus, it is incumbent upon the state legislatures to develop the rules and methods for voting that are to be followed during any election. It is also the responsibility of state legislatures to determine the times for voting (see Article I, Section 4, Clause 1). However, this responsibility is limited, particularly where federal elections are concerned. It would be impractical for presidential elections to take place on different dates in each of the states. Therefore, the dates for federal elections are established at the federal level. Specific locations and hours for voting are generally determined at the state level.

It is also the responsibility of Congress to decide when Electors will cast their votes. This is to be the same date for each state and is generally set for mid-December following the general election held in early November.

Clause 5: *No Person except a natural born Citizen, or a Citizen of the United States, at the time of the Adoption of this Constitution, shall be eligible to the Office of President; neither shall any Person be eligible to that Office who shall not have attained to the Age of* *thirty five Years, and been fourteen Years a Resident within the United States.*

Like the qualifications for members of Congress, the qualifications for the office of president are simple. First, an individual must be a natural born citizen of the United States or a citizen at the time of the ratification of the Constitution. This begs the question: **How was citizenship to be determined given the fact that the United States was a new-born nation?**

In fact, citizenship was loosely defined and even arbitrary prior to the ratification of the Constitution. For instance, immigrants who had fought on the side of the colonies in the Revolutionary War were generally considered citizens along with those who, in some fashion, had shown their allegiance to the United States. Prior to the Constitution, a person's citizenship, or lack thereof, was decided at the state level and was often determined in the courts.

In 1790, Congress passed a Naturalization Act defining citizenship. In that act, they followed the general rules that had served as a guideline in those early years as the Constitution was written. According to The Naturalization Act, citizenship was awarded to those naturally born in the colonies and children born in foreign lands to citizens of the United States. Additionally, individuals could apply for citizenship if they were a "…free white person, who shall have resided within the limits and under the jurisdiction of the United States for the term of two years."[37]

---

[37] Immigration History, *Nationality Act of 1790*, https://immigrationhistory.org /item/1790-nationality-act/, Accessed October 3, 2023

The qualifications for president not only required citizenship, but residency within the borders of the United States of not less than fourteen years. Additionally, no one who had not attained the age of thirty-five years would be eligible for the office. Note that no educational or professional requirements were established for the office.

Clause 6: *In Case of the Removal of the President from Office, or of his Death, Resignation, or Inability to discharge the Powers and Duties of the said Office, the Same shall devolve on the Vice President, and the Congress may by law provide for the Case of Removal, Death, Resignation or Inability, both of the President and Vice President, declaring what Officer shall then act as President, and such Officer shall act accordingly, until the Disability be removed, or a President shall be elected.*

Not every president has been able to serve his full term(s) in office. A few presidents have died while in office (e.g., Abraham Lincoln, Franklin D. Roosevelt). One President, Richard M. Nixon, resigned from the office in 1974. No president has been forcibly removed from office. This clause provides for consistency in the discharge of presidential responsibilities if, for some reason, the president cannot carry out those duties.

On any occasion when the president is unable to fulfill his obligations in that office, the Constitution requires that those responsibilities fall upon the shoulders of the vice president until such time that the president is able to return to the office. Upon the president's death or permanent removal from office, the vice president will assume the office of President until the end of the current presidential term.

142

Who assumes the office of president if the vice president cannot? Assorted lines of succession have been in place over the course of time. However, in 1947, Congress passed a statute placing the resumption and responsibilities of the office of president on the Speaker of the House of Representatives if, for any reason, both the president and vice president are unavailable.

Clause 7: *The President shall, at stated Times, receive for his Services, a Compensation, which shall neither be encreased nor diminished during the Period for which he shall have been elected, and he shall not receive within that Period any other Emolument from the United States, or any of them.*

The president, as with all government employees, is entitled to be compensated for his services. This clause provides for that compensation. However, no increase in the salary of the president is allowed to take place during a single four-year term. If Congress increases the amount of compensation to be received by the president, that increase cannot take effect until the beginning of the presidential term following the passage of that increase. The current presidential salary stands at $400,000 annually, having been increased from $200,000 in 2001. There are, of course, substantial perks and sizeable expense and travel allowances that are available to the office of the president.

Clause 8: *Before he enter on the Execution of his Office, he shall take the following Oath or Affirmation:– I do solemnly swear (or affirm) that I will faithfully execute the Office of President of the United States, and will to the best of my Ability, preserve, protect and defend the Constitution of the United States.*

Upon election to office, but prior to stepping into the office of president, the newly elected chief executive is generally referred to as *president elect*. Prior to taking the reins of the executive arm of the government, the president elect is required to take an oath concerning his execution of the duties of that office. Specifically, he must swear to execute the duties that the office requires. Those duties include *preserving, protecting, and defending the Constitution of the United States*. Because this duty concerning the Constitution is embedded within the presidential oath, it stands to reason that the founders believed this to be the *primary* role of the president. All other presidential functions stem from his responsibility to "preserve, protect, and defend the Constitution."

Section 2

Clause 1: *The President shall be Commander in Chief of the Army and Navy of the United States, and of the Militia of the several States, when called into the actual Service of the United States; he may require the Opinion, in writing, of the principal Officer in each of the executive Departments, upon any Subject relating to the Duties of their respective Offices, and he shall have Power to grant Reprieves and Pardons for Offences against the United States, except in Cases of Impeachment.*

The Commander in Chief Clause, it might be said, resulted from lessons learned both during the Revolutionary War and from history generally. First, the founders understood that making the military an independent branch of government was a dangerous proposition. English history had demonstrated the pitfalls of vesting military authority in an individual or group outside political leadership.

Additionally, the Revolutionary War had taught them that spreading that authority too thin could have catastrophic consequences.

It was decided that authority over the military complex should be vested in the President of the United States and that this person, having been chosen by the people, should be relied upon to make decisions where the use of the military is concerned. That authority is limited, at least to a certain extent, in that Congress establishes guidelines for military use. Also, only Congress can formally declare war against another nation. Other than these provisions, the president has plenary authority over the military forces of the United States.

When necessary, the president also has constitutional authority to call into federal service the militia (National Guard) from the states when their use by the federal government is required. When this happens, members of the militia fall under the direct supervision of the federal government and the President of the United States.

Coupled with the Advice and Consent of the Senate, the president may nominate candidates to head the various major departments of the Executive Branch of the federal government (e.g., Department of Treasury, Department of Defense, etc.). Upon Senate approval, the nominee takes charge of the department for which that person was selected. The heads of these major departments serve as the president's Cabinet, offering advice on matters of the state.

The president also has the authority to grant reprieves and pardons for crimes committed or to commute (reduce) someone's sentence. This authority, however, extends only to federal criminal offenses. The president may not offer pardons in instances of impeachment or crimes prosecuted under state laws. The president's authority to pardon is broad and many presidents have, at the end of their terms in office, made liberal use of the ability to pardon those convicted of crimes.

Many people have questioned the wisdom of this clause. Placing in the hands of one individual the power to release convicted criminals without question or reason has been challenged in the Supreme Court. However, in *Ex Parte Garland* (1866), the Court ruled that:

> The power of pardon conferred by the Constitution upon the President is unlimited except in cases of impeachment. It extends to every offence known to the law, and may be exercised at any time after its commission, either before legal proceedings are taken or during their pendency, or after conviction and judgment. The power is not subject to legislative control.

When asked to consider judicial review after a presidential pardon in *Connecticut Board of Pardons v. Dumschat* (1981), the Supreme Court ruled that presidential pardons:

> …have not traditionally been the business of courts; as such, they are rarely, if ever, appropriate subjects for judicial review.[38]

Of note is the fact that a presidential pardon does not prevent a state from prosecuting the same individual if the crime committed has broken a state law. In fact, an individual may be prosecuted at the state level even after that person has been pardoned. Also, while a pardon relieves an individual of the penalties resulting from a committed crime, a person is not obligated to accept a pardon if it is offered.

---

[38] Howe, Amy, *The Supreme Court and the president's pardon power* - SCOTUSblog, citing the Supreme Court, Accessed January 31, 2024.

This right of refusal was first recognized by the Court in 1833 when a man by the name of George Wilson refused to accept the pardon that was offered by President Andrew Jackson. Wilson had committed numerous crimes and was facing twenty years in prison. However, for one particular crime he was facing the death penalty. Evidently the pardon only covered that crime where the death penalty was in view so Wilson rejected the President's offer. The Court ruled in favor of Wilson, finding:

> A pardon is a deed, to the validity of which delivery is essential, and delivery is not complete without acceptance. It may then be rejected by the person to whom it is tendered, and if it be rejected, we have discovered no power in a court to force it on him." (Strangely, the details of whether or not Wilson was ever executed are lost to time.)[39]

This finding was upheld in *George Burdick v. United States* (1915). In a case where accepting the pardon would require him to testify against himself in matters not covered by the pardon, the Court found that:

> Acceptance, as well as delivery, of a pardon is essential to its validity, if rejected by the person to whom it is tendered the court has no power to force it on him.[40]

Clause 2: *He shall have Power, by and with the Advice and Consent of the Senate, to make Treaties, provided two thirds of the Senators present concur; and he shall nominate, and by and with the Advice and Consent of the Senate, shall appoint Ambassadors, other public Ministers and Consuls, Judges of the supreme Court, and all other*

---

[39] Thompson, Austin, *Can a Person Refuse a Presidential Pardon?* | Mental Floss, Accessed January 31, 2024.

[40] Casetext, *Burdick v. United States*, https://casetext.com, Accessed January 31, 2024

Officers of the United States, whose Appointments are not herein otherwise provided for, and which shall be established by Law: but the Congress may by Law vest the Appointment of such inferior Officers, as they think proper, in the President alone, in the Courts of Law, or in the Heads of Departments.

Two powers are here granted to the chief executive, but those powers are, at least in part, shared with the Senate. The first is the power to make treaties with other nations. The president has the authority to negotiate treaties between the United States and other nations. However, the Advice and Consent Clause limits that authority since such a treaty cannot become effective unless and until it is approved by at least two-thirds of the Senate. Currently, sixty-seven of the one-hundred members of the Senate must concur for an international treaty to take effect.

The president is also authorized to appoint individuals to certain offices and governmental posts with the concurrence of a majority of the Senate. As with the Cabinet positions, with the Advice and Consent of the Senate, the president may nominate individuals to fill positions like ambassadorships and other federal roles. The president may also nominate judges to the federal court system, including the Supreme Court, following the same rules of Advice and Consent.

It is noteworthy that, while the Supreme Court and subsidiary federal courts constitute an entirely independent third branch of the federal government, appointment to the bench follows the same procedure as appointment to other executive positions. The president offers a candidate to the Senate and, upon approval of a majority of the Senate the justice takes their position in an independent branch of government where they are not subject to oversite by the executive or legislative branches.

Clause 3: *The President shall have Power to fill up all Vacancies that may happen during the Recess of the Senate, by granting Commissions which shall expire at the End of their next Session.*

The Recess Appointment Clause grants the president the power to make temporary appointments to key federal positions when the Senate is not in session and, therefore, unable to give approval. At such a time, the president, at his own discretion, may fill vacancies without the consent of the Senate. These appointments, however, must be approved by the Senate by the end of the next session otherwise the position becomes vacant again.

The phrase "Recess of the Senate" is not open to casual interpretation. It does not refer to Senators simply retiring to their homes for the evening after a long day on Capitol Hill. The term points specifically to those times when the Senate is officially in recess for a longer period and naturally unable to convene.

This clause was at the center of a decision in *National Labor Relations Board v. Noel Canning*, (2014). In that case, President Obama determined that the Senate was in recess and, in accordance with this clause, made some appointments to the National Labor Relations Board. When these appointments were challenged, the Court determined that the President had exceeded his authority under this clause since the Senate was, in fact, still in session when the appointments were made. According to the ruling, only the Senate may declare when it is officially in recess.

Section 3

Clause 1: *He shall from time to time give to the Congress Information of the State of the Union, and recommend to their Consideration such Measures as he shall judge necessary and expedient; he may, on extraordinary Occasions, convene both Houses, or either of them, and in Case of Disagreement between them, with Respect to the Time of Adjournment, he may adjourn them to such Time as he shall think proper; he shall receive Ambassadors and other public Ministers; he shall take Care that the Laws be faithfully executed, and shall Commission all the Officers of the United States.*

This section mandates that, on occasion, the president inform Congress of the general status of the Union. This responsibility has historically been fulfilled through an annual *State of the Union Address* to a joint session of Congress. The clause does not specify the form of the information provided to Congress, so it could easily be given in written form. However, the practicality and political convenience of this annual public address has proven valuable over the years as all eyes are on the president during the address. This political benefit explains why presidents have been consistent in taking advantage of this opportunity.

Historically, in the *State of the Union Address*, each president has sought to lay out an agenda for Congress for the coming year where the welfare of the nation is concerned. The president generally highlights those issues deemed most significant in his eyes, encouraging Congress to join with him to accomplish his goals.

George Washington, who was the first President of the United States, taking the office on April 30, 1789, was the first to offer a *State of the Union Address*, which he delivered on January 8, 1790, in New

150

York City. With rare exceptions, each president has similarly addressed Congress annually to fulfill this obligation.

Section 4

Clause 1: *The President, Vice President and all civil Officers of the United States, shall be removed from Office on Impeachment for, and Conviction of, Treason, Bribery, or other high Crimes and Misdemeanors.*

The removal of a federal official is a serious matter. This is true whether that official is elected by the people or appointed to a civil position in accordance with the appointment process discussed earlier through the joint efforts of the president and the Senate (see Article II, Section 2, Clause 2).

Using this clause, even the president or vice president could face removal, although members of the House of Representatives and the Senate are excluded. These chambers have their own rules to deal with errant members. A member of Congress can be expelled, but not through the impeachment process.

The House of Representatives is responsible for the impeachment of any federal official, whether elected or appointed. In the case of impeachment, the members of the House must first investigate the situation to decide if there is sufficient evidence to carry out an impeachment trial. If it is determined that the evidence is sufficient, members of the lower chamber will be selected to take the evidence to the Senate to make their case.

Once the evidence has been presented to the Senate, the Senators will determine via a vote, whether the evidence rises to the level of guilt that the person should be removed from office. Two-thirds of the Senate must agree that the evidence is sufficient to remove that individual from office (see Article I, Section 2, Clause 5)

Treason is a term that is often thrown around in cavalier fashion, but it does have a specific constitutional definition (see Article III, Section 3, Clause 1). Similarly, bribery is easily and clearly defined as, "...the offering, giving, soliciting, or receiving of any item of value as a means of influencing the actions of an individual holding a public or legal duty."[41] This definition is generally accepted among legal and constitutional scholars. Indeed, it seems reasonable that a person guilty of treason or bribery, which are both criminal offenses, should be removed from the office they hold.

While identifying treason and bribery seems to be a straightforward matter, determining what *high Crimes and Misdemeanors* qualify as impeachable offenses has been a sticking point where this section is concerned. Two questions have been naturally raised concerning this phraseology in connection with impeachment. The first question is: **Must a high Crime and Misdemeanor involve an actual crime, legally speaking?** The second question that has been raised asks: **Does any and every (felony) crime rise to the level of impeachability?** Legal scholars have struggled with these questions pretty much since Article II, Section 4, was penned.

---

[41] Cornell Law School Legal Information Institute, *Bribery*, https://www.law.cornell.edu/wex/bribery#:~:text=Overview%3A,a%20public%20or%20legal%20duty. Accessed October 5, 2023

Men will undoubtedly continue this debate, but it is unlikely that these questions will ever be answered to everyone's satisfaction for one simple reason. Over the course of time, impeachment has proven to be grounded primarily in politics rather than criminality.

It takes a majority of votes in the House of Representatives to engage in the impeachment process, so it is generally the party with more representatives in the House that will move to impeach. Historically, the party with the most members in the House of Representatives has never sought to impeach someone from their own party. This says much about the nature of impeachment. A few judges have been removed from office through the impeachment process over crimes or misconduct, but those impeachments tend to be viewed as apolitical since their position is purportedly apolitical.

The definition of *high Crimes and Misdemeanors* depends largely on who committed the offensive act and who is in charge in the House of Representatives. For this reason, the questions concerning *high Crimes and Misdemeanors* are inconsequential. These words are most often viewed as the means to an end. The phrase will be narrowly defined or broadly defined depending on the circumstances and the characters involved. The definition of this terminology will always be fluid and grounded in the convenience or inconvenience of political conditions.

Chapter 7
The Judicial Branch

Article III
Section 1

Clause 1: *The judicial Power of the United States, shall be vested in one supreme Court, and in such inferior Courts as the Congress may from time to time ordain and establish. The Judges, both of the supreme and inferior Courts, shall hold their Offices during good Behaviour, and shall, at stated Times, receive for their Services, a Compensation, which shall not be diminished during their Continuance in Office.*

King George III had insisted that judges receive their compensation from England rather than the local governmental bodies. This allowed the King to tip the scales of justice when he saw fit. With this history in view, and given the fact that federal judges receive their compensation from the federal coffers, the founders deemed it necessary to remove heavy-handed congressional and executive influence over the court system.

The solution was to establish the federal court system as an equal and independent branch of the federal government. This branch would consist of a Supreme Court, in which primary judicial authority would be vested. However, since a single court could not possibly address every issue that might arise, the founders recognized that it would be necessary to establish courts that were inferior to the Supreme Court.

This would provide a means of filtering so that only the cases dealing with exceptional constitutional issues might end up on the docket of the Supreme Court.

It was important to the founders that judges should be sheltered, as much as possible, from political influences and interference. It was believed that the decisions of judges facing reappointment may well be swayed by political winds. The solution was that federal judges should receive lifetime appointments. However, they would be subject to the impeachment process if it was determined that their behavior warranted it.

The original Supreme Court assembled in 1790 and consisted of six justices. John Jay served as the first Chief Justice. He was considered one of the Founding Fathers and was highly influential in the successful ratification of the Constitution as the author of several of the Federalist Papers.

Where the Supreme Court is concerned, the Constitution does not establish the number of justices who are to serve at any one time. That number is set by Congress. When the Supreme Court first met in 1790, six justices had been appointed to the Court. From 1790 to 1869 that number varied. However, in 1869, Congress set the figure at nine justices and that number has remained in place since that time.

Section 2

Clause 1: *The judicial Power shall extend to all Cases, in Law and Equity, arising under this Constitution, the Laws of the United States, and Treaties made, or which shall be made, under their Authority;—to all Cases affecting Ambassadors, other public*

Ministers and Consuls;—to all Cases of admiralty and maritime Jurisdiction;—to Controversies to which the United States shall be a Party;—to Controversies between two or more States;—between a State and Citizens of another State,—between Citizens of different States,—between Citizens of the same State claiming Lands under Grants of different States, and between a State, or the Citizens thereof, and foreign States, Citizens or Subjects.

The Constitution delineates the types of *cases* or *controversies* to which the federal judicial power "shall extend." These include "all Cases, in Law and Equity," arising under the Constitution, cases "of admiralty and maritime jurisdiction," controversies in which the parties come from different states (diversity jurisdiction), and more. The jurisdiction of the federal court system is very broad and can include anything from maritime controversies and cases involving treaties and ambassadors to issues with land grants.

While federal courts have far-reaching jurisdiction, not every case that falls under that jurisdiction makes it to the federal court system. Most trials begin and are settled at the county or state level. The losing party may choose to appeal the case to a higher court, which often happens. Once the highest state court has heard a case, it can be appealed to the lower federal court system.

As a final move, a case may be appealed to the U.S. Supreme Court, but the likelihood of the Supreme Court accepting the case is slight. The Supreme Court receives requests for between five-thousand and seven-thousand cases each year and must decide which cases rise to the level of magnitude that they should be decided by the Supreme Court.

Generally, the Supreme Court limits its hearings to cases involving constitutional issues. This might include questions about what constitutes governmental encroachment upon an individual's civil rights or larger questions involving constitutional application. Constitutional cases serve to address jurisprudence on a grand level, potentially impacting the larger citizenry and setting precedents for future cases.

Often, the Supreme Court will refuse an appeal if the lower court has given solid constitutional reasoning for their decision and there is little or no reason to believe that the Supreme Court will arrive at a different conclusion. In such a case, the ruling of the lower court will stand.

> **Clause 2:** *In all Cases affecting Ambassadors, other public Ministers and Consuls, and those in which a State shall be Party, the supreme Court shall have original Jurisdiction. In all the other Cases before mentioned, the supreme Court shall have appellate Jurisdiction, both as to Law and Fact, with such Exceptions, and under such Regulations as the Congress shall make.*

There are certain types of cases where the U.S. Supreme Court has "original Jurisdiction." In other words, some cases may be taken directly to the Supreme Court, bypassing the lower court system, and dodging the many appeals that may be required for the case to reach the highest court. Other times, the Supreme Court may deem a case to be of critical importance and set aside the Court's schedule to hold an emergency hearing. These cases often involve governmental issues where a timely decision is vital (e.g., matters involving elections).

Some controversy has developed over the final statement in this clause. The question has arisen as to the meaning of the words, "...the supreme Court shall have appellate Jurisdiction, both as to Law and Fact, with such Exceptions, and under such Regulations as the Congress shall make." This statement has raised questions about the extent to which Congress may involve itself in the Supreme Court's appellate jurisdiction. Some believe this clause opens the door to congressional input while others have argued that, according to this clause, Congress could choose to limit, or even eliminate, the Court's appellate jurisdiction over certain types of cases (e.g., cases involving moral questions such as abortion or same sex marriage).

According to Alexander Hamilton in Federalist No. 80, the purpose of this statement was to provide "the national legislature...ample authority to make such exceptions, and to prescribe such regulations as will be calculated to obviate or remove [the] inconveniences"[42] arising from the constitutional powers awarded to the federal judiciary. In other words, Congress could choose to *lighten the load* for the federal court system by reducing the courts' range of jurisdiction. Could Congress stretch this clause into an opportunity to interfere in cases they do not want before the court for political reasons? Arguably, the answer is yes, but that was not the intent of the Founding Fathers.

Congress has, at times, sought to limit federal court jurisdiction. For instance, in 1789, Congress passed a statute limiting certain cases

---

[42] Hamilton, Alexander, Federalist No. 80.

with a small *amount at stake* and other minor matters. Still, federal court jurisdiction remains vast.

> **Clause 3:** *The Trial of all Crimes, except in Cases of Impeachment, shall be by Jury; and such Trial shall be held in the State where the said Crimes shall have been committed; but when not committed within any State, the Trial shall be at such Place or Places as the Congress may by Law have directed.*

Except for cases of impeachment, where the Senate serves as jury, all federal crimes must be tried before a jury, unless the defendant waives their right to a jury trial. Additionally, a federal case must be tried in the state where the crime was committed. For this reason, each state has a plethora of federal courts. If, however, the crime was not committed in a single state (perhaps bridging state lines), the trial is to be held in a location determined by the Congress. Impeachment trials are exempt from this clause since only the Senate is constitutionally empowered to hear cases of impeachment (see Article I, Section 3, Clause 6).

Certain amendments to the Constitution have served to strengthen this clause. For instance, in *Hamilton v. Alabama* (1961), the Supreme Court ruled that the Sixth Amendment included certain federal rights for an individual facing criminal prosecution in a state court by combining it with the Due Process clause in the Fourteenth Amendment. Also, the Seventh Amendment expands the right of trial by jury to include certain civil cases.

Section 3

Clause 1: *Treason against the United States, shall consist only in levying War against them, or in adhering to their Enemies, giving them Aid and Comfort. No Person shall be convicted of Treason unless on the Testimony of two Witnesses to the same overt Act, or on Confession in open Court.*

The crime of treason is narrowly defined here, and that narrowness is intentional. This clause was included, not so much to highlight the severity of the crime, but to provide protection against historical use of the charge of treason by repressive governments seeking to silence political opposition. With this clause, the framers sought to remove that temptation from the political hands and minds of Congress, restricting it to actual acts of treason.

Despite the attempt to avoid ambiguity, the clause is still open for discussion. For instance, what constitutes "levying War" and what actions may be deemed "giving Aid and Comfort?" To a certain degree, the Supreme Court has seen the opportunity to address these questions from time to time.

An early case of treason charged former Vice President Aaron Burr (V.P. to Thomas Jefferson) with treason in 1807, accusing him of attempting to persuade certain western states to desert the Union and join with him to colonize new lands. In that instance, the Supreme Court upheld the Constitution's narrow definition of treason. Chief Justice John Marshall wrote:

However flagitious may be the crime of conspiring to subvert by force the government of our country, such conspiracy is not treason. To conspire to levy war, and actually to levy war, are distinct offences. The first must be brought into open action by the assemblage of men for a purpose treasonable in itself, or the fact of levying war cannot have been committed.. . . it has been determined that the actual enlistment of men to serve against the government does not amount to levying war.[43]

Acts of treason can extend beyond "levying War" and can include "Giving Aid and Comfort" to enemies of the United States. The terminology "Aid and Comfort" is admittedly more general than those words used to define "levying War," but courts have historically held a narrow view of the term.

What if the treasonous character of an action is unknown when committed? For instance, suppose someone helps an individual without knowing that person is the enemy? It partly depends on the nature of the actions and how much those actions served to assist the enemy's purpose. The Supreme Court addressed this issue in *Haupt v. United States*, (1947) where a father had gone to *great lengths* in assisting his son, who was deemed a traitor at the time. In that case, Justice Jackson wrote:

> No matter whether young Haupt's mission was benign or traitorous, known or unknown to the defendant, these acts were aid and comfort to him." These acts, Justice Jackson continued, "were more than casually useful; they were aids in steps essential to his design for treason.[44]

---

[43]FindLaw, *Treason Under the Constitution,* https://constitution.findlaw.com/article3/ annotation24.html

[44] Cornell Law School Legal Information Institute, *Haupt v. United States,* https://www.law.cornell.edu/constitution-conan/article-3/section-3/clause-1/aid-and-comfort-to-the-enemy-as-treason, Accessed October 11, 2023

The term "enemies," as it appears in the second clause was written with a settled meaning in view at the time the Constitution was written. The term applied specifically to subjects of a foreign power that was in the process of carrying on open hostilities against the United States. It did not, and does not apply to those citizens who simply rebel against their own government.

Where treason is concerned, a guilty verdict is not permitted based upon purely circumstantial evidence. A person may be found guilty of treason based on three possible requisites. First, the testimony of two or more witnesses may suffice, particularly where substantive evidence supports that testimony. Second, the accused may willingly confess to the act. Finally, as in any case, jurisprudence recognizes that a court may naturally return a guilty verdict if the action is so egregious, so overt, and evidence is so incontrovertible, that no other verdict is reasonable.

Clause 2: *The Congress shall have Power to declare the Punishment of Treason, but no Attainder of Treason shall work Corruption of Blood, or Forfeiture except during the Life of the Person attainted.*

It is left to Congress rather than the court to "declare the Punishment" for treasonous acts against the United States. Current statutory law states that such person "shall suffer death or shall be imprisoned for not less than five years and fined under this title but not less than $10,000, and shall be incapable of holding any office under the United States."[45]

---

[45] U.S. Code, Chapter 115, §2381, *Treason, Sedition, and Subversive Activity*, https://uscode.house.gov/view.xhtml, Accessed October 15, 2023

What is meant by the terms "Attainder of Treason" and "Corruption of Blood?" The concepts are both simple and complicated. Attainder refers to the figurative *stain* on the person convicted of the crime. In English law, this entailed not only the loss of life, but forfeiture of property and titles. Forfeiture of property includes the loss of a person's ability to pass on property to descendants.

The combination of "Attainder of Treason" and "Corruption of Blood" is slightly more complicated. Historically, "Corruption of Blood" has to do with bloodline inheritances. For instance, a man found guilty of treason forfeits property and, as a result, cannot leave anything to his descendants. However, suppose that man dies first, and his father dies afterward. According to the "Corruption of Blood" principle, since the man's descendants would only receive an inheritance from the grandfather through the son ship of the father, they would not be allowed any inheritance from the grandfather due to the stain on the bloodline.

The Attainder of Treason clause seeks to prevent the penalizing of innocents that is grounded in the conduct of the guilty. The clause allows the attainder to be in effect only during the life of the individual convicted of the crime. Upon the death of that person, the attainder is vacated.

Chapter 8

The Federalist Structure

Article IV
Section 1

Clause 1: *Full Faith and Credit shall be given in each State to the public Acts, Records, and judicial Proceedings of every other State. And the Congress may by general Laws prescribe the Manner in which such Acts, Records and Proceedings shall be proved, and the Effect thereof.*

The Constitution holds accountable those who may attempt to escape a state's legal system. It prevents someone from moving to a different state to escape the findings of the courts in the state where a crime was committed. The courts of each state must honor the state laws and court orders of other states, even if their own laws are contrary. In other words, each state must honor legally binding directives from other states. If a court in State A orders a cease-and-desist order, the courts in State B must recognize and enforce the order from State A. An individual may not escape the order by crossing the state line. Additionally, State A's binding of a legal contract or relationship (e.g., adoption) cannot be overturned by State B.

Also in this clause, Congress is given the power to legislate how each state must recognize records and laws from other states and how one state is to enforce the court orders of other states. It stands to reason that these laws can, at times, become very detailed since state laws vary widely and honoring of the laws of each state may become complicated. After all, these cases may involve anything from personal wills and child custody to multi-billion-dollar business dealings in multiple states. Writing laws sufficient to cover such a vast array of disputes can be challenging.

Section 2

Clause 1: *The Citizens of each State shall be entitled to all Privileges and Immunities of Citizens in the several States.*

Put simply, the Privileges and Immunities Clause recognizes that a citizen's rights may not be infringed anywhere within the borders of the United States. The citizens of each state enjoy the same rights and privileges of citizenship even when visiting states not considered their home state.

Clause 2: *A Person charged in any State with Treason, Felony, or other Crime, who shall flee from Justice, and be found in another State, shall on Demand of the executive Authority of the State from which he fled, be delivered up, to be removed to the State having Jurisdiction of the Crime.*

Clause 2 has an inverse effect from the Privileges and Immunities Clause. When an interstate traveler is a fugitive from criminal justice, the Extradition Clause compels the state to which that person has fled to return that individual to the state where the alleged crime took place. However, the return of such a fugitive does not occur automatically. It requires a formal request from the chief executive officer (governor) of the state where the individual was charged with the crime.

> **Clause 3:** *No Person held to Service or Labour in one State, under the Laws thereof, escaping into another, shall, in Consequence of any Law or Regulation therein, be discharged from such Service or Labour, but shall be delivered up on Claim of the Party to whom such Service or Labour may be due.*

The Fugitive Slave Clause, which became obsolete on January 1, 1863, with the enactment of the Emancipation Proclamation, expanded this idea of *fugitive* to those who had escaped from slavery. Although slavery was an abhorrent act of injustice, it was legal at the time and treated as legally binding where the law was concerned. However, there was a strong tendency among abolitionists in the northern states to disregard Clause 3 and authorities rarely enforced it. It is noticeable that no congressional involvement or enforcement is delineated in this section of Article IV.

Section 3

> **Clause 1:** *New States may be admitted by the Congress into this Union; but no new State shall be formed or erected within the Jurisdiction of any other State; nor any State be formed by the Junction of two or more States, or Parts of States, without the Consent of the Legislatures of the States concerned as well as of the Congress.*

Given the wealth of seemingly endless acreage between the Mississippi River and the Pacific Ocean, it is not surprising that the framers anticipated the growth of the Union. Recognizing that new states would likely be formed and seek admission into the Union, Congress made provision, but with certain limitations.

Congress has admitted many new states to the Union. However, it was made clear in this clause that no group could form a new independent state fully within the boundaries of an established state. Additionally, no two states could combine to form a new, larger state, nor could a state split itself into two separate states absent the consent of the state(s) involved and the permission of Congress.

Clause 2: *The Congress shall have Power to dispose of and make all needful Rules and Regulations respecting the Territory or other Property belonging to the United States; and nothing in this Constitution shall be so construed as to Prejudice any Claims of the United States, or of any particular State.*

The framers realized that it would be necessary for the federal government to take title of some land within the borders of various states for the government to fully accomplish federal responsibilities (e.g., positioning/training of military, etc.). This clause does not establish the right for the federal government to own property, but simply recognizes the necessity.

Over the course of time, Congress has authorized the federal government's purchase of land for assorted causes including the construction of federal buildings (courts, etc.), national parks, wildlife refuge, and more. Additionally, where rules and regulations are concerned, Congress has full jurisdiction over any and all property owned by the federal government, notwithstanding that property's location within a particular state.

Section 4

Clause 1: *The United States shall guarantee to every State in this Union a Republican Form of Government, and shall protect each of them against Invasion; and on Application of the Legislature, or of the Executive (when the Legislature cannot be convened) against domestic Violence.*

Historically, it has been understood that the remark concerning "a Republican Form of Government" applies at both the federal and state levels. In other words, the federal government assures that not only will the Union remain a representative republic under the Constitution, but the individual states who make up that Union must maintain a representative form of government.

There have been times when the actions of the federal government have been challenged under Section 4. Cases have come before the Supreme Court claiming that the federal government has, on occasion, ignored this clause. While the history of the U.S. is strewn with complaints concerning judicial activism (where the court effectively writes laws, which is the role of Congress), this clause has been the object of what may be called judicial restraint.

The courts have generally remained uninvolved in questions concerning Section 4. In the case of *Luther v. Borden*, (1849), the Court determined that "questions arising from this section are political, and not judicial, in character," and "it rests with Congress to decide what government is the established one in a state...as well as its republican character."[46] In that same case, "the court indicated that it

---

[46] Justia U.S. Law, *Luther v. Borden*, https://law.justia.com/constitution/us/article-4/21-guarantee-of-republican-form-of-government.html, accessed October 23, 2023

rested with Congress to determine the means proper to fulfill the guarantee of protection to the states against domestic violence."[47]

Article V

Clause 1: *The Congress, whenever two thirds of both Houses shall deem it necessary, shall propose Amendments to this Constitution, or, on the Application of the Legislatures of two thirds of the several States, shall call a Convention for proposing Amendments, which, in either Case, shall be valid to all Intents and Purposes, as Part of this Constitution, when ratified by the Legislatures of three fourths of the several States, or by Conventions in three fourths thereof, as the one or the other Mode of Ratification may be proposed by the Congress;*

The prudence of the Founding Fathers is reflected here. While they were very wise men, they realized that they were not all-knowing and there would be times when the citizenry might consider changes (additions or subtractions) to the Constitution. This clause provides the methodology by which the document may be amended. The procedure was intentionally designed to be cumbersome. The framers fully understood the depth of the principles established in the Constitution and wanted to assure that these were not easily dismissed for transient reasons.

The clause establishes assorted methods for amending the Constitution. Historically, the first method mentioned here is the one used most often. In that scenario, one of the two congressional chambers (the House of Representatives or the Senate) may propose an amendment. That amendment is then voted upon by the two chambers

---

[47] ibid

and must be approved by at least two-thirds of the members of each chamber. Once approved by the House and the Senate, the proposed amendment is forwarded to each state in the Union for consideration. If the legislatures of three-quarters of the states ratify the amendment, it is added to the Constitution. Given that the United States currently consists of fifty states, the proposal would require ratification by thirty-eight states to be added to the Constitution.

This method of ratification reveals a difference between a democracy and a republic. In a democracy, the majority always wins. However, the Constitution provides for a method whereby a simple majority cannot impose their will on the minority. Where amending the Constitution is concerned, it is necessary to have what is called a *super-majority* of the states in agreement.

The clause also provides a method whereby the states can bypass Congress in proposing amendments. With this method, two-thirds of the state legislatures may organize a convention with the goal of amending the Constitution. According to this clause, "on the Application of two-thirds of the Legislatures of the several States, [Congress] shall call a Convention for proposing amendments." Once the states have settled on their proposed amendment(s), the proposal is forwarded to all the states for approval. If three-quarters of the states ratify the amendment(s), it becomes part of the Constitution.

Congress has the option available to require each state to call a convention for the purpose of deciding whether to ratify an amendment. This would take the decision out of the hands of the legislature of each state, although the framework for such a convention is left to the states. The Twenty-first Amendment, which overturned the prohibition of alcohol that was established in the Eighteenth Amendment, is the single occasion where Congress called for state conventions.

May a state rescind its vote of ratification? This is not spelled out in the Constitution. In one instance, a state's citizens sought to override their legislature's ratification of an amendment, but the Supreme Court determined that the Constitution made no provision for such a move (see Eighteenth Amendment for details).

Whether a state's legislature may rescind its ratification of an amendment has not yet faced constitutional scrutiny. Naturally, each constitutional scholar has his/her own point of view. Some say that once a state has ratified an amendment, that decision is irreversible. Others insist that ratification may be rescinded if it happens prior to the completion of the ratification process. Such a case has not yet arisen. If that happens, it will undoubtedly be challenged, and the Supreme Court will be faced with deciding an issue where the constitutional wording is unclear.

> **Clause 2:** *Provided that no Amendment which may be made prior to the Year One thousand eight hundred and eight shall in any Manner affect the first and fourth Clauses in the Ninth Section of the first Article; and that no State, without its Consent, shall be deprived of its equal Suffrage in the Senate.*

Two specific constitutional items were deemed by the framers to be unalterable and, therefore, shielded from the amendment process.

Article I, Section 9, Clause 1, deals specifically with the issue of slavery. It is stated there that the importing of slaves "shall not be prohibited by the Congress prior to the Year one thousand eight hundred and eight." Since that clause had an expiration date, the founders were assuring slaveholders that this would be allowed to run its course and that Congress would not address the topic for the next twenty years.

The second matter that was considered unchangeable is each state's representation in the Senate. A state's representation in the House of Representatives may change since that number is dependent on the population of the state. As some states grow in population and others decrease, the number of representatives is adjusted based on the census that is taken every ten years in the United States.

Senate representation is not based on population, but on statehood. Each state is entitled to representation by two Senators without respect to size of population. No state may increase that number. However, the wording of the clause suggests that a state could (foolishly) choose to reduce its number of Senators, although such a self-destructive decision seems unimaginable.

Article VI

Clause 1: *All Debts contracted and Engagements entered into, before the Adoption of this Constitution, shall be as valid against the United States under this Constitution, as under the Confederation.*

Originally, the existence of the federal government of the United States was grounded in the Articles of Confederation, which was seen as the nation's first Constitution. Under the Articles of Confederation, those who represented the states in Congress could, when necessary, borrow money on behalf of the Union to operate the government as they saw fit. Borrowing was especially critical during the war with England, and some of those debts would need to carry over under the new Constitution. By ratifying the Constitution, the states agreed that those debts would, indeed, remain the responsibility of the United States of America.

> **Clause 2:** *This Constitution, and the Laws of the United States which shall be made in Pursuance thereof; and all Treaties made, or which shall be made, under the Authority of the United States, shall be the supreme Law of the Land; and the Judges in every State shall be bound thereby, any Thing in the Constitution or Laws of any State to the Contrary notwithstanding.*

Under the Articles of Confederation, state laws superseded federal law. According to Article II of that document, "Each state retains its sovereignty, freedom and independence, and every Power, Jurisdiction and right, which is not by this confederation expressly delegated to the United States, in Congress assembled."[48] This treatment of law was reversed under the Supremacy Clause. Upon ratification, federal law would be considered supreme and would supersede state law. This meant that state laws that conflicted with federal law or the Constitution would need to be vacated or rewritten to harmonize with federal statutes and the Constitution.

---

[48] Articles of Confederation

Judges in the various states had, under the Articles of Confederation, made legal judgments based on the laws of the states in which they presided, and those laws varied widely from state to state. Upon ratification of the Constitution, state judges would be required to adjust their judicial approach, assuring that the outcomes of their cases were in keeping with constitutional principles and federal law.

> **Clause 3:** *The Senators and Representatives before mentioned, and the Members of the several State Legislatures, and all executive and judicial Officers, both of the United States and of the several States, shall be bound by Oath or Affirmation, to support this Constitution; but no religious Test shall ever be required as a Qualification to any Office or public Trust under the United States.*

Elected members and appointed officers of both federal and state government are required to take an oath supporting the Constitution of the United States. Note that it is not an oath regarding the people, but a pledge in support of the Constitution. The reason for this is grounded in the notion that emotions and circumstances can cloud judgment. The roller coaster of demands from politicians' constituents may vary widely without measuring the wisdom of those actions. However, constitutional principles are written and unchanging. It stands to reason that government decisions should be grounded in wise constitutional principles rather than satisfying the peoples' fleeting desires.

There is a certain amount of irony in a clause that prohibits any religious test for a person to hold public office. In today's secular world, many people in office are criticized if it is believed that their religious views may impact their decisions or performance in office.

The argument has even been made that people of certain faiths should not be allowed to hold public office out of concern that their religious views may sway them in a way unacceptable to their co-workers or constituents.

What is ironic is that, at the time this clause was written things were much different. Faith in God was common among the citizenry, many of whom had journeyed to the U.S. specifically so they could practice their faith without reprisal. The framers were more concerned that a person's *lack of belief* in God may be the very thing that could hinder their appointment to public office. This clause was intended to remove that obstacle.

Article VII

Clause 1: *The Ratification of the Conventions of nine States, shall be sufficient for the Establishment of this Constitution between the States so ratifying the Same.*

One certain standard is prevalent through the pages of the Constitution, and it is the worth of a *super-majority*. The founders wanted to ensure that the majority, whether among the citizenry or their representatives, could not run roughshod over the minority. From this standard, the super-majority was born.

Part of the logic behind this clause was concern that if ratification required a simple majority of the states, the Constitution might be ratified by the seven least populated states. If that occurred while the six most populous states rejected the document, it could be seen as the majority being out-voted. Alexander Hamilton addressed this concern in Federalist No. 22.

> The smaller States, considering how peculiarly their safety and welfare depend on union, ought readily to renounce a pretension which, if not relinquished, would prove fatal to its duration. It may be objected to this, that not seven but nine States, or two thirds of the whole number, must consent to the most important resolutions; and it may be thence inferred that nine States would always comprehend a majority of the Union. But this does not obviate the impropriety of an equal vote between States of the most unequal dimensions and populousness; nor is the inference accurate in point of fact; for we can enumerate nine States which contain less than a majority of the people; and it is constitutionally possible that these nine may give the vote.[49]

It is this two-thirds principle that serves as the standard for things like impeachments or constitutional amendments (although ratification of an amendment requires three-fourths of the states). It is not surprising, then, that this same standard was applied for ratification of the Constitution. At the time the Constitution was submitted for ratification, the U.S. consisted of thirteen separate states. The framers determined that, for the Constitution to be fully accepted, it would require ratification by more than a simple majority of states. Therefore, to provide full constitutional legitimacy, it was determined that adoption of the Constitution should only take place if the document was ratified by at least two-thirds (9) of the states.

As an observation, the founders might have done themselves a favor had they altered slightly the manner of ratification. Their concern was that if the nine least populated states ratified the

---

[49] Hamilton, Alexander, Federalist No. 22

Constitution and the four largest states did not, the document would have been ratified by a minority of the population. This issue could have been resolved had they insisted that the U. S. Constitution be ratified by both a super-majority of the states *and* a sufficient number of states to represent a majority of the citizenry. Fortunately, their minds were eased when the document was unanimously ratified by the states.

Delaware was the first state to ratify the Constitution. They held their state convention in December of 1787 and ratification was completed on December 7, 1787. Other states soon followed and on June 21, 1788, New Hampshire became the ninth state to ratify the Constitution. Unanimous ratification by the states was completed when Rhode Island, on May 29, 1790, in a 34-32 vote of the delegates, gave final approval.

Section 3

The Constitution:
The Amendments

Chapter 9
The Bill of Rights

Proposal of Twelve Amendments

Most Americans have heard of The Bill of Rights. At least, most are familiar with the terminology even if they are unaware of what those words represent. The Bill of Rights is the designation that has been given to the first ten amendments to the U.S. Constitution. These amendments enumerate certain rights of the U.S. citizenry including freedom to practice religion, freedom of speech, the right to bear arms, etc. They were submitted to the states for ratification as a group in 1789 and ratified by the states in 1791.

Most people are not aware, however, that Congress initially submitted twelve amendments to the states and what is currently known as the First Amendment was listed third in that submission. The amendment that originally topped the list was a proposal that no congressional district should consist of more than 50,000 citizens. This amendment was not ratified, and hindsight indicates that this was a wise choice. Given the current population of the U.S., which is more than 300 million, ratification of that amendment would have resulted in a current Congress of well over 6,000 members.

Unlike more recent amendment proposals that include a time limit for ratification, the timeline for the original submission of twelve amendments was open-ended. The second of the proposed twelve amendments, known as the Compensation Amendment, was not ratified in the late 1700's, nor was it ratified at any time in the 1800's. The amendment was finally adopted when, on May 7, 1992, the state of Michigan joined the cause as the 38th state to ratify the Compensation Amendment. It is now known as the Twenty-seventh amendment, currently the last adopted amendment.

First Amendment

Congress shall make no law respecting an establishment of religion, or prohibiting the free exercise thereof; or abridging the freedom of speech, or of the press; or the right of the people peaceably to assemble, and to petition the Government for a redress of grievances.

The First Amendment of the U.S. Constitution, adopted in 1791, provides for the protection of certain civil rights associated with life as an American, including freedom of religion, freedom of speech, and freedom of the press. It also addresses the rights to assemble peacefully and to petition the government. This amendment was added to the Constitution along with nine other amendments, which together became known as the Bill of Rights.

The colonists had grown accustomed to England where the Church of England and the throne of England were essentially indistinguishable. The Church of England was launched during the sixteenth century Reformation Movement by King Henry VIII in protest against the Roman Catholic Church who refused to issue him a divorce from Catherine of Aragon.

The fact that the Church of England was formed by the government should provide some insight into the character of the church. It was government-run, and its practices could be forced upon the citizenry. This was the kind of situation the founders sought to avoid in America. In this First Amendment, it was determined that what Henry VIII had done in England must not be allowed to happen in America. Therefore, the U. S. government is prevented from establishing a state religion and forcing it upon the citizenry. Individuals may worship (or not worship) as they see fit within the confines of the law and without intruding on the rights of others (e.g., heinous religious acts like child sacrifices and other barbarous practices are unacceptable).

It can be successfully argued that freedom of speech lies at the very heart of the American experiment. America was born partly out of the colonists' frustration as they were taxed heavily by England without being allowed a voice in the political conversation. Indeed, King George III and Parliament often sought to quiet the voices of their opposition. Freedom of speech holds that any American should be able to speak his/her mind, particularly on topics that are political in character, unfettered by governmental persecution or prosecution.

Freedom of speech is generally understood to focus on speech involving opinions, especially political opinions, but the term is used in a broad sense. There are, of course, some exceptions where freedom of speech is concerned. The Supreme Court has held that certain types of speech are not acceptable. For instance, the common man cannot issue a medical prescription. That requires professional licensing.

No one is permitted, under the guise of freedom of speech, to place others in imminent danger. As an example, it has been determined that falsely yelling "fire!" in a crowded building may result in panic, leading to possible pandemonium where people could be injured. This possibility was addressed by Justice Oliver Wendell Holmes in *Schenk v. United States,* (1919), when he wrote:

> The question is whether the words are used in such circumstances and are of such a nature as to create a clear and present danger that they will bring about the substantive evils that Congress has the right to prevent. It is a question of proximity and degree.[50]

Still, where ideology, politics, religion, and other topics are concerned, freedom of speech is a core principle in the United States. Congress sought to assure the uninhibited expression of ideas, knowing that, once speech was regulated, other freedoms would soon follow.

This amendment also holds that the press, whose purpose is to keep Americans informed, should remain unencumbered when reporting the news or offering opinions. Since it is individuals who report the news and offer opinions, this right might well be covered by the individual's right to free speech, but Congress saw fit to award the press its own right to freedom from government interference.

---

[50] American Library Association, *Foundations of Free Expression: Historic Cases:Schenk v. United States,* https://www.ala.org/advocacy/intfreedom/censorship/courtcases, accessed October 28, 2023.

Like the freedom of speech awarded to individuals, freedom of the press is not without limitations. First, members of the press are equally vulnerable to lawsuits for language of a slanderous or malicious nature. Additionally, as with individuals, the press is subject to laws concerning language that poses "a clear and present danger." However, beyond these, there are few restrictions where the press is concerned.

Americans also have the right to peacefully assemble for any reason they deem worthy. As with all other rights, this may be done so long as the assembly does not infringe on the rights of other people. For instance, no one has the right to assemble in the middle of the highway and block traffic. Once a person or group begins to infringe upon the rights of other people, they have eclipsed the intent behind the words of this amendment.

Lawsuits involving the right to assembly are plentiful and the courts have steadily upheld this right with little restriction. The attempts of state and local governments to constrict freedom of assembly in cases like *DeJonge v. Oregon*, (1937), *Bates v. Little Rock*, (1960), *Edwards v. South Carolina*, (1963), *Cox v. Louisiana*, (1965), and *Coates v. City of Cincinnati*, (1971), have consistently failed.

Finally, Americans have the right to address the government with grievances and seek redress for infringement of rights or any other grievance they may have experienced. Depending on the nature and seriousness of the grievance, this may involve as little as a letter to a congressman or as much as a lawsuit in federal court. Nonetheless, this amendment designates that right to citizens of the United States. This right was likely included here as the members of Congress recalled the futility they had experienced when addressing their grievances to England.

Second Amendment

A well regulated Militia, being necessary to the security of a free State, the right of the people to keep and bear Arms, shall not be infringed.

Arguably the most controversial and most debated of the amendments, a person's right to "bear arms" is clearly delineated here. At the time these words were penned, it was customary for the common man to not merely own a firearm, but to carry it freely and openly in the public arena. Yet, if these words so clearly express the intent of the framers, some may wonder exactly what it is that is open to discussion. The conversation incorporates several issues including just how some of the words of the amendment should be applied.

This amendment experienced virtually no scrutiny in the early years following its ratification and federal courts did not hear serious challenges concerning gun rights. Most Second Amendment legal challenges in the 1800's were raised in the years following the Civil War. Late in the nineteenth century some courts held that the intent here was to bar the federal government from enacting gun restriction laws, but that the actions of individual states might not be considered a violation of this amendment. An example is found in *The United States v. Cruikshank*, (1875).

A few years later, in *Presser v. Illinois*, (1886), the state of Illinois was challenged concerning a statute that confined the definition of "militia" to the organized state militia. The Supreme Court found in favor of Presser, holding that the Second Amendment barred the states from "prohibit[ing] the people from keeping and bearing arms, so as to deprive the United States of their rightful resource for maintaining the public security."[51]

The National Firearms Act of 1934 sought three primary results. First, Congress chose to tax both the manufacture and sale of firearms. In *The United States v. Miller*, (1939), the Supreme Court ruled that such taxation did not constitute infringement of a person's right to bear arms. It simply impacted the cost of exercising that right. Second, it was determined by Congress that all firearms should be registered with the Secretary of the Treasury. Finally, the statute placed restrictions on the interstate transport of firearms. Later, Congress also required the licensing of manufacturers and sellers of firearms in The Federal Firearms Act of 1938.

The assassination of President Kennedy in November of 1963, followed by the assassinations of Martin Luther King, Jr. and Robert Kennedy in 1968 raised the temperatures of gun control advocates and the debate over the wisdom of the Second Amendment reached a fever pitch. On October 22, 1968, President Johnson signed The Firearms

---

[51] Britannica, *Presser-v-Illinois*, https://www.britannica.com/topic/ Accessed, October 27, 2023

Act of 1968. This statute repealed The Federal Firearms Act of 1938, but it also included many of the provisions of that earlier law. This new law restricted the ownership of firearms by criminals, aliens, and certain other individuals and again required licensing for those in the gun trade.

The twenty-first century has seen a number of gun rights cases rise to the Supreme Court. Perhaps the most significant of these cases is *The District of Columbia v. Heller*, (2008). In that case, the Supreme Court determined that "The Second Amendment protects an individual right to possess a firearm unconnected with service in a militia, and to use that arm for traditionally lawful purposes, such as self-defense within the home."[52]

The debate over the Second Amendment will continue. However, if someone wonders why the framers would propose such an amendment, an explanation can be seen in their hard-fought conflict with England. They believed men should always be prepared to defend their own interests. This is surely what George Washington had in view with these words from his first annual address to Congress:

> A free people ought not only to be armed, but disciplined; to which end a uniform and well-digested plan is requisite; and their safety and interest require that they should promote such manufactories as tend to render them independent of others for essential, particularly military, supplies."[53]

---

[52] Justia U.S. Supreme Court, *District of Columbia v. Heller*, 554 U.S. 570 (2008) https://supreme.justia.com/cases-by-topic/gun-rights/, accessed October 28, 2023.
[53] Founders Online, *From George Washington to the United States Senate and House of Representatives*, https://founders.archives.gov/documents/Washington/ 05-04-02-0361, accessed October 28, 2023.

Third Amendment

No Soldier shall, in time of peace be quartered in any house, without the consent of the Owner, nor in time of war, but in a manner to be prescribed by law.

In the years prior to the American Revolution, King George III made a practice of posting standing armies in American cities even in times of peace. With The Quartering Acts of 1765 and 1774, England had compelled the colonists to provide nourishment, housing, and transportation to British troops stationed in their towns and cities. This was a major sticking point where the colonists were concerned and served to galvanize colonial opposition, which ultimately led to their separation from England (see the Declaration of Independence, Grievance No. 14).

Following the Revolution, as America's focus turned toward the development of a U.S. Constitution, these actions by England were still fresh in the minds of the colonists. Recognizing the characteristic injustice of forcing citizens to relinquish their rights to privacy and property without justifiable cause or reasonable compensation, the framers constitutionalized protection against such abuses with this amendment.

Fourth Amendment

The right of the people to be secure in their persons, houses, papers, and effects, against unreasonable searches and seizures, shall not be violated, and no Warrants shall issue, but upon probable cause, supported by Oath or affirmation, and particularly describing the place to be searched, and the persons or things to be seized.

Here the framers sought to protect individuals from over-zealous federal and state governments. The goal was to protect the citizens from what is termed "unreasonable searches and seizures." The idea was that the rights of property and privacy are subtly embedded within the unalienable rights of liberty and the pursuit of happiness (see the Declaration of Independence).

Whether a search of an individual's effects is reasonable or not is often a matter of perspective. There are certainly occasions when such intrusion into a person's life is justified. It was the role of the founders to establish guidelines for determining when such searches and seizures are reasonable.

The framers decided that the U.S. Constitution should lean heavily in favor of the individual and that avoiding unreasonable governmental intrusion should be the priority. As a result, it was decided that a reasonable search should include permission from a court with jurisdiction. That permission should only be granted upon presentation of evidence or credible testimony (of a person's activity) supporting the claim that the state's interest legitimately outweighs the individual's rights. Even then, searches must be limited in character to the specifics the state deems relevant to the case in question.

Not every case of "unreasonable search and seizure" involves a warrant issued by a court. The Supreme Court has held that there are times when a police officer's search of an individual may be warranted without the court's initial involvement. Such was the case of *Terry v.*

Ohio, (1968). On that occasion, an officer witnessed what he considered suspicious behavior by three men. Suspecting they were planning to rob the store where they were assembled, he approached the three and questioned them, but the men apparently mumbled and failed to provide coherent answers. He then searched the three men and found that Terry and one other man were carrying concealed guns. The officer promptly arrested the men.

At trial, Terry was convicted of carrying a concealed weapon. Claiming that his Fourth Amendment right of protection from unreasonable search and seizure had been violated, he then appealed to the Supreme Court. He lost that appeal. In that case, the Court held that:

> … an officer's interest in the safety of himself and others outweighs an individual's Fourth Amendment right. In addition, when an individual is stopped on the street, the police may conduct a proper search for weapons if based on the facts and circumstances, the officer reasonably believes the person is armed.[54]

This incident is considered a landmark case. In legal circles it is referred to as the *Terry Stop*. It was this case that served to establish the constitutionality of an officer's authority to carry out a limited search and seizure on the basis of reasonable suspicion that public safety may be at stake and/or the commission of a crime may be imminent.

---

[54] Legal Dictionary, *Terry v. Ohio - Case Summary and Case Brief*, legaldictionary.net, accessed November 1, 2023.

Fifth Amendment

No person shall be held to answer for a capital, or otherwise infamous crime, unless on a presentment or indictment of a Grand Jury, except in cases arising in the land or naval forces, or in the Militia, when in actual service in time of War or public danger; nor shall any person be subject for the same offence to be twice put in jeopardy of life or limb; nor shall be compelled in any criminal case to be a witness against himself, nor be deprived of life, liberty, or property, without due process of law; nor shall private property be taken for public use, without just compensation.

Like the First Amendment, the Fifth Amendment is comprised of five distinct clauses, with each clause outlining a specific right. The first four clauses deal specifically with criminal accusations and criminal trials. In each of these four clauses, the burden for protection of these rights lies with the accuser (the government).

The first clause states that "No person shall be held to answer for a capital, or otherwise infamous crime, unless on a presentment or indictment of a Grand Jury, except in cases arising in the land or naval forces or in the Militia, when in actual service in time of War or public danger." The intent of this provision is to prevent over-enthusiastic law enforcement. It is the role of the grand jury to review the government's case against the accused to determine if the evidence is sufficient to carry the case to trial. If the grand jury determines that the evidence is, indeed, sufficient, an indictment is issued and the trial may proceed.

The Grand Jury Clause makes exceptions in cases "…arising in the land or naval forces, or in the Militia." Where military personnel are concerned, crimes are heard by military courts where a separate set of rules apply. Those rules are far more stringent and are grounded in necessary military disciplinary principles. When it comes to criminal prosecution, military personnel cannot claim many of the procedural rights afforded the common citizen.

Most people have heard the term *double jeopardy* even if they are unaware of its exact meaning. The term derives from the Fifth Amendment and serves to protect an individual from further prosecution once the trial has been held and he/she has been acquitted by a judge or jury. That is the meaning of the clause in the amendment where it is stated that no person shall "…be subject for the same offence to be twice put in jeopardy of life or limb." This also protects the individual, once guilt is established, from receiving multiple punishments for the same crime once sentencing is concluded.

Certain caveats exist where *double jeopardy* is concerned. For instance, when the criminal act violates both state and federal laws, a person may be subject to prosecution at both levels, although this rarely occurs. Additionally, whether acquitted or convicted, this amendment does not protect the accused from facing a civil law suit by those who may have been harmed as a result of the crime committed.

Protection from *self-incrimination* is served up in the third clause of this amendment. In other words, individuals accused of crimes cannot be forced to testify against themselves. This right was clarified in *Miranda v. Arizona*, (1966). In that case, Ernesto Miranda confessed to kidnapping and rape charges, unaware of his rights to remain silent and have an attorney present. The Supreme Court determined that his confession was inadmissible in court, insisting that an individual must be informed of these rights before what is said may be admissible. From that ruling came what is known as the *Miranda Warning*, which is given to anyone arrested for a crime: In the case of an arrest, the police officer must inform the accused:

> You have the right to remain silent. Anything you say can and will be used against you in a court of law. You have the right to an attorney. If you cannot afford an attorney, one will be provided for you.

Police officers commonly carry a card with this warning printed out so that the card may be handed to the accused upon their arrest as a complement to the verbal warning. It is interesting to note that, in the case of Ernesto Miranda the man was retried for his crime without the benefit of his confession and was again found guilty.

The fourth clause of the Fifth Amendment bundles a person's rights of *life, liberty*, and *property* into a package. Since these directly reflect the unalienable rights of *life, liberty, and the pursuit of happiness* (which seems to encompass a right to personal property) named in the Declaration of Independence, some may wonder why they should be repeated here. The Declaration of Independence is a general document reflecting human rights common to all. This amendment serves to incorporate those rights into the American legal process, stipulating how they must apply in the case of someone who has been accused of criminal activity.

No one may be "...deprived of life, liberty, or property, without due process of law." Known as the Due Process Clause, this statement seeks to protect these basic rights even in the face of an accusation of criminal activity, ensuring that these rights are protected by inserting some procedural safeguards. The preservation of these rights within the legal system is built on the principle that an individual is presumed innocent until proven guilty. Failure to protect these rights for an accused person may do irreparable harm to someone who is later determined to be innocent.

The Fifth Amendment was ratified in 1791 along with the rest of the Bill of Rights. Yet, in the American court system, presumption of innocence as a legal standard was not *formally* established until late in the nineteenth century with the case of *Coffin v. United States,* (1895). Still, it had long been held as a general legal principle historically. The French phrase *item quilbet presumitir innocens nisi probetur nocens* (a person is presumed innocent until proven guilty) purportedly originated with Jean Lemoine, a thirteenth century lawyer and Cardinal, although the idea and application of this standard seems to have predated Lemoine by several centuries.

The second mention of a person's right to property in the final clause of this amendment deals with the topic outside the framework of criminal law. At the time this amendment was ratified, and even in modern times, the idea of owning property has been seen as a component of a person's right to pursue happiness. The founders also understood that there would be times when a person's individual right to ownership of property, specifically real estate, must sometimes yield to the *greater good* where the whole of society is concerned.

There would inevitably be times when what is best for the community infringes on the individual right to property. This understanding is what led to this clause, known as the Takings Clause.

A growing country and the government's responsibility in providing for the development of that growth would certainly end up challenging property lines that were established in the earliest days of the colonies. The Takings Clause empowers the government to use what is known as *eminent domain*, allowing the government to take private property for public use. However, such taking must be for *public use* and include *just compensation* (presumably fair market value) for the property owner.

While the courts have generally been faithful to the *public use* principle (highways, parks, etc.), there have been exceptions. For instance, in *Kelo v. City of New London*, (2005), the Supreme Court upheld the city's use of this clause to take ownership of certain private property for a commercial development that, it was argued, would have a positive impact on the community and provide huge benefits to its citizenry. This case seems to have redefined the Court's position on what constitutes *public use*.

Sixth Amendment

In all criminal prosecutions, the accused shall enjoy the right to a speedy and public trial, by an impartial jury of the State and district wherein the crime shall have been committed, which district shall have been previously ascertained by law, and to be informed of the nature and cause of the accusation; to be confronted with the witnesses against him; to have compulsory process for obtaining witnesses in his favor, and to have the Assistance of Counsel for his defence.

In the Sixth Amendment, the framers established guidelines for the prosecution of an individual charged with criminal activity. In keeping with the theme of the Bill of Rights, this amendment focuses on safeguarding the rights enjoyed by the accused. The purpose was to hold the legal system accountable for the reasonable treatment of a defendant.

The first right to which an accused individual is entitled is a speedy trial and this is conjoined with a right to a public trial. Note that a public trial is not a *requirement*, but an *opportunity*. An accused person may forego a public trial if he/she wishes.

The right to a speedy trial has a rich history. Twelfth century England was known for having itinerant judges. As these judges made their rounds, certain locations were not on the regular schedule, due either to the infrequency of crimes and lawsuits or the remoteness of their locations. This became a problem in that a person charged in one of these places may be subjected to an unreasonably long wait before standing trial.

Assize (Law) of Clarendon, (1166) was a series of ordinances developed by King Henry II of England. Seeking to improve criminal law procedures, the King met with a *convocation of lords* in Clarendon, England. That meeting saw the establishment of the grand, or presenting, jury (consisting of 12 men in each 100 and 4 men in each township). It became the responsibility of the grand jury to inform the King's itinerant judges of the most serious crimes committed in each local district and to assure a speedy trial.

These ordinances also included the idea of trial by jury, replacing antiquated methods such as *trial by ordeal*. This was an approach where the accused was subjected to a dangerous and painful test to determine guilt or innocence. It was believed that the outcome of the test would reveal a divine (God-ordained) verdict. Also replaced was the rarely employed *trial by battle*. In that case, the accused could agree to battle one of the people's champions. It was held again that the outcome would be up to God. Also eliminated was a mundane method known as *trial by compurgation*. This method simply involved the accused swearing to his/her own innocence and the witness of twelve individuals of good repute swearing that they believed the claim of innocence.

The Assize of Clarendon had its flaws and the process was abused by the inclusion of many false accusations and miscarriages of justice. It was replaced by the Assize of Northampton, (1176), which sought to solidify people's rights, although it dealt primarily with property rights and claims of inheritance. Nonetheless, this seemed to mark the beginning of the notion that individuals have rights and the government should recognize those rights. The reasoning behind this effort was that recognition of rights, especially property rights, might help curb lawlessness that was so rampant in the kingdom.

Similar recognition of individual rights can be found in the Magna Carta (England, 1215). In it, a statement of subjects' rights was issued by King John. Chapter 39 of that document provided that "[n]o free man shall be arrested or imprisoned . . . except by lawful judgment of his peers or by the law of the land." This language, it is said, gave rise to the concept of "due process of law" that was incorporated into the Due Process Clause of the Fifth Amendment.

The Supreme Court has heard many cases related to the Sixth Amendment. This is understandable since the amendment names multiple rights (e.g., right to a speedy trial, right to assistance of counsel, etc.). A person's right to a speedy trial was tested in *Barker v. Wingo*, (1972). This, too, is considered a landmark case. The court used it to develop four guidelines for courts to follow in determining whether this right had been violated. Those guidelines are 1) the length of the delay, 2) the reason for the delay, 3) when the defendant asserted this right, and 4) the degree of harm to the defendant due to the delay.

Gideon v. Wainright, (1963), was a milestone case with respect to the Assistance of Counsel clause. Clarence Gideon was convicted of breaking and entering in Florida, He requested a court-appointed attorney, but the request was denied. At the time, it was understood that the right to counsel applied only in federal courts. The Supreme Court used that case to reason that right to counsel was intended to apply universally and must be recognized at every level of the legal system. The conviction was overturned.

These are but two examples of the abundance of Sixth Amendment cases brought before the Supreme Court. It is highly worthwhile to review cases like these, not merely to learn how individual rights have been applied historically, but to appreciate how modern courts rely on history in their reasoning concerning assorted rights.

Seventh Amendment

In Suits at common law, where the value in controversy shall exceed twenty dollars, the right of trial by jury shall be preserved, and no fact tried by a jury, shall be otherwise re-examined in any Court of the United States, than according to the rules of the common law.

Drafted by James Madison, the Seventh Amendment is designed to protect a person's right to a trial by a jury of his/her peers in any civil suit in federal court where the value of the plaintiff's claim exceeds $20. In the twenty-first century, people generally scoff at the notion that a lawsuit for such a miniscule amount could be taken seriously. However, in 1791, when the Constitution was ratified by the states, $20 constituted roughly one month's wages for the average citizen. Depending on how it is calculated, that 1791 $20 threshold translates to somewhere between $500 and $700 in modern terms. However, because the process of amending the Constitution is onerous, the wording of this amendment has remained. Appreciating the fact that the framers had understandably failed to consider the impact of inflation when drafting this amendment, the Supreme Court has supported modern statutes setting a threshold in federal court cases for damages exceeding $75,000.

Why did the framers deem *trial by jury* to be essential as a basic right? The colonists had experienced considerable injustices under the English court system where King George III appointed, and effectively *owned*, American judges. As a result, rulings in both criminal and civil cases tended to favor the view of the King or Parliament. Even with England out of the picture, the framers thought it would be unwise to have government judges decide the outcome of all cases, particularly where civil suits were concerned.

The U. S. Supreme Court has traditionally held that constitutional matters that impact federal courts equally apply to the courts of each state, but that is not true where this amendment is concerned. In *Minneapolis & St. Louis Railroad Co. v. Bombolis*, (1916), the court ruled that the Seventh Amendment "…applies only to proceedings in courts of the United States; it does not in any manner govern or regulate trials by jury in state courts."[55] Still, most states have included the right to civil jury trial in certain cases in their state constitutions.

Of note is the fact that, according to the Supreme Court, a jury trial in a federal court requires a unanimous verdict by the jury. This decision was based on the use of the term "common law," which appears twice in the amendment. First, the amendment points to "Suits at common law…" The amendment then closes with the statement, "…no fact tried by a jury, shall be otherwise re-examined in any Court of the United States, than according to the rules of the common law."

[55] Justia US Supreme Court Center, *Minneapolis & St. Louis R. Co. v. Bombolis* :: 241 U.S. 211 (1916) :: https://supreme.justia.com , accessed November 15, 2023.

How should the term *common law* be understood and how does it impact the application of this amendment? In *Parsons v. Bedford*, (1830), the Supreme Court ruled that in the Seventh Amendment, the framers had in view the *common law* of England that required unanimous verdicts from the jury. More than a century later, in *Dimick v. Schiedt*, (1935), this ruling was upheld.

The Seventh Amendment does not specify the number of jurors required to hear a case. Traditionally, the most common number of jurors stood at twelve. However, given that the amendment does not specify the number of jurors, flexibility has been the norm in civil cases. This reflects the Courts position as stated in *Colgrove v. Battin*, (1973). Consequently, civil cases are often heard by six jurors rather than the traditional twelve jurors.

Eighth Amendment

Excessive bail shall not be required, nor excessive fines imposed, nor cruel and unusual punishments inflicted.

The Eighth Amendment is both straightforward and mysterious. It is grounded in the reasonable notion that no individual should be over-punished when they are in violation of the law or found liable in a civil suit. This amendment prohibits courts from imposing an excessive bail or an excessive fine. The amount of a bail or fine should befit the nature and scope of the crime or liability and should not exceed it.

The amendment also prohibits the courts from inflicting "cruel and unusual punishment." This is the mystery feature of the amendment. It begs the question: **What constitutes cruel and unusual punishment in any given case?** It stands to reason that a standard must be used to reason whether a punishment is cruel and unusual.

There is some observable history to lean on when it comes to the term *cruel and unusual punishment*. In 1689, a century before the drafting of the U.S. Constitution, England had adopted a similar Bill of Rights. That document also prohibited the infliction of "cruell and unusuall punishments." Later, in 1776, the Commonwealth of Virginia developed a Declaration of Rights for its citizens. Borrowing from the English Bill of Rights, that document also prohibited the employment of cruel and unusual punishments.

The Constitution, in its original seven articles, did not specify that cruel and unusual punishments were prohibited. This raised concerns since the proposed Constitution would place in the hands of the government much more power over the lives of the citizens than was afforded in the Articles of Confederation. This understandably led to concern and some serious debate over ratification. Abraham Holmes insisted that without this protection, Congress might easily replicate the abuses of "...that diabolical institution, the Inquisition."[56] The eloquent Patrick Henry, in a debate in Virginia over the ratification of the Constitution, made the following argument, stating:

> Congress, from their general powers, may fully go into business of human legislation. They may legislate, in criminal cases, from treason to the lowest offence--petty larceny. They may define crimes and prescribe punishments. In the definition of crimes, I trust they

---

[56] The National Constitution Center, *Interpretation and Debate: The Eighth Amendment* | https://constitutioncenter.org,, Accessed November 15, 2023

will be directed by what wise representatives ought to be governed by. But when we come to punishments, no latitude ought to be left, nor dependence put on the virtue of representatives. What says our [Virginia] bill of rights?--"that excessive bail ought not to be required, nor excessive fines imposed, nor cruel and unusual punishments inflicted." Are you not, therefore, now calling on those gentlemen who are to compose Congress, to . . . define punishments without this control? Will they find sentiments there similar to this bill of rights? You let them loose; you do more--you depart from the genius of your country. . . .

In this business of legislation, your members of Congress will loose the restriction of not imposing excessive fines, demanding excessive bail, and inflicting cruel and unusual punishments. These are prohibited by your declaration of rights. What has distinguished our ancestors?--That they would not admit of tortures, or cruel and barbarous punishment.

But Congress may introduce the practice of the civil law, in preference to that of the common law. They may introduce the practice of France, Spain, and Germany--of torturing, to extort a confession of the crime. They will say that they might as well draw examples from those countries as from Great Britain, and they will tell you that there is such a necessity of strengthening the arm of government, that they must have a criminal equity, and extort confession by torture, in order to punish with still more relentless severity. We are then lost and undone.[57]

The character of these and other debates serves to clarify, at least in part, the meaning of cruel and unusual punishments. The phrase is juxtaposed against "the Inquisition" and "the practice of France, Spain, and Germany of torturing." This indicates that the concern was a return to what may be considered *barbaric* practices of earlier societies where torturous methods were used to induce confessions and/or inflict physical and mental pain on one's enemies. Eighth Amendment

---

[57] University of Chicago Press, *Amendment VIII: Debate in Virginia Ratifying Convention*, https://press-pubs.uchicago.edu.com, Accessed November 15, 2023.

cases are determined on an individual basis, since no *exact* standard exists. For instance, in *Whitley v. Albers*, (1986), the Court ruled that this amendment provides constitutional protection against inhumane conditions of confinement.

A legitimate argument can be made that prohibition of cruel and unusual punishment might be a concern when it comes to maintaining equity between the punishment and the crime. As an example, it is fair to say that the crime of jaywalking should not translate into a sentence of life in prison. Courts have also given serious consideration to how this amendment impacts the sentencing of minors. For instance, where first degree murder is concerned, Alabama law called for a sentence of mandatory life in prison with no opportunity for parole. As a result, a convicted fourteen-year-old was given that sentence. Upon appeal, in *Miller v. Alabama,* (2012), the Supreme Court returned the case to Alabama for more equitable sentencing, stating:

> The mandatory penalty schemes at issue prevent the sentencing court from considering youth and from assessing whether the harshest term of imprisonment proportionately punishes a juvenile offender. Life-without-parole sentences share characteristics with death sentences, demanding individualized sentencing.[58]

Does this amendment prohibit the death penalty? Some have insisted that capital punishment should be considered cruel and unusual. Moral and legal arguments have been raised on both sides of the issue and societal views abound. While it may be difficult to come to a consensus on the topic in a diverse society, most states have

---

[58] Justia US Supreme Court Center, *Miller v. Alabama* :: 567 U.S. 460 (2012) :: https//supreme.justia.com, Accessed November 15, 2023.

passed statutes allowing the death penalty in certain cases. No doubt, the discussion over what constitutes cruel and unusual punishment will continue for the foreseeable future.

Ninth Amendment

The enumeration in the Constitution, of certain rights, shall not be construed to deny or disparage others retained by the people.

As with the previous amendment's use of the undefined term *cruel and unusual punishment*, the Ninth Amendment is seasoned with a dash of mystery. The U.S. Constitution, in its original form, did not include a Bill of Rights (the first ten amendments) when it was initially submitted to the states for ratification. Only the seven articles appeared in that document. This fact may lead some to believe that these rights were added as an afterthought, the framers having realized the error of their ways by omitting a statement protecting individual rights, but that was not the case. The framers were fully aware of the Bill of Rights established in England in the previous century and the same in the Constitution in the state of Virginia.

The ratification process for the seven articles saw vigorous debate across the Union, and a big part of those debates involved spirited discussion concerning the enumeration of rights (or absence thereof) within the four corners of the document. Some like James Wilson, who was a signer of the Constitution and served as a justice on the original U. S. Supreme Court (1789-1798), raised concerns about the consequences of incorporating these rights into the Constitution.

Wilson argued that by enumerating specific rights in the Constitution, it may be construed (by diabolical minds) to justify the government's power to limit any unnamed liberties of the people and that any rights not listed were automatically surrendered. According to Wilson, it would be impossible to itemize a comprehensive list of every right of the citizens. He believed the country would best be served by presuming the citizens had *all* rights (living, as much as possible, a life free from government interference) and that the limiting of a person's rights should be an extreme matter.

The topic of a Bill of Rights was given serious attention in the Federalist Papers. Addressing the overall nature of the debates over ratification, James Madison remarked pointedly about the divide over a Bill of Rights in Federalist No. 38.

> This one tells us that the proposed Constitution ought to be rejected, because it is not a confederation of the States, but a government over individuals. Another admits that it ought to be a government over individuals to a certain extent, but by no means to the extent proposed. A third does not object to the government over individuals, or to the extent proposed, but to the want of a bill of rights. A fourth concurs in the absolute necessity of a bill of rights, but contends that it ought to be declaratory, not of the personal rights of individuals, but of the rights reserved to the States in their political capacity. A fifth is of opinion that a bill of rights of any sort would be superfluous and misplaced, and that the plan would be unexceptionable but for the fatal power of regulating the times and places of election.[59]

A strong argument can be made that, absent a pledge from James Madison and others that a Bill of Rights would be forthcoming once

---

[59] Madison, James, Federalist No. 38.

the Constitution was adopted, the framers may well have fallen short of the nine states necessary for ratification.

Madison's initial plan was to rephrase/improve some of the wording of the Constitution itself. For instance, he proposed that the Preamble of the Constitution might be amended to reinforce the unalienable rights of *life, liberty, and the pursuit of happiness* delineated in the Declaration of Independence. He also wished to insert a list of specific rights into Article I, Section 9, and, as a matter of assurance, conclude with a safeguarding provision as follows:

> The exceptions here or elsewhere in the constitution, made in favor of particular rights, shall not be so construed as to diminish the just importance of other rights retained by the people; or as to enlarge the powers delegated by the constitution; but either as actual limitations of such powers, or as inserted merely for greater caution.

Madison's ideas were submitted to a congressional Select Committee to which Madison was also appointed. From that committee, the Ninth Amendment to the Constitution was born. That, however, is not the end of the story where this amendment is concerned since it naturally raises the question: **What unnamed rights are covered under this amendment and how are those rights recognized and preserved?**

Politicians and courts have continued to debate this question over the course of time. In those debates, four primary trains of thought have been offered, particularly over the past few decades, in an effort to identify the unspecified rights mentioned here.

- Some have asserted that *other rights* are those granted by state constitutions or state statutory laws, which could, of course, be preempted by federal laws under the Supremacy Clause.

- Others have contended that the amendment indicates "residual" rights that are not surrendered by the enumeration of powers. The idea is that, if Congress is working within the confines of the powers offered by the Constitution, they would not be in danger of infringing on any unnamed rights of individuals..

- Still others believe that, at its core, this amendment refers to the "collective" rights of the people, for example, to alter or abolish their government.

- The final argument is that the amendment alludes to the natural rights of the people as individuals (as opposed to citizens), which are also delineated in the Declaration of Independence, in various states' bills of rights, and Madison's proposed addition to the Preamble.

It has also been suggested that, although these unnamed rights may be unidentifiable in an affirmative sense, perhaps the framers intended for the courts to ascertain those rights as they come into question in the framework of society. The late Justice Antonin Scalia (1936-2016), who served on the Supreme Court for nearly thirty years (1986-2016), challenged the opinion that it was the Court's place to *name* rights. He believed rights should be delineated through either constitutional amendments or statutory methods at either the state or federal level. In keeping with the first of the four arguments given above, he denied that this amendment empowered the courts to proclaim individual rights via judicial decree, stating that:

> ...the Constitution's refusal to 'deny or disparage' other rights is far removed from affirming any one of them, and even further removed from authorizing judges to identify what they might be, and to enforce the judges' list against laws duly enacted by the people.

It is important, at this juncture, to distinguish between *rights* and *privileges*, since many confuse these two concepts. It could be said that the distinguishing factor is that participating in a privilege involves meeting certain qualifications, and that rights do not. Yet, that would be a false assertion. For instance, citizens have the right to vote in America, but to exercise that right one must meet an age qualification. The age qualification generally applies to statutory rights while unalienable rights (e.g., the right to life) are not limited by age.

Perhaps the best way to differentiate between a right and a privilege is to recognize that the qualifications for exercising rights differ from exercising privileges. While the primary qualification for exercising a right involves a person's age, exercising a privilege (e.g., attaining a driver's license), involves a demonstration of a level of skill where that privilege is concerned.

Similarly, it stands to reason that an individual has a right to seek out a means to earn a living based on his/her own *right to life, liberty, and the pursuit of happiness*. However, that same person does not have a right to be employed by the company of their choice. The employer will hire only those they deem sufficiently skilled for the position they wish to fill. Working for a company is a privilege even for the person who has a right to seek employment.

This amendment has had very little impact on American life, and specifically on the court system of the United States since few Ninth Amendment cases have reached the courts. Even on those occasions when the Ninth Amendment has been raised, it is generally paired with another amendment in seeking to identify (or deny the claim of) an unnamed right. For instance, in *Munn v. Illinois*, (1877), the Ninth Amendment served as support in the Supreme Court's ruling that the state of Illinois may, to a certain extent, regulate industry for the common good. Also, in *United States v. Jones*, (2012), the Ninth Amendment was used as support when the Supreme Court ruled that the government placing a tracker on a person's vehicle and recording information from the tracker was a violation of that person's Fourteenth Amendment right to property.

Generally, the Court has treated the Ninth Amendment as a guideline in the application of other amendments rather than a standalone guarantee of any specific rights. Disagreements over the identification of the Ninth Amendment's *other rights* will not be easily settled; nor will everyone soon agree on just how to construe this amendment. The debate will surely continue while much of the mystery presented by this amendment will remain unresolved. It will, however, continue to provide fodder for discussion among constitutional enthusiasts.

Tenth Amendment

The powers not delegated to the United States by the Constitution, nor prohibited by it to the States, are reserved to the States respectively, or to the people.

The process for ratification of the U.S. Constitution was arduous and debates over the pros and cons were often heated. One of the strongest opposing voices was that of Patrick Henry, who argued that the Constitution, as written, placed far too much power in the hands of the federal government. The Tenth Amendment was intended to assuage those concerns.

The divide over the meaning of the Tenth Amendment can be seen in the original discussion over the precise wording of the text. Those who hoped to minimize the role of the federal government (known as Anti-Federalists) sought slightly different wording than ultimately appeared in this amendment. They argued in favor of the wording: **The powers not *expressly* delegated to the United States...**, which had been included in the Articles of Confederation. They believed inclusion of this wording would serve to prevent the federal government from overstepping. There were others (known as Federalists) who feared that such wording could handicap the federal government.

Is there a significant difference between *powers not delegated* and *powers not expressly delegated*? Both sides saw a clear difference between these two statements. However, Federalists assured Anti-Federalists that, while providing the federal government with some flexibility, the less restrictive language was sufficient to block federal overreach. It is evident, given the final wording of the text, that those who believed in a less restrictive role for the federal government won the day.

Federalists claimed that the concerns of the Anti-Federalists were unwarranted. In fact, the limited scope of federal authority was used as a major selling point to affect ratification of the Constitution. James Madison, in Federalist No. 14, wrote explicitly about the founders' vision of a national government whose authority would be limited to those matters requiring a federal solution.

> ...the general government is not to be charged with the whole power of making and administering laws. Its jurisdiction is limited to certain enumerated objects, which concern all the members of the republic, but which are not to be attained by the separate provisions of any. The subordinate governments, which can extend their care to all those other subjects which can be separately provided for, will retain their due authority and activity.[60]

Disagreement over the scope of federal authority has led to a plethora of court actions where the Tenth Amendment is concerned. The results have been mixed as the amendment is weighed against the Necessary and Proper Clause of the Constitution (Article I, Section 8, Clause 18) authorizing Congress:

> To make all Laws which shall be necessary and proper for carrying into Execution the foregoing Powers, and all other Powers vested by this Constitution in the Government of the United States, or in any Department or Officer thereof.

The Anti-Federalists, whose concerns about federal overreach had been described as baseless, did not need to wait long for vindication. The tension between the Tenth Amendment and the Necessary and Proper Clause was tested early in the Supreme Courts and the Court's ruling focused precisely on the absence of the term *expressly* in this amendment. In *McCulloch* v. *Maryland*, (1819), the state of Maryland sought to thwart the establishment of a national bank, which had been

---

[60] Madison, James, Federalist No. 14.

a pet project of Alexander Hamilton. Ruling against the state of Maryland, Chief Justice John Marshall wrote the following in the majority opinion:

> Even the 10th Amendment, which was framed for the purpose of quieting the excessive jealousies which had been excited, omits the word "expressly," and declares only that the powers "not delegated to the United States, nor prohibited to the States, are reserved to the States or to the people," thus leaving the question whether the particular power which may become the subject of contest has been delegated to the one Government, or prohibited to the other, to depend on a fair construction of the whole instrument. The men who drew and adopted this amendment had experienced the embarrassments resulting from the insertion of this word in the Articles of Confederation, and probably omitted it to avoid those embarrassments.[61]

Following *McCulloch v. Maryland*, the Supreme Court upheld the federal government's authority to regulate interstate commerce in *Gibbons v. Ogden*, (1824). Over the course of the next century, the courts largely endorsed the principle expressed in John Marshall's opinion. As a result, the scope of federal authority grew substantially through the nineteenth century.

The early twentieth century saw some court decisions that seemed to challenge the reasoning employed in *McCulloch v. Maryland*, although the results were mixed. For instance, in *Hammer v. Dagenhart*, (1918), the Supreme Court struck down a federal law prohibiting child labor as an infringement on state sovereignty. However, two years later, the Court upheld a federal law that

---

[61] Britannica, *Tenth Amendment, United States Constitution*, www.britannica.com/topic/tenthamendment, Accessed November 20, 2023

implemented a treaty to protect migratory birds in *State of Missouri v. Holland*, (1920), rejecting the Tenth Amendment challenge. Then, in *United States v. Sprague*, (1931), a case dealing with the topic of prohibition, the Supreme Court stated that federal power was strictly limited to only what was contained in the U.S. Constitution and that anything further violated the Tenth Amendment. It is evident from these rulings that the Court has been inconsistent in its application of this amendment

The Great Depression, which began in 1929, saw Franklin D. Roosevelt replace Herbert Hoover in 1933 as President of the United States. Roosevelt believed it was the role of the federal government to get intimately involved in economic restoration and, as a result, between 1933 and 1937, Congress passed his economic plan involving public work projects, banking reforms, the establishment of Social Security, and other programs, all under the umbrella of what was termed The New Deal.

The Supreme Court blocked many of Roosevelt's proposals, insisting that they far exceeded the limits placed on the federal government by the Constitution. The Tenth Amendment was a critical component in those decisions. However, Roosevelt won a landslide reelection in 1936. Relying on this political capital, he threatened to pack the Supreme Court with justices who would do his bidding. As a result, the Tenth Amendment was disregarded and most of the programs in The New Deal were implemented.

In the ensuing years, The Supreme Court seemed to support a view of government that aligned with Roosevelt's ideas. In *United States v. Darby Lumber*, (1941), the Supreme Court upheld the federal Fair Labor Standards Act of 1938, finding that the federal government did, indeed, have constitutional support to implement a federal minimum wage and assorted other labor-related laws.

In the late twentieth century, the Court seemed to rely on the Tenth Amendment in certain cases, limiting intrusion by the federal government into state sovereignty. In *New York v. United States,* (1992), the Court found in favor of the state of New York as the federal government attempted to force upon the states certain responsibilities concerning low-level radioactive waste. Also, in the case of *Printz v. United States*, (1997), the Supreme Court found that The Brady Handgun Violence Prevention Act, which required state agencies to perform background checks on buyers before issuing handguns, was unconstitutional. According to the Court, this act "forced participation of the State's executive in the actual administration of a federal program."[62]

A more recent and better-known example of Tenth Amendment challenges involved a statute passed by Congress called The Patient Protection and Affordable Care Act (ACA), commonly known as Obamacare. Questions about the constitutionality of this law have reached the Supreme Court several times. The most notable of these cases, and the first to reach the Supreme Court, is *National*

---

[62] The Tenth Amendment – Definition and Famous Cases, infotracer.com, Accessed February 2, 2024.

Federation of Independent Businesses v. Sebelius, (2012). As captivating as the political arguments surrounding this case may be (and it is always viewed through a political lens), the goal here is to set aside any judgment of the virtues or vices where the statute is concerned and review the Court's decision strictly in terms of constitutionality.

At issue were questions about the federal government's authority to mandate healthcare for individuals, including a mandate for employers to provide healthcare for their employees. Another issue involved the statute's expansion of Medicaid, which made a state's federal funding for Medicaid contingent upon the state's expansion of eligibility requirements for that program. The primary question before the Court was whether Congress had the authority to declare a *mandate to purchase*, which seemed to stretch congressional authority into the arena of "powers not delegated."

The ACA established financial penalties for those who did not participate and were not otherwise covered by health insurance. This penalty was ruled unconstitutional by the Supreme Court, but the ruling then took a curious turn. The Court determined that the penalty could survive constitutional scrutiny if it was deemed a tax rather than a penalty.

> While the court rejected the claim that the individual mandate was within Congress's commerce power, the mandate was found to be constitutional as a tax...Moreover, while the individual mandate is clearly intended as an incentive to purchase health insurance, many other taxes are also in place to promote certain behaviors—for example, the government taxes cigarettes to reduce nicotine consumption. Thus the Court found the mandate well within

Congress's power to tax. While Congress doesn't have the power to require individuals to purchase health insurance, it *does* have the power to tax those individuals who do not.[63]

The Supreme Court used what many have described as creative reasoning to circumvent the unconstitutionality of the measure. The mandate was ruled unconstitutional, but the mechanism to enforce the mandate was upheld. Thus, the Court left in place what it understood to be an unconstitutional statute.

The Court's comparison of ACA penalties to other taxes is strained since the taxes mentioned involve no *mandate to purchase*. For instance, taxes on cigarettes and alcohol (drolly referred to as sin taxes) involve no such mandates. They are intended only to influence free will choices. In other words, if no purchase is made, no tax is due. However, the Court upheld the ACA despite the fact that the statute was, by the Court's own admission, unconstitutional. The strongest argument is that the Supreme Court should have returned the statute to Congress for reconsideration and rewording in order to make it constitutionally palatable.

The political problem for the Court was that the make-up of the body of Congress had changed since the statute had passed in 2010. It was clear that no reworking of the ACA would survive a congressional vote in 2012. The Supreme Court's rather creative solution was to read into the statute something that the statute itself rejected. In this instance, a strong case can be made that the Court

---

[63] AMA Journal of Ethics, *The Constitutionality of the Affordable Care Act*: https://journalofethics.ama-assn.org/ Accessed November 21, 2023.

overstepped its own constitutional authority by essentially rewriting the law on behalf of Congress.

The decision to uphold the individual mandate was based partly upon an earlier questionable application of the Commerce Clause (Article I, Section 8, Clause 3) by Judge Laurence Silberman, an Appeals Court Judge from the District of Columbia, in *Seven-Sky v. Holder*, (2011). It is an explanation that has been highly criticized by many legal scholars. Current Supreme Court Justice Bret Kavanaugh, who was a member of the panel of judges who heard *Seven-Sky v. Holder*, wrote in his dissenting opinion:

> The Anti-Injunction Act, a part of the Internal Revenue Code, only bars pre-enforcement challenges to the assessment and collection of *taxes*. As is well known, Congress, in passing the Affordable Care Act, pointedly rejected proposals to designate the shared responsibility payment as a "tax," instead labeling it a "penalty." That Congress called numerous other provisions in the Act "taxes" indicates that its decision to use the word "penalty" here was deliberate. And congressional findings never suggested that Congress's purpose was to raise revenue. The Government estimates the penalty would raise $4 billion, but congressional findings emphasize that the aim of the shared responsibility payment is to encourage everyone to purchase insurance; the goal is universal coverage, not revenues from penalties.[64]

The assenting Supreme Court Justices adopted Silberman's progressive elucidation of the text and allowed the mandate to stand. This alternate meaning of the word *penalty* was applied despite the fact that the statute itself purposely eschewed that label, specifically identifying the charge as a penalty rather than a tax. Justice Antonin

---

[64] Casetext, *Seven-Sky v. Holder*, https://casetext.com, Accessed November 21, 2023

Scalia recognized the Tenth Amendment implications in his dissenting opinion.

> What is absolutely clear, affirmed by the text of the 1789 Constitution, by the Tenth Amendment ratified in 1791, and by innumerable cases of ours in the 220 years since, is that there are structural limits upon federal power—upon what it can prescribe with respect to private conduct, and upon what it can impose upon the sovereign States. Whatever may be the conceptual limits upon the Commerce Clause and upon the power to tax and spend, they cannot be such as will enable the Federal Government to regulate all private conduct and to compel the States to function as administrators of federal programs.[65]

It is interesting that the Supreme Court ruled against the statute with respect to the Medicaid mandate. What makes the decision exceptional is that the logic employed to strike down the Medicaid mandate seemed to directly conflict with the reasoning used by the Court to uphold the individual mandate. The contradiction can be seen in the fact that the required penalty in the Medicaid mandate was expressly deemed by the Court to be a penalty rather than a tax. In contrast to the decision concerning the individual mandate, the Court determined that the Constitution would not allow penalization of the states for refusing to participate.

> Striking down as unconstitutional a penalty on nonparticipating states, the court reasoned that Medicaid originally intended to cover four types of needy persons: the blind, the disabled, the elderly, and families with children. It argued that, while Congress has the right to redefine who may fall into the categories of those covered and to provide monetary incentives to states to cover certain populations of persons, the Medicaid expansion changed the original goal of the

---
[65] Legal Information Institute, *National Federation of Independent Business v. Sebelius* | www.law.cornell.edu, Accessed November 21, 2023.

program itself—making it not just a program to cover needy persons, but a national health care plan intended to provide universal coverage that, moreover, uses penalties rather than incentives to encourage compliance. Deeming the provision too coercive, the court held instead that the government cannot penalize those states that choose not to expand Medicaid in this way.[66]

In 2017, Donald Trump stepped into the office of President, having campaigned on a promise to repeal the ACA. As a result, The Tax Cut and Jobs Act of 2017 introduced considerable changes to the Internal Revenue Code. One of those changes was the reduction of the ACA penalty to $0. This effectively eliminated the *mandate to purchase* that had been the primary sticking point for those who deemed the statute unconstitutional. Still, the debate over whether it is constitutional for the federal government to be the arbiter of health care remains contentious as it appears to be an authority "not delegated to the United States by the Constitution."

What this case demonstrates is that the Supreme Court, as in the case of The New Deal in the late 1930's, will occasionally abandon constitutional principles in favor of political interests. Whether or not a federal action is ruled to be constitutional tends to be less dependent on the words of the Constitution and more dependent on the political leanings of a majority of the justices at the time a case is heard. While not true in every situation, conservative justices tend to view the federal government's role through a strict application of the

---

[66] AMA Journal of Ethics, *The Constitutionality of the Affordable Care Act*: https://journalofethics.ama-assn.org/ Accessed November 21, 2023.

Tenth Amendment while more liberal justices often rely on the fact that the amendment does not *expressly* limit specific powers.

Chapter 10
Amendments 11-16

Eleventh Amendment

The Judicial power of the United States shall not be construed to extend to any suit in law or equity, commenced or prosecuted against one of the United States by Citizens of another State, or by Citizens or Subjects of any Foreign State.

It is fascinating that the Constitution, along with the amendments, may be viewed differently by the Court depending on the philosophical character of the justices hearing a case. The Eleventh Amendment serves as a prime example. It also demonstrates how the wording of the Constitution, amendments, or statutes may be construed differently by those who are most directly impacted by a particular meaning (plaintiffs and defendants). Often the imagination of the Court and others strains the meaning of an amendment (or statute) well beyond what a plain reading of the text allows.

At its core, the scope of this amendment is very narrow. It states that federal courts are prohibited from hearing any case where an individual sues a state when the individual is either a citizen of another state or a citizen or resident/subject of a foreign country. For instance, federal courts may not entertain a law suit where a citizen of Maryland sues the state of New York. Based on a candid reading of the text, it is difficult to imagine anyone deriving an application beyond this.

This amendment was birthed when concerns arose over a certain provision of Article III which, it was argued, allowed federal courts to adjudicate cases where a dispute arose between a state and a citizen of another state. The article reads that federal jurisdiction covers cases "between a State and Citizens of another State" (Article III, Section 2).

Some questioned whether this language was intended to limit federal jurisdiction in the case of a state suing a citizen from another state or if it could be used to allow an individual from one state to bring suit against another state. The disputed meaning of Article III allowed *Chisholm v. Georgia*, (1793), to appear on the docket of the Supreme Court. The executors of the estate of Alexander Chisholm, who was a citizen in South Carolina, sued the state of Georgia over unpaid war-related debts the state had incurred during the Revolutionary War.

The state of Georgia took issue, denying that Article III allowed the case to be heard by a federal court and, as a result, refused to appear. The state argued that the State of Georgia, like other states, had sovereign immunity. This meant that the state could only be sued if the state consented.

Testing what many considered to be a questionable application of Article III, the Supreme Court, in a 4-1 ruling, determined that the case should proceed at the federal level. This finding, at least at the time, also answered the unsolicited question: **May a state be sued?** The

Supreme Court determined that with the wording of Article III where is stated "between a State and Citizens of another State," that the word *between* should be construed to include not only law suits brought *by* the State, but also law suits brought *against* the State.

The details of the case are complicated and will not be reviewed here. Suffice it to say that the Supreme Court ruled in favor of Chisholm's estate, but that decision was dwarfed by the grander implications of the lawsuit. In the majority ruling, Chief Justice John Jay reasoned, in finding that states may be sued and are subject to federal jurisdiction, that the state of Georgia had misconstrued the concept of state sovereignty. He insisted that sovereignty belongs, not to each individual state *government*, but to the *people* of each state, indicating that he believed the two were not the same.

Associate Justice Iredell, who was the sole dissenting voice, defended the concept of independent state sovereignty. He insisted that federalism was loosely designed in the likeness of English common law where a sovereign state (government) may not be sued without giving its own consent.

The backlash from several states, infuriated by the Court's verdict in *Chisholm v. Georgia*, was swift and spirited. Georgia's governor, Edward Telfair, proclaimed that if this is the kind of decision that could be expected from the Supreme Court, it would eventually lead to "an annihilation of [the state's] political existence."[67] Officials from

---

[67] National Park Service, *The Supreme Court Decides in Chisholm v. Georgia, https//*nps.gov, Accessed November 27, 2023.

other states also vigorously voiced their frustration since comparable suits against some of those states were pending at the time.

Responding to the voices of discontent, on March 4, 1794, the U. S. House of Representatives passed a resolution for an amendment to be added to the Constitution. That proposal specifically forbade suits against states from individuals residing in other states. The following January, Senator Caleb Strong of Massachusetts, offered a similar proposal to the Senate, which easily passed. The House soon adopted the Senate's version and the Eleventh Amendment was quickly submitted to the states for ratification. Perhaps not surprisingly, within a month (February 1795), the amendment had been ratified by the state legislatures.

Despite what seemed to be the straightforward intent of Congress, this amendment has been applied variously over the course of time. For instance, in *Cohens v. Virginia*, (1821), the state of Virginia turned to the Eleventh Amendment challenging the Court's jurisdiction to review a state court decision in a criminal case. Virginia had prosecuted two brothers from Virginia for the crime of selling lottery tickets. The defendants argued that a federal statute allowed the lottery and ticket sales. The Court determined, in that case, that the Eleventh Amendment did not apply since the defendants were citizens of Virginia. Second, the Court found that, since the Eleventh Amendment did not apply, jurisdiction reverted to the words of Article III where is stated that federal courts have appellate jurisdiction "in all cases arising under the Constitution, laws, or treaties of the United States."

In its decision in *Hans v. Louisiana*, (1890), the Supreme Court seems to have countered the ruling in *Cohens v. Virginia*. In this case, the Court delivered an imaginative treatment of the Eleventh Amendment. The Court found somewhere in its reading of the amendment that not only were citizens from another state prohibited from filing suit against a state, but the state's own citizens were equally prohibited from suing their own state.

The Court ruled in *Alden v. Maine*, (1990), that states do, indeed, enjoy immunity in state court from suits that are based on federal law. However, a state may, if it so chooses, *allow* a suit that is barred by the Eleventh Amendment. These decisions suggest that the Court regards a state's sovereign immunity from law suit without its own consent as a fundamental constitutional principle.

Sundry Eleventh Amendment cases have resulted in a variety of rulings with the Supreme Court applying the amendment narrowly on occasion, as in *Cohens v. Virginia*, and broadly at other times, as in *Hans v. Louisiana*, depending on the Court's leaning at the time. In the case of *Pennsylvania v. Union Gas Co.*, (1989), the Court (at least provisionally) held that Congress, acting in accord with its Article I powers, may override a state's immunity from suit that is established in the Eleventh Amendment, so long as Congress offers reasonable and clear justification for its action.

The *Pennsylvania v. Union Gas* decision was short-lived. In fact, it lasted a mere seven years before the Court overruled it in *Seminole Tribe of Florida v. Florida*, (1996). Writing for the majority in this 5-4 decision, Chief Justice Rehnquist concluded that Union Gas had taken undue advantage of the *Hans v. Louisiana* ruling that treated the Eleventh Amendment as the establishment of the "fundamental principle of sovereign immunity [that] limits the grant of judicial authority in Article III."[68] According to this new ruling, since "the Eleventh Amendment restricts the judicial power under Article III . . . Article I cannot be used to circumvent the constitutional limitations placed upon federal jurisdiction."[69] Subsequent court decisions have reinforced this reversal of the *Pennsylvania v. Union Gas* ruling.

Twelfth Amendment

The Electors shall meet in their respective states and vote by ballot for President and Vice-President, one of whom, at least, shall not be an inhabitant of the same state with themselves; they shall name in their ballots the person voted for as President, and in distinct ballots the person voted for as Vice-President, and they shall make distinct lists of all persons voted for as President, and of all persons voted for as Vice-President, and of the number of votes for each, which lists they shall sign and certify, and transmit sealed to the seat of the government of the United States, directed to the President of the Senate;–the President of the Senate shall, in the presence of the Senate and House of Representatives, open all the certificates and the votes shall then be counted;–The person having the greatest number of votes for President, shall be the President, if such number be a majority of the whole number of Electors appointed; and if no person have such majority, then from the persons having the highest numbers not exceeding three on the list of those voted for as

---

[68] Justia U. S. Law, *Suits Against States*, https://law.justia.com, accessed December 3, 2023
[69] Ibid.

President, the House of Representatives shall choose immediately, by ballot, the President. But in choosing the President, the votes shall be taken by states, the representation from each state having one vote; a quorum for this purpose shall consist of a member or members from two-thirds of the states, and a majority of all the states shall be necessary to a choice. [And if the House of Representatives shall not choose a President whenever the right of choice shall devolve upon them, before the fourth day of March next following, then the Vice-President shall act as President, as in case of the death or other constitutional disability of the President.–]The person having the greatest number of votes as Vice-President, shall be the Vice-President, if such number be a majority of the whole number of Electors appointed, and if no person have a majority, then from the two highest numbers on the list, the Senate shall choose the Vice-President; a quorum for the purpose shall consist of two-thirds of the whole number of Senators, and a majority of the whole number shall be necessary to a choice. But no person constitutionally ineligible to the office of President shall be eligible to that of Vice-President of the United States.

Article II of the Constitution lays out the process for selecting the President of the United States. Rather than selection by a national popular vote of the people, it was decided that the president should be chosen by the states. Each state was awarded a number of electoral votes, equivalent to the state's representation in Congress (number of representatives in the House plus two Senators). The idea was that the candidate who receives the majority of the citizens' votes in a state would receive the electoral votes from that state.

George Washington was unanimously elected as the first President of the United States in 1789 and served for eight years, having been reelected in 1792. It was the hope of George Washington and many other Founding Fathers that the U. S. could avoid the trappings of political parties and Article II was designed with that in mind. For this reason, the Constitution was written such that, in an election, the individual who received the most electoral votes would become president and the person receiving the second highest number of electoral votes would serve as vice president.

While some in modern times might consider this an encumbrance, since the two would have necessarily been adversaries both vying for the same position, the thought behind it was not unreasonable. The founders were concerned about having a vice president, an individual a heartbeat away from the office of president, who got there on another person's coattails. They believed the office of vice president should be filled by someone who was selected based on that individual's own standing with the people. It would be the person the citizenry viewed as second-most-qualified for the office. Their concern was that a person who was selected as a vice presidential candidate by a political party or via a presidential candidate's personal choice might not have the character the office of president demands, since they would not receive votes for that office based on personal merit.

Those concerns may have been justified. In the history of the United States, fifteen vice presidents have also served as president. Eight of those took the presidential reins upon the death of the president under whom they served, yet many of those who inherited the presidency seem to have struggled in office. For example, Andrew Johnson was impeached (unsuccessfully) and Lyndon Johnson's presidency was so weighed down by the Vietnam War that he chose very early to end his campaign for a second term and remove his name from consideration.

Since the ratification of the Twelfth Amendment, only seven vice presidents have subsequently been *elected* to the office of president, and many of those saw limited success. Of those elected to the office, only three (Theodore Roosevelt, Harry S. Truman, and Richard Nixon) were elected to a second presidential term.

The single example of rivals for the office of president ultimately serving together in the roles of president and vice president occurred during the election of 1796 as George Washington relinquished the office, having served two terms. Unfortunately, Washington waited until two months before Election Day to announce that he was stepping down, which triggered considerable anxiety where the upcoming election was concerned.

George Washington loathed, and warned against, the idea of political parties. He believed they would only serve to foment division within communities. He also foresaw a time when men would begin to choose party over community and warned that partisan factions tended to provide opportunists with political tools that could be used to thwart the will of the people. Washington's concern about the dangers posed by political parties seems eerily prophetic when viewed through a modern-day lens. He spoke of his concerns in his Farewell Address to the nation on November 4, 1796.

> They serve to organize faction, to give it an artificial and extraordinary force; to put, in the place of the delegated will of the nation the will of a party, often a small but artful and enterprising

minority of the community, They are likely, in the course of time and things, to become potent engines, by which cunning, ambitious, and unprincipled men will be enabled to subvert the power of the people and to usurp for themselves the reins of government, destroying afterward the very engines which have lifted them to unjust dominion.[70]

Despite Washington's warnings, early in his first term, as the proposals for constitutional amendments were being shaped, members of Congress as well as certain members of the executive branch began drawing distinct ideological lines. These conflicting philosophical views led to the formation of two political parties. One group became known as Federalists[71] and consisted of some well-known personalities like John Adams, Alexander Hamilton, and John Jay. Although George Washington did not identify with either party, many Federalists saw him as their natural (albeit unofficial) leader since John Adams served as his Vice President and he appeared to espouse their views.

The coalition on the other side of the political aisle became known as Democratic-Republicans – arguably an awkward term in the twenty-first century when the primary rival parties are known as Democrats and Republicans. They originally called themselves Republicans, but the hyphenated designation, which seemed to stick, was thrust upon them by the opposition in hopes of linking the party to the excessive brutalities carried out during the French Revolution

---

[70] National Constitution Center, *On This Day: The first bitter, contested presidential election takes place* | https://constitutioncenter.org, Accessed November 5, 2023.
[71] Federalist views were witnessed in the political divide over the wording of the Tenth Amendment that was mentioned in the discussion of that amendment.

where similar terminology was used. This party consisted of equally famous men like Thomas Jefferson, who had served as Washington's Secretary of State, and James Madison, who would later serve as the fourth President of the United States.

While disagreements between the two factions involved both international and domestic issues, most of those divisions were grounded in differences over how they perceived the respective roles of the federal and state governments. Democratic-Republicans believed primary authority should be vested in the states with the federal government serving more as a coordinator than an authority. Federalists thought primary authority should be centralized (in the federal government), insisting that this would provide for a stronger, more cohesive Union.

In the 1796 election, John Adams was selected as the presidential candidate for the Federalists and Thomas Jefferson ran as a Democratic-Republican. Diving into the sordid details of those two months in 1796 would be a formidable task. It is sufficient to say that the venomous nature of political campaigning has neither improved nor deteriorated in the more than two hundred years that have passed since Adams faced Jefferson.

The campaign saw twelve candidates throw their hats into the ring. John Adams, Thomas Pinkney, Oliver Ellsworth, and James Iredell ran as Federalists. In contrast, Thomas Jefferson, Aaron Burr, Samuel Adams, and George Clinton took up the Democratic-Republican mantle. John Jay, Samuel Johnson, and Charles Pinkney ran as

Independent Federalists. One final contestant by the name of John Henry ran as a true Independent.

A total of 276 electoral votes were up for grabs in November 1796. It was John Adams who won the day, garnering 71 votes. Jefferson followed closely with 68 votes. Thomas Pinkney took third place with 59 votes, the remaining 78 going to other candidates. Although he was not running, even George Washington received 2 votes. However, it was John Adams and Thomas Jefferson, the top two vote-getters, who were installed as President and Vice President respectively.

Adams and Jefferson had been friends and allies during the early days of the Union and had worked together through the separation from England. However, their political differences proved problematic and, in the aftermath of a vicious political campaign, it is fair to say that their working relationship was strained. Jefferson settled into the menial tasks afforded his office, anxiously anticipating the election of 1800.

As the next election drew close, Jefferson again challenged Adams for the presidency. Aaron Burr ran as Jefferson's vice presidential running mate while Adams was joined on the Federalist ticket by Charles Pinkney. Abiding by Article II, Electors each cast two votes for president and the result of those votes in 1800 changed the course of history. Jefferson and Burr tied with 73 votes each while Adams received 65 votes. This meant that, in keeping with Article II of the Constitution, the decision of who should be installed as president fell to the House of Representatives.

The tie vote between Jefferson and Burr revealed what many saw as weaknesses in the selection process established in Article II. First, there was considerable dismay that, in practicality, the one-state/one-vote system gave Delaware's sole Representative, James Bayard, who was a devoted Federalist, the same voting power as the state of Virginia. Not only was Virginia the largest state at the time, but it was also Jefferson's home state. Additionally, if a state had an even number of representatives and those representatives chose to split their votes equally between two candidates, the state's vote was forfeit.

At the time of the election of 1800, the Union consisted of sixteen states. To reach a majority, nine states had to come to agreement in their choice for president. This task was found to be more daunting than expected. The House was in session for several days without reaching agreement. Finally, on the 36th ballot, Representative Bayard acquiesced and switched his vote to Thomas Jefferson, ending the stalemate. One could argue that Bayard's decision was simply pragmatic since, after several days of deadlock the Jeffersonian governors from Pennsylvania and Virginia were threatening to have their state militias march on Washington, D.C. Perhaps that threat provided the motivation that swayed Bayard's decision.

On the heels of the awkwardly divided Adams/Jefferson administration, the challenges presented by the election of 1800 caused the nation's leaders to realize that the system was flawed. It was the embittered election of 1800, with its twists and turns, that served as a catalyst for the development of the Twelfth Amendment.

It became evident, as a result of the election of 1800, that Article II did not provide sufficient protection against the calamity that had occurred. In 1800 and in previous elections, each vote cast by Electors was understood to be a vote for the office of president. The candidate who received the most votes would be declared the winner. However, in 1800, Jefferson had run for the office of president and Burr ran as his running mate, seeking the office of Vice president. Had things gone differently in the House of Representatives, their roles may well have been reversed.

The Twelfth Amendment sought to improve on the process established in Article II. Congress reasoned that, going forward, electoral votes should be split between the office of president and the office of vice president. That way a candidate running for vice president could only be elected to that office. Similarly, a candidate for president could only be chosen to fill that particular role. As before, in the case of an electoral tie, the decision would again fall on the House of Representatives with each state casting a single vote.

Each state is responsible for certifying the accuracy of the votes it sends to the vice president, who serves as President of the Senate and is responsible for the counting of the ballots. After the ballots are received, they are opened before the members of both the Senate and the House of Representatives and counted. The current Electoral College consists of 538 Electors, so a candidate must receive 270 votes to be declared the winner. Yet, it is possible for two candidates to be tied at 269 votes each, in which case, the decision concerning the

Presidency would move to the House of Representatives where procedures could be followed and the office would be filled.

As in the days prior to the adoption of the Twelfth Amendment, it is not that unusual in modern times to have additional candidates for the Presidency beyond the two major parties. This begs the question: **What would happen if no candidate receives the minimum 270 votes?** In such a case, the newly elected members of the House of Representatives would need to choose from the three candidates who received the most electoral votes. The House members would vote, each state being allowed a single vote. Naturally, the party holding the majority of seats in the majority of states would be in a position to control the outcome of the vote.

In similar fashion, if no candidate for vice president receives the necessary 270 electoral votes, responsibility for the selection of the vice president would fall to the newly elected Senate. In that case, it would be the Senate's role to consider the two individuals who received the highest number of votes for that office. With one vote allowed from each state, the Senate would vote to choose who would serve as vice president.

The Twelfth Amendment primarily changed the manner in which electoral votes were cast. Electors were now required to cast one vote for president and a second vote for vice president. They could no longer cast two votes for presidential candidates. This assured that the newly elected president would not be saddled with a vice president who had been a presidential candidate from an opposing party.

This amendment did not address every issue that some people considered to be constitutional flaws. For instance, the one-state/one-vote formula in the House of Representatives and Senate remained intact. Nonetheless, the amendment was approved by Congress on December 8, 1803, and subsequently submitted to the states for ratification. It was ratified by the states and inserted into the Constitution on June 4, 1804, just in time for the election to be held later that year.

Thirteenth Amendment
Section 1

Neither slavery nor involuntary servitude, except as a punishment for crime whereof the party shall have been duly convicted, shall exist within the United States, or any place subject to their jurisdiction.

During the drafting of the U.S. Constitution, the framers recognized that the issue of slavery was problematic. If, within the framework of the Constitution, they sought to eliminate slavery, southern states would never agree to ratification, forcing the Union to continue to operate under the insufficient Articles of Confederation. Thus it was necessary to reach a compromise. The result was Article I, Section 9, which prohibited the federal government from passing slavery-related legislation until the year 1808 – roughly twenty years in the future from the writing of the document.

As the date of opportunity approached, many in Congress were eager to address the issue, but they also realized that an immediate, outright ban on slavery could easily destroy the fragile, newly established Union. It was decided that it would be wise to begin by taking small bites. They determined that eliminating the importation of new slaves would be a good start. In 1807, Congress passed a statute, enthusiastically signed by President Jefferson, eliminating the import of new slaves. That statute took effect on January 1, 1808.

Fifty-five years later, in the middle of the Civil War, Abraham Lincoln issued the Emancipation Proclamation on January 1, 1863, freeing all slaves in the Confederate States of America. While the proclamation sought to free those slaves that was only part of Lincoln's objective. In fact, it may have been a secondary goal. At least in part, he sought to weaken the South by removing a major slice of the southern economy – cheap human labor = hopefully limiting their war time resources. He was convinced that emancipating enslaved people in the South would help the Union squash the Confederate revolt and win the Civil War.

The legality of freeing slaves via presidential fiat was highly disputed, and slave owners in southern states were not particularly impressed. They would not, as the proclamation demanded, release their slaves so easily and the institution of slavery continued mostly unchecked through the end of the war. In the aftermath of the war, Congress knew it was time to fully eliminate the institution of slavery through legislative action. Amending the Constitution was the reasonable approach since it would give the abolition of slavery a sense of permanence that a statute would not provide.

The Thirteenth Amendment was actually approved by Congress prior to General Lee's surrender at Appomattox on April 9, 1865. The Senate passed this amendment on April 8, 1864. However, given that 1864 was an election year, there was resistance in the House of Representatives. The amendment did not pass in the House until January 31, 1865, after the election. Abraham Lincoln added his signature on February 1, 1865, and the amendment was submitted to the states for ratification shortly thereafter.

Some may wonder how this amendment garnered sufficient support among southern states to be adopted. A little known fact is that they were given no choice. During the war, southern states forfeited their congressional representation. In the aftermath, Congress required the former Confederate states to ratify the Thirteenth and Fourteenth Amendments or they would fully relinquish their representation in the federal government.

Abraham Lincoln had seen the nation through one of the bloodiest wars in history, so it stands to reason that he drew a measure of satisfaction from the passage of the Thirteenth Amendment. Unfortunately, he did not survive to witness its ratification, which was completed on December 6, 1865. His life was taken from him on April 14, 1865, when he was assassinated by John Wilkes Booth just days after the war had ended.

Section 2

Congress shall have power to enforce this article by appropriate legislation.

The Thirteenth Amendment was the first amendment where the legislature chose to attach an Enforcement Clause. There was concern that an edict of this magnitude (the abolition of slavery) would be rendered meaningless absent an enforcement mechanism. This clause was included as part of the product ratified by the states. Therefore, ratification by the states meant accepting Congress's right to hold accountable those who failed to act upon the provisions of the amendment.

Until recently, the Supreme Court applied this Enforcement Clause very narrowly. For more than a century after the ratification of the Thirteenth Amendment, the Supreme Court denied that Congress's power of enforcement should be so loosely defined that it might extend to the legislation impacting personal opinions. Attitudes that were descended from the era of slavery and led to discriminatory actions were not seen as congressional concerns. That perspective began to change when, in *Jones v. Alfred H. Mayer* Co., (1968), the Court ruled that Congress could regulate the sale of private property to prevent racial discrimination. Since that time, Congress has passed a multitude of statutes to address these kinds of discriminatory practices.

Fourteenth Amendment
Section 1

All persons born or naturalized in the United States, and subject to the jurisdiction thereof, are citizens of the United States and of the State wherein they reside. No State shall make or enforce any law which shall abridge the privileges or immunities of citizens of the

United States; nor shall any State deprive any person of life, liberty, or property, without due process of law; nor deny to any person within its jurisdiction the equal protection of the laws.

U. S. citizenship was mentioned on occasion in the Articles of the Constitution (i.e., Article I, Section 2, Clause 2; Article II, Section 1, Clause 5; Article III, Section 2, Clause 1; Article IV, Section 2, Clause 1). Complementing the use of this term in the Articles, U.S. citizenship is also referenced in the Eleventh Amendment. The inescapable conclusion drawn from the previous uses of this term is that the Founding Fathers presumed the existence of citizenship at both the state and federal levels in the United States of America. However, while citizenship was recognized by those men, it was never clearly defined. This clause in the Fourteenth Amendment sought to remedy that oversight a full seventy-five years after the Constitution was ratified.

In the days following ratification of the Constitution, the idea of citizenship at both the state and federal levels was widely discussed. Citizenship was important since the Constitution recognized certain rights, privileges, and protections afforded the citizenry at each level. The Constitution had placed upon Congress the responsibility for developing a process for naturalization (Article I, Section 8, Clause 4).

In the early stages of Washington's Presidency, Congress devised a system in The Naturalization Act of 1790. However, at the time slavery was still a common practice and foreigners (especially those who were not White Caucasian) were viewed with skepticism. Thus, the naturalization process was limited to "...any alien, being a free white person, who shall have resided within the limits and under the jurisdiction of the United States for the term of two years."[72]

The violence of the French Revolution in the early 1790's raised concerns that some of those responsible for what became known as the *Reign of Terror* in France might try to sneak into the U.S. and attempt to gain citizenship. As a result, Congress upped the ante and passed the 1795 Naturalization Act, increasing the residency requirement to five years. Three years later, in The Naturalization Act of 1798, the residency requirement was increased to fourteen years.

Believing a majority of naturalized citizens would likely share their political views, Democratic-Republicans opposed the fourteen year waiting period, insisting that it was much too long. When Jefferson won the Presidency in 1800, his party also wrested control of Congress from the Federalists. They then restored the five year residency requirement in The Naturalization Act of 1802.

In the earliest days of the Union, citizenship was male-centered. While the term "all persons" in The Naturalization Act of 1790 included women, the law also stated that "the right of citizenship shall not descend to persons whose fathers have never been resident in the United States...." Thus, even if the mother was an American citizen, a child born abroad whose father had not resided in the United States was not automatically granted citizenship. Until 1934, when Congress

---

[72]Immigration History, *Nationality Act of 1790*, https://immigrationhistory.org/item/1790-nationality-act/, Accessed October 3, 2023

corrected this evident inequity, a person's descendant citizenship was realized solely through the father.

In the years leading up to the Civil War, both state and national citizenships were again serious topics for discussion. While many agreed on certain aspects of citizenship (e.g., those born in the U. S. were generally considered citizens of the U.S. as well as citizens of the state where they resided), there were differences of opinion on certain matters. One divisive issue concerned the citizenship of those individuals who had been freed from slavery.

The conversation concerning the citizenship of former slaves took a dramatic turn following the Supreme Court's decision in *Dred Scott v. Sandford*, (1857). The case was originally brought in 1846 in the state courts of Missouri. It wound its way through the courts, finally reaching the Supreme Court on appeal in the late 1850's. This case thrust the topic of citizenship to the forefront of political discussion in the United States.

Dred Scott, a slave, sued the executor of his former master's estate who insisted that Scott *belonged* to the estate. Scott had claimed his freedom since he had accompanied his previous owner, Dr. John Emerson, into the free territories of Illinois and Wisconsin in the mid 1830's. Living in Missouri with Emerson's widow, Scot sued based on a Missouri statute which stated that any person taken to a free territory automatically became free and could not be re-enslaved upon returning to a slave state. He insisted that he was both a federal and state citizen and deserved all rights and privileges that citizenship afforded him.

In the final analysis, Chief Justice Taney concluded that Scott could not claim his freedom since he was not considered a citizen of any state. According to Taney, the Constitution *implicitly* limited both state and national citizenship on racial grounds. Therefore, Scott was excluded from citizenship since he was of African descent. Based on his lack of citizenship, Taney insisted that Scott lacked standing to sue in federal court. The ruling was highly disputed by dissenters on the Court and others, noting that free Blacks had in fact been accepted as citizens by many states as early as the very founding of the nation.

The *Dred Scott v. Sanford* decision is often credited with injecting new life into the anti-slavery movement just prior to the Civil War. The political character of Taney's decision can be seen in the fact that, in his ruling, he also insisted that Congress had no authority to restrict slavery in federal territories. This aspect of the ruling made it clear that the Justice had little regard for the Missouri statute on which Scott's claim was based.

The Republican Party (descended from the Democratic-Republicans) decried the *Dred Scott* decision. It was well-known that eliminating slavery from the territories was a principal goal of the Republican Party. The Chief Justice's ruling besmirched that goal, suggesting that the party was organized for an unconstitutional purpose. Soon after, led by Abraham Lincoln, the Republican Party won control of the White House and Congress in the election of 1860. Rebuffing the Supreme Court's ruling in *Dred Scott*, the Lincoln administration took the legal position that free Blacks were indeed American citizens.

Following the Civil War and Abraham Lincoln's assassination, the Republican Party controlled the Thirty-ninth Congress, which began its first session in December 1865. At the same time, former Confederate states had been busy forming new state governments, predominantly consisting of White males, who passed laws, commonly referred to as "Black Codes," limiting the rights of former slaves. It was in response to those controversial laws that Congress passed The Civil Rights Act of 1866, recognizing *all persons* born or naturalized in the United States as citizens of the United States and the state in which they lived. The act also recognized the rights of all citizens to own property, make contracts, etc. President Johnson, a former slave owner who was sympathetic to the confederate states, vetoed the bill, but Congress was successful in overriding the veto in April of 1866.

After the passage of The Civil Rights Act of 1866, it was decided that recognition of citizenship should be given constitutional weight, which led to the inclusion of this clause in the Fourteenth Amendment. The Joint Committee on Reconstruction in the House of Representatives drafted the document. However, in its original form, the Fourteenth Amendment did not explicitly deal with the citizenship issue. The Senate added what is now the first clause of Section 1, known as the Citizenship Clause, granting both national and state citizenship in language comparable to that of the Civil Rights statute.

The House of Representatives subsequently agreed to the inclusion of this clause. President Johnson openly opposed the amendment, but the Republicans' veto-proof majority in Congress gave him little say in the matter.

The Due Process Clause constitutes a subtle but critical entry in Section 1. It pertains to citizens' rights and the government's responsibilities with respect to those rights. The intent was to protect citizens from an overbearing government's infringement on almost every conceivable individual right.

The clause, to a large degree, echoes the principles found in the Fifth Amendment. However, the earlier amendment served to protect citizens from *federal* overreach. The Due Process Clause sought to extend those protections to include actions by other levels of government. This resulted in the wording that "No State shall make or enforce any law which shall abridge the privileges or immunities of citizens of the United States; nor shall any State deprive any person of life, liberty, or property, without due process of law."

It was originally understood that the purpose of the Due Process Clause was to prevent government from depriving a person of rights and/or property without legal due process as the law was applied by the courts. Over the course of time, however, the Supreme Court has taken liberties to expand upon the meaning of the clause, including such matters as a citizen's right to be informed of governmental decisions that may impact their lives. For instance, in *Goldberg v. Kelly*, (1970), the Court ruled that certain governmental benefits

246

amount to "property" with due process protections. The specific case focused on welfare benefits, but the principle has been broadly applied.

The rights protected under the Fourteenth Amendment can now be understood to fall into three categories: Constitutional experts have identified those categories as (1) procedural due process; (2) the individual rights listed in the Bill of Rights, "incorporated" against the states; and (3) substantive due process.

Procedural due process focuses on the procedures that the government is required to follow before depriving an individual of life, liberty, or property. It is important to understand (1) what procedures serve to satisfy the due process requirement and (2) what constitutes life, liberty, or property.

Where procedural satisfaction is concerned, a jury trial will generally suffice, but the idea of *procedure* has evolved over time. For instance, in *Chicago v. Morales*, (1999), it was determined that due process included the dissemination of proper information. In that case, the law in question was deemed to be too vague. The Court ruled that "A criminal law is unconstitutionally vague if an ordinary person could not understand what conduct is criminalized, and if the vagueness of the law encourages arbitrary and potentially discriminatory enforcement."[73]

The clause has also been applied to actions by entities other than the government who are responsible for disseminating information. In

---

[73] Justia US Supreme Court Center, *Chicago v. Morales* :: 527 U.S. 41 (1999) :: https//supreme.justia.com, Accessed December 9, 2023

Mullane v. Central Hanover Bank, (1950), the Court relied on this clause in determining what effort would be required of the bank in informing investors in a Trust about changes that impacted the Trust. Specifically, it was decided that "Notice must be reasonably calculated under the circumstances to inform interested parties of a pending action and give them an opportunity to respond. Notice by publication may be insufficient if the names and addresses of the parties are known."[74]

Incorporating the principles of the Bill of Rights into the Fourteenth Amendment was a monumental step. These rights originally protected individuals from an aggressive federal government as decided in *Barron v. Baltimore*, (1833). However, a person who sought protection from a state government could only rely on the state's constitution or applicable state statutes. Fortunately, certain states, like Virginia, provided a comparable Bill of Rights in their state constitution.

Questions have risen as to whether all rights in the first ten amendments apply to the states or if this is only true of certain amendments. For instance, the Third Amendment restricts the quartering of soldiers in private homes. Yet, it is unlikely that a state would seek to quarter soldiers. Additionally, questions have arisen about whether the Fifth Amendment's right to a grand jury trial, the Seventh Amendment's right to jury trial in civil cases, and the Eighth Amendment's prohibition of excessive fines should be applied at the

---

[74] Justia US Supreme Court Center, *Mullane v. Central Hanover Bank & Trust Co.* :: 339 U.S. 306 (1950), https//supreme.justia.com, Accessed December 9, 2023.

state level. These questions are mostly irrelevant since these same rights are echoed in most state constitutions.

The Court has also determined that the due process clauses of the Fifth and Fourteenth Amendments are intended to guarantee the protection of certain *substantive* rights that are not specifically enumerated in the Constitution (see Ninth Amendment). The idea is that certain freedoms are so critical to *life, liberty, and the pursuit of happiness* that they cannot be infringed without an exceptionally persuasive reason no matter how much process is involved.

Over the years the Court has been barraged with Due Process cases and, it may be argued, the Court's rulings have been a bit inconsistent. At times the Court has been charged with taking license as in *Lochner v. New York*, (1905). In that case, the state of New York accused the Court of political activism as the justices determined that the state could not limit an individual's right to engage in a business contract by restricting his ability to fulfill the contract. Other times the Court has been accused of tiptoeing around the serious nature of the clause as in the *Slaughterhouse Cases*, (1873), when the Court insisted that the Fourteenth Amendment did not apply. In that instance, the Court held the amendment had "one pervading purpose" and that purpose was the protection of the newly emancipated Black community.

The Equal Protection Clause speaks to the idea of *blind justice*. That is to say, each individual is to receive equal treatment where the law is concerned. Whether in criminal or civil law, factors such as race, religion, education, political position, social standing, wealth, etc., should have no bearing on the outcome. Each citizen, according to this clause, must be seen as equal in the eyes of the law.

The Equal Protection Clause has been tested in the courts on occasion. For instance, *Plessy v. Ferguson*, (1896), dealt with a Louisiana statute, passed in 1892, requiring Black and White residents to ride separate but equal train cars. In that case, Plessy argued that the statute violated the Thirteenth and Fourteenth Amendments. It is not surprising that Plessy lost in every Louisiana state court. Appealing to the Supreme Court, the plaintiff was hopeful, but those hopes were dashed. In a 7-1 decision, the Court ruled that the equality of the facilities satisfied the Fourteenth Amendment. Justice John Marshall Harlan, who was the lone dissenter on the Court, feared that this decision would, in the future, be notoriously ranked with the *Dredd Scott* decision of 1857.

Over the course of the next several decades, views about segregation began to change. A notable case that recognized those changes was *Brown v. Board of Education*, (1954). Following the Court's 1896 ruling, public school segregation was deemed acceptable as long as facilities could be shown to be equal. In *Brown*, the Court determined that equality of the facilities did not satisfy the Fourteenth Amendment since racial segregation, in itself, was inherently unequal.

In certain cases, the Supreme Court has been forced to walk a fine line between racial equality and racial discrimination. In *Regents of the University of California v. Bakke*, (1978), Allan Bakke insisted that he had been denied entrance into the University of California Medical

School based strictly on his status as a White male. His claim was based on the fact that the school had specifically reserved sixteen positions in that program for minority students, thus limiting the acceptance of White students. In a divided Court, it was ruled that the university must admit Bakke, stating that the school's rigid use of racial quotas violated the Equal Protection Clause of the Fourteenth Amendment.

Section 2

Representatives shall be apportioned among the several States according to their respective numbers, counting the whole number of persons in each State, excluding Indians not taxed. But when the right to vote at any election for the choice of electors for President and Vice-President of the United States, Representatives in Congress, the Executive and Judicial officers of a State, or the members of the Legislature thereof, is denied to any of the male inhabitants of such State, being twenty-one years of age, and citizens of the United States, or in any way abridged, except for participation in rebellion, or other crime, the basis of representation therein shall be reduced in the proportion which the number of such male citizens shall bear to the whole number of male citizens twenty-one years of age in such State.

The manner by which states would be represented on a federal level is detailed here. Federal representation for each state would be apportioned based on "the whole number of persons in each state, excluding Indians not taxed." Each state would receive representation based on its percentage of population measured against the population of the whole Union with a minimum of one representative per state (see Article I, Section 2). Native Americans, who paid no taxes, were omitted from that formula.

Section 2 of the Fourteenth Amendment had the additional effect of changing how a state's congressional representation was calculated where former slaves were concerned. According to Article I, Section 2, of the Constitution, each slave was counted as three-fifths of a person for purposes of representation. Ratification of this amendment eliminated that calculation and those who had originally been counted as fractional were now recognized in full. This resulted in stronger congressional representation for those southern states whose former slaves decided to remain rather than moving to friendlier territories.

Equal representation goes deeper than merely determining a state's federal representation based on population. The Supreme Court has held, in cases like *Reynolds v. Sims*, (1964) and *Wesberry v. Sanders*, (1964), that it was equally important for representation within a state to be equitable. The Supreme Court has determined that *one person, one vote*, a phrase popularized by the National Municipal League and applied by the courts in the first half of the twentieth century, meant that the populations of districts within a state must be comparable. This would prevent under-representation of individuals in a heavily populated district when compare to over-representation in a less populated district. Some states have also sought to calculate representation based, not on a district's population, but on the number of voters in each district. The Supreme Court ruled, in *Evenwell v. Abbott*, (2016), that representation must be based on population rather than number of voters.

Voting rights on a federal level were not directly addressed in the Articles of Confederation. Instead voting rights were considered a state matter and were generally established at the state level. That is because individual citizens were not directly involved in the election of federal representatives at the time.

The Articles of Confederation, where the executive and judicial branches of the government were not yet established, stipulated that a state's delegates to the United States Congress were to be selected in a manner defined by the legislature of that state. In most cases, U. S. congressional representatives were appointed by their state legislatures who had been selected by a vote of the people of that state. That system continued until the ratification of the U. S. Constitution.

During the Constitutional Convention, many members supported maintaining that system of selecting representatives. However, James Madison and James Wilson argued that direct elections by a popular vote of the people of each state would provide a more meaningful connection between House members and their constituents. They argued that, while state legislatures were selected by the people, having their national representatives selected by their state legislature served as an unnecessary buffer between the people and their representatives at the federal level. Consequently, it was determined that members of the House of Representatives should be selected by a direct vote of citizens (see Article I, Section 2).

Eighteenth century societal norms were quite different from modern day perspectives. At the time, voting rights were generally reserved to White men who were property (real estate) owners as well as some freed slaves. Women, Native Americans, and slaves were excluded. Beginning with the ratification of the Fourteenth Amendment, the right to vote could not be "denied to any of the male inhabitants of such State, being twenty-one years of age, and citizens of the United States, or in any way abridged, except for participation in rebellion, or other crime, the basis of representation therein shall be reduced in the proportion which the number of such male citizens shall bear to the whole number of male citizens twenty-one years of age in such State.." Admittedly, this portion of the text is worded strangely and can be a bit confusing. The Travis Translation of the Constitution offers the following, easy to understand paraphrase.

> If a State will not let any male citizen over 21 years old vote freely (unless he commits a crime, or takes part in a rebellion), the number of Representatives for that state will be reduced.[75]

States could not restrict the voting rights of eligible citizens, but exceptions were allowed for criminals and those who had participated in rebellions against the United States. In *Richardson v. Ramirez*, (1974), a California case that shed light on this section, the Supreme Court ruled that The Fourteenth Amendment allowed the state to deny a convicted felon the right to vote.

The section also authorized Congress to reduce a state's congressional representation if groups of eligible voters were denied that right. This was aimed primarily at southern states where there was

---

[75] Constitutional Law Reporter, *Amendment 14: Section 2*, https//constitutionallaw reporter.com, Accessed December 11, 2023

a tendency in the post-Civil War era to deny the vote to otherwise eligible Black Americans. History holds no record of congressional enforcement of this clause and Black Americans were regularly denied the right to vote in some southern states until ratification of the Fifteenth Amendment.

Some delegates to the Constitutional Convention thought it would be prudent to keep property ownership in place as a requisite for voting, as was the case in most states. Benjamin Franklin and others were able to successfully challenge that notion. Franklin told the assembly that many individuals who were not fortunate enough to own property had fought courageously for America's freedom from England. Denying those people a right to vote in the nation for which they had sacrificed much may be seen as an affront and could easily prevent ratification of the Constitution. As a result, that qualification was removed.

Section 3

No person shall be a Senator or Representative in Congress, or elector of President and Vice-President, or hold any office, civil or military, under the United States, or under any State, who, having previously taken an oath, as a member of Congress, or as an officer of the United States, or as a member of any State legislature, or as an executive or judicial officer of any State, to support the Constitution of the United States, shall have engaged in insurrection or rebellion against the same, or given aid or comfort to the enemies thereof. But Congress may by a vote of two-thirds of each House, remove such disability.

The founders were not unfamiliar with the idea of insurrection. After all, they were themselves guilty of insurrection/rebellion against

England. Congress addressed the issue in the early years of the Union by passing The Insurrection Act of 1807. The statute did not address the political side of the issue, known as the Ineligibility Clause (the prohibition of holding public office), that is addressed in Section 3. The Insurrection Act of 1807 dealt primarily with the manner in which the federal government can respond to an insurrection at the time it occurs. The text of the statute authorized the president to deal swiftly and decisively with rebellious activity.

10 U.S. Code Chapter 13 – INSURRECTION §251: Whenever there is an insurrection in any State against its government, the President may, upon the request of its legislature or of its governor if the legislature cannot be convened, call into Federal service such of the militia of the other States, in the number requested by that State, and use such of the armed forces, as he considers necessary to suppress the insurrection.

10 U.S. Code Chapter 13 – INSURRECTION §252: Whenever the President considers that unlawful obstructions, combinations, or assemblages, or rebellion against the authority of the United States, make it impracticable to enforce the laws of the United States in any State by the ordinary course of judicial proceedings, he may call into Federal service such of the militia of any State, and use such of the armed forces, as he considers necessary to enforce those laws or to suppress the rebellion.

10 U.S. Code Chapter 13 – INSURRECTION §253: The President, by using the militia or the armed forces, or both, or by any other means, shall take such measures as he considers necessary to suppress, in a State, any insurrection, domestic violence, unlawful combination, or conspiracy, if it—

> **(1)** so hinders the execution of the laws of that State, and of the United States within the State, that any part or class of its people is deprived of a right, privilege, immunity, or protection named in the Constitution and secured by law, and the constituted authorities of that State are unable, fail, or refuse to protect that right, privilege, or immunity, or to give that protection; or

(2) opposes or obstructs the execution of the laws of the United States or impedes the course of justice under those laws.

In any situation covered by clause (1), the State shall be considered to have denied the equal protection of the laws secured by the Constitution.

10 U.S. Code Chapter 13 – INSURRECTION §254: Whenever the President considers it necessary to use the militia or the armed forces under this chapter, he shall, by proclamation, immediately order the insurgents to disperse and retire peaceably to their abodes within a limited time.

10 U.S. Code Chapter 13 – INSURRECTION §255: For purposes of this chapter, the term "State" includes Guam and the Virgin Islands.

It is clear from this text that the statute focused on insurrection/rebellion *within one of the states* of the Union. Congress, in The Posse Comitatus Act of 1878, barred domestic use of the federal military. However, where insurrection is concerned, The Insurrection Act of 1807 represents an exception to that prohibition. This statute fails to provide a clear definition of insurrection/rebellion. Yet, the implication is that to be considered an insurrection an event must reach a level that warrants the threat of military action to bring it under control.

After the Civil War, and after the passage of the Fourteenth Amendment, Congress recognized that the language of The Insurrection Act of 1807 specified rebellion within a state or against a state government. It was then decided that the same principle should apply where the federal government is concerned. With that in view, Congress passed The Insurrection Act of 1869, which reads as follows:

18 U.S. Code § 2383: Rebellion or insurrection: Whoever incites, sets on foot, assists, or engages in any rebellion or insurrection against the authority of the United States or the laws thereof, or gives aid or comfort thereto, shall be fined under this title or imprisoned not more than ten years, or both; and shall be incapable of holding any office under the United States

This statute, unlike The Insurrection Act of 1807, addressed the issue of holding office after participating in an act of insurrection/rebellion...echoing the prohibition found in Section 3. Also, with the passage of this statute, Congress provided for additional punishment for insurrection, which may include fines and/or imprisonment.

Where Section 3 of the Fourteenth Amendment is concerned, with the Civil War behind them, Congress was faced with the challenge of reintegrating southern states into the Union. This included decisions about how those states might again be represented on a federal level. It seemed unwise to place in the higher echelons of the federal government individuals who had led the rebellion in an effort to secede from the Union.

One factor was that President Johnson, who had been unsuccessfully impeached in early 1868, was a sympathizer where the Confederacy was concerned. Congress weighed the possibility that he might pardon members of the rebellion, allowing them to be placed in critical federal positions where they might regain power and wreak havoc. This concern was evidently warranted since, on December 25, 1868, President Johnson granted unconditional amnesty to all participants of the rebellion who had not yet been pardoned by either himself or Abraham Lincoln.

Section 3 was not intended to prevent someone from holding public office simply because they had fought on the side of the Confederacy. It specifically targeted those who had, at one time, served as public officials in the U. S. prior to the war. In any public position, they would have been required to pledge support for the U. S. Constitution. Participation in the rebellion was considered a breaking of that oath. This section made them ineligible for public service in the aftermath of the war. According to Kira Cummings, writing for legalknowledgebase.com:

> Another section dealing directly with the aftermath of the Civil War, section 3 of the 14th Amendment prohibits those who had "engaged in insurrection or rebellion against the same [United States], or given aid or comfort to the enemies thereof" from serving in the government.[76]

Although it is not specifically stated in the text, it is clear that the amendment had a singular focus; it was directed at those public figures who had served to rebel against the government during the Civil War. This is evident in that the amendment offers no mechanism for identifying (1) who is guilty of rebellion, (2) who is responsible for determining guilt, and (3) what action could trigger a vote by Congress to "remove such disability."

The fact that these issues were not addressed in the text suggests that (1) the list of offenders was relatively short and had already been

---

[76] Cummings, Kira, Legal Knowledge Base, *Has the 14th Amendment Section 3 ever been used?* www.legalknowledgebase.com, Accessed November 12, 2023.

identified and (2) any attempt by one of these individuals to re-enter public service would be easily recognized. The ambiguity of the amendment suggests that these matters were already settled and there was no need to expound on them. Congress regularly received from President Johnson the list of names of those pardoned for their offenses. While Johnson pardoned more than 12,000 Confederates, only a small fraction would have been impacted by the contents of Section 3.

While guilt or innocence is generally determined in the courts, this amendment does not address criminality since it does not address what might be considered war crimes. Instead, it is about a unique moment in history and appears to place responsibility on Congress to determine guilt or innocence since Congress alone is charged with deciding whether to "remove such disability." Where the Civil War was concerned, the amendment did not leave it to the courts to decide whether an individual may return to public office. A person's ability to return to office relied only on the actions of Congress.

The bitter Civil War had ended in 1865 and it would be years before the nation would know the kind of healing that was necessary to begin to restore unity. When the Fourteenth Amendment was ratified in 1868, the atrocities of the war were still fresh in the minds of citizens on both sides of that war. The amendment was written partly as a protective measure to avoid future conflicts and partly as a punishment for public officials who had participated in the rebellion.

Its direct application to Confederate agitators is also recognized in National Archives records.

> Both chambers of the 40th–41st Congresses (1867–1871) established temporary select committees to consider petitions for the removal of legal and political disabilities imposed on former Confederates by the 14th Amendment. The Select Committee on Reconstruction handled such business in the House, while the Select Committee on the Removal of Political Disabilities considered amnesty petitions in the Senate.[77]

That Section 3 was uniquely written with Civil War agitators in mind is seen in The Amnesty Act of 1872. For the most part, Section 3 was utilized only between July 28, 1868, and May 22, 1872. The Amnesty Act of 1872, passed by a two-thirds majority of Congress in keeping with the terms of the amendment, removed the ineligibility for office detailed in Section 3. This was done in an effort to begin the national healing that was needed to restore unity.

Historically, it has been generally accepted that the Civil War-related provisions of Section 3 were fully satisfied with The Amnesty Act of 1872. The Fourteenth Amendment had saddled Congress with the responsibility of preventing certain Confederates from returning to public office without the approval that only Congress could provide. The Amnesty Act of 1872 was meant to relieve Congress of that burden.

---

[77] National Archives, *Presidential Pardons and Congressional Amnesty to Former Confederate Citizens, 1865–1877*, https://www.archives.gov/files/research/naturalization/411-confederate-amnesty-records, Accessed December 12, 2023

Is Section 3 applicable beyond <u>The Amnesty Act of 1872</u>? The section remains a valid component of a constitutional amendment. It stands to reason, then, that one who is deemed guilty of insurrection in accord with this amendment could be faced with the monumental task of getting two-thirds of the House of Representatives and two-thirds of the Senate to agree to lift that person's ineligibility.

> Section 3 of the Fourteenth Amendment was last used in 1919 to refuse to seat a socialist congressman accused of having given aid and comfort to Germany during the First World War, irrespective of the Amnesty Act.[78]

Concerning the earlier mentioned issues where the amendment fails to identify (1) who is guilty of rebellion and (2) who is responsible for determining guilt, it is not that these questions have never been contemplated. Indeed, they have been considered and answered, at least to a degree. According to Congressional Research Service:

> **What Activities Trigger the Bar?** Determining who has engaged in either of the two disqualifying activities—that is, engaging in insurrection or rebellion or giving aid or comfort to an enemy—is likely to be a difficult task given the scarcity of precedents and lack of clear definitions.
>
> **Engaging in Insurrection and Rebellion:** The U.S. Constitution does not define insurrection or rebellion. Article 1, Section 8, clause 15, of the U.S. Constitution does empower Congress to call forth the militia "to suppress Insurrection." It seems to follow that Congress has the authority to define insurrection for that purpose…Once an insurrection is deemed to have occurred, the question becomes whether a specific person engaged in it. Section 3 does not establish

---

[78] Legal Knowledge Base, *Has the 14th Amendment Section 3 ever been used?* www.legalknowledgebase.com, Accessed November 12, 2023.

a procedure for determining who is subject to the proscription on holding office, instead providing only a process by which the disability may be removed (i.e., by twothirds vote in both houses). Congress has also not set forth a procedure for determining who is subject to the disability imposed by Section 3.[79]

Congress either thought it unnecessary to repeal Section 3 given the passage of The Amnesty Act of 1872 or they decided it may be a useful instrument in the future. Nonetheless, after more than one-and-one-half centuries, the section remains. Still, seeking to apply this section in the twenty-first century would involve some heavy lifting.

- A person must first be declared ineligible for office under Section 3, but there is no precise mechanism for determining guilt or how the use of Section 3 might be triggered.

- Indicting an individual and finding that person guilty of insurrection in a court of law might be considered a first step in banning someone from office. However, that would be a high hurdle given the absence of a precise criminal definition of insurrection.

- If an individual was found guilty of insurrection or rebellion by a criminal court, that verdict would need to stand through the appeals process. Even then, only Congress could decide if such conviction rose to Section 3 levels. Such a decision would be beyond the authority of the Court.

- It stands to reason that the initial decision to apply Section 3 to a specific case would require a majority vote in both the House of Representatives and the Senate. Since the decision concerning the triggering of Section 3 would almost certainly be political in character, the decision to deny an individual access to public office may well depend on the composition of Congress at the time. Even then, in the Senate, the minority party has the tool of the filibuster to block any such decision.

---

[79] Congressional Research Service, *The Disqualification Clause*, https//crsreports.congress.gov., Accessed December 12, 2023

These are serious impediments that must be overcome to apply the Ineligibility Clause of Section 3 in modern America. The reason it is so difficult to apply this section now is that it was written for a unique purpose under circumstances that are foreign to the political economy of the twenty-first century. It seems unlikely that Section 3 obstacles would be easily navigated in a highly divided United States Congress.

Section 4

The validity of the public debt of the United States, authorized by law, including debts incurred for payment of pensions and bounties for services in suppressing insurrection or rebellion, shall not be questioned. But neither the United States nor any State shall assume or pay any debt or obligation incurred in aid of insurrection or rebellion against the United States, or any claim for the loss or emancipation of any slave; but all such debts, obligations and claims shall be held illegal and void.

At times it is necessary for the federal government to borrow money to accomplish what Congress deems necessary for the good of the country. Quite often this happens in times of war when costs tend to elevate dramatically. This section was written (1) to assure that the federal government would have access to necessary funds when they were needed and (2) to ensure lenders to the federal government that they could be confident in their investment.

In the post-Civil War era, some southern states reneged on much of the debt they had accumulated during the war. One such Court case was mentioned earlier in *Chisolm v. Georgia* (see discussion on the Eleventh Amendment). One of the primary sources for the government to borrow money is the people of the United States. The government generally offers bonds to the citizenry with a promise to repay those bonds with interest at some point in the future. Yet, the default on debt by certain Confederate states had made many people uneasy when it came to investing in government bonds. Section 4 was intended to alleviate those concerns.

The primary purpose of this section was to ensure investors that any money loaned to the federal government was a safe investment. However, Congress also took this opportunity to vacate all war-related obligations of those Confederate states who had amassed debt either through direct loans or via credit extended from suppliers to cover the expense of the war. Neither those states nor the federal government would be held accountable for debts that resulted from a rebellion against the United States.

Congress was careful to draw a clear line of distinction between debts of the Confederate states and those accumulated by the federal government during the Civil War. Whatever concerns the public may have had with respect to war-related obligations of the federal government, debtors could rest assured that those commitments would be met.

The war had been costly not only for the federal government, but also for citizens. Many slave owners believed they should be compensated by the federal government for the loss of property (slaves) they had experienced as a result of the emancipation. This section made clear that any "claim for the loss or emancipation of any slave" was not the responsibility of the federal government.

Section 5

The Congress shall have the power to enforce, by appropriate legislation, the provisions of this article.

As with the Thirteenth Amendment, Congress added an Enforcement Clause to the Fourteenth Amendment. With its ratification, the states were recognizing Congress's authority to enforce the provisions of the amendment. Nearly a century later, Congress relied on this authority in passing The Civil Rights Act of 1964 and The Voting Rights Act of 1965.

The Fourteenth Amendment had a powerful impact on the balance of power between federal and state governments. Section 1 not only iterated the Citizenship Clause, the Due Process Clause, and the Equal Protection Clause, but states would now be held to account by Congress for adherence.

Section 2 of the amendment fine-tuned the states' congressional representation, going so far as to change the very manner in which members of the House of Representatives were selected. This change was accompanied by assurances to the citizenry of the government's respect for a person's right to vote. Voting rights were reinforced with the inclusion of possible retribution for states who sought to interfere with that right.

In Section 3 of the amendment, Congress saw fit to address federal representation for southern states during Reconstruction. Concerns over undue Confederate influence within the walls of the federal government led Congress to deny certain members of the Confederacy the opportunity to seek any position in the federal government without the approval of Congress.

The Fourteenth Amendment was submitted to the states for ratification on June 16, 1866. Due to the dramatic changes proposed in the amendment, there was considerable debate. States wrestled with what was perceived by many to be a power grab by the federal government as the amendment weakened authority that was previously understood to be vested with the states. It took more than two years, but the amendment was finally ratified by a sufficient number of states and was adopted on July 28, 1868.

Fifteenth Amendment
Section 1

The right of citizens of the United States to vote shall not be denied or abridged by the United States or by any State on account of race, color, or previous condition of servitude–

The right to vote was not addressed in the Articles of Confederation, the Articles of the U. S. Constitution, or the Bill of Rights. In pre-Constitution America, sundry voting rules, including who should have the right to vote and how the voting process should be carried out, were developed in the states and those rules varied dramatically from state to state. Additionally, during that period, citizens did not vote directly for their federal representatives. They voted only for their state representatives who, in turn, selected the state's federal representatives. For this reason, there was little concern at the federal level about the details of state elections.

While Article I, Section 1, of the Constitution established that members of the House of Representatives should be chosen via a vote of the people of each state, the subject of voting rights remained a tangential issue. Only after the passing of the Fourteenth Amendment, which included the Equal Protection Clause, did Congress seriously consider how disparate voting rules and practices in the states impacted the citizenry as a whole. The Equal Protection Clause, combined with the Fourteenth Amendment's recognition of full citizenship for former slaves, helped prompt movement on the issue of voting rights.

In post-Civil War America, as Congress dealt with Reconstruction, it was painfully obvious that former slaves, who were now counted as full citizens of the United States, were not always treated equally where voting was concerned. In many southern states, Black American citizens, particularly those who were former slaves, were often denied the opportunity to vote. Viewed by many as the man who had freed the slaves, Ulysses S. Grant won the Presidency in 1868 and it was largely the votes of Black men in the southern states that solidified his victory. On the heels of ratification of the Fourteenth Amendment, he encouraged Congress to address the disparity where voting rights were concerned. The Fifteenth Amendment was designed to tackle that issue.

While the provisions of the Fourteenth Amendment were heavily debated at the state level during the ratification process, the Fifteenth Amendment was highly debated within the halls of Congress. The amendment was written and supported by the Republican Party. However, the Democrats in Congress were decidedly opposed. With no favorable votes from the Democrat side of the aisle, the amendment passed the Republican controlled Congress on February 26, 1869. The amendment was ratified on February 3, 1870, and ratification was certified on March 30, 1870.

The final wording of the Fifteenth Amendment represents a concession by those who wanted far more sweeping language addressing the suffrage of the former slave community. However, the Democrats wanted no such amendment. Although the amendment was watered down from its original proposals in an effort to seek additional support, Democrats failed to accept what was seen by many as a reasonable compromise.

The nineteenth century saw little court action with respect to the newly ratified Fifteenth Amendment. One notable case was *United States v. Reese*, (1876). In that case, a Kentucky electoral official was indicted for denying a Black American the opportunity to register to vote in a municipal election. The government, on the shoulders of The Enforcement Acts of 1870 and 1871, accused the official of denying the vote to a Black man. The Court's decision was complex, finding that the man's voting privilege was denied on factors other than race. The Court also insisted that The Enforcement Acts were too broadly worded and that the Fifteenth Amendment did not specifically confer the right to vote on anyone in particular. The amendment simply stated that no one could be denied participation in the voting system based on their race.

> In an 8-1 decision authored by Chief Justice Morrison Waite, the Court concluded that the relevant sections of the Enforcement Act lacked the necessary, limiting language to qualify as enforcement of the Fifteenth Amendment. The Chief Justice first stated that the Fifteenth Amendment "does not confer the right of suffrage upon any one," but "prevents the States, or the United States, however, from giving preference…to one citizen of the United States over another on account of race, color, or previous condition of servitude." In examining the language of the Enforcement Act, the Court noted that, while the first two sections of the act explicitly referred to race in criminalizing interference with the right to vote, the relevant third and fourth sections refer only to the "aforesaid" offense. [80]

The Court's decision in *United States v. Reese* remained virtually unchallenged for nearly a century. However, in the 1960's, the Supreme Court took serious aim at voting restrictions that were being applied in questionable fashion among the states. For instance, in *Harper v. Virginia Board of Elections*, (1966), *Dunn v. Blumstein*, (1972), and other cases, the Court ruled that any restrictions impacting a person's right to vote must consider the *spirit* of the right to vote (one person, one vote) and thus be subject to the highest scrutiny. This announcement by the Court limited any government actions denying the vote to those who were eligible. Thereafter,

---

[80] Oyez, *United States v. Reese*. https://www.oyes.org/cases/1850-1900/92us214, Accessed December 18, 2023

essentially all restrictions on voting other than citizenship, residency in the jurisdiction where the individual votes, and the 18 years of age limit were deemed unconstitutional.

Section 2

The Congress shall have the power to enforce this article by appropriate legislation.

As with earlier amendments, Congress believed it would be wise to include an Enforcement Clause here, likely because they anticipated resistance. They believed there would be those, particularly in former slave states, who disagreed with the principles laid out in the amendment.

Congress penned The Enforcements Acts of 1870 and 1871 in an attempt to give teeth to the amendment. The Court initially determined that those laws were too broadly written. While they were intended to support Congress's belief that the Fifteenth Amendment conferred upon the former slave community the right to vote, the Court construed the statutes very narrowly, denying that the Amendment *conferred* the right to vote on anyone in particular. It simply restricted a state's ability to deny the vote to any individual based on that person's race. A further finding of the Court in *United States v. Reese* was that where the Enforcement Act(s) were concerned:

> ...the language does not sufficiently tailor the law to qualify as "appropriate legislation" under the Enforcement Clause of the Fifteenth Amendment.[81]

---

[81] Ibid.

Sixteenth Amendment

The Congress shall have power to lay and collect taxes on incomes, from whatever source derived, without apportionment among the several States, and without regard to any census or enumeration.

Taxation without representation was a charge the early colonists leveled against England in the mid-eighteenth century. In fact, unjust taxation was a major factor that eventually led the colonists to separate from England (see Declaration of Independence, Grievance No. 17). The Stamp Act (1765), The Townshend Act (1767), and The Tea Act (1773) were prime examples of what the colonists saw as unreasonable taxation.

Upon separation from England, the Second Continental Congress drafted the Articles of Confederation (1777), establishing a limited government that was designed to guide the colonies through that separation. The Articles said little about taxation, placing the primary financial burden upon the states whose responsibility it was to collect from the citizenry through various methods of taxation (e.g., property taxes) and, in turn, supply funds to the federal government to support the war effort. The only reference to taxation in the Articles read as follows:

Article VIII: All charges of war, and all other expenses that shall be incurred for the common defence or general welfare, and allowed by the United States in Congress assembled, shall be defrayed out of a common treasury, which shall be supplied by the several States, in proportion to the value of all land within each State, granted to or surveyed for any person, as such land and the buildings and improvements thereon shall be estimated according to such mode as the United States in Congress assembled, shall from time to time direct and appoint.

The taxes for paying that proportion shall be laid and levied by the authority and direction of the Legislatures of the several States within the time agreed upon by the United States in Congress assembled[82]

This section in the Articles of Confederation was not a demand for funds, but more of a request, since Congress had no authority to collect taxes and no enforcement mechanism was in place. Still, some revenue was received from the states. However, the war was funded largely through tariffs (taxes on imports) and excise taxes (similar to a sales tax or value added tax) along with loans from other European countries like France and Spain. That funding was complemented by donations from wealthy French donors like Marquis de Lafayette and Baron of Kalb who supported the colonists in their quest for independence.

Once independence was secured and the war ended (1783), Congress settled in to the tasks assigned to the federal government by the Articles of Confederation. At the time, the government continued to receive funding primarily through tariffs, excise taxes, and participation by the states in supporting the federal functions. It was in the summer of 1787 that Congress undertook the monumental task of forming a more permanent government through the U. S. Constitution.

---

[82] Constitution Annotated, *Article I, Section 8, Clause 1*, constitution.congress.gov, Accessed December 21, 2023

The Constitution placed the responsibility for the imposition and collection of federal taxes on Congress. Article I, Section 8, of the Constitution authorizes Congress to "lay and collect Taxes Duties, Imposts and Excises, to pay the Debts and provide for the common Defence and general Welfare of the United States; but all Duties, Imposts and Excises shall be uniform throughout the United States." Additionally, Article I, Section 9, states that "No Capitation, or other direct, Tax shall be laid, unless in Proportion to the Census or Enumeration herein before directed to be taken."

The term *impost* refers to any obligatory or compulsory tax, particularly "a tax; esp., a duty on imported goods."[83] Capitation, on the other hand, is a flat tax that is charged per person by those performing certain services such as doctors. Webster's defines it as "a tax or fee of so much per head; payment per capita."[84]

Income taxes were not part of the American financial landscape until the time of the Civil War. In 1861, in anticipation of a costly war, Congress passed The Revenue Act of 1861. The act levied a 3% tax on personal income exceeding $800 annually (approximately $24,000 in today's dollars) and a 5% tax on income earned abroad. This was later adjusted to a graduated tax in 1864 when the rate charged on income between $600 and $10,000 was 3% and a rate of 5% was levied on income in excess of $10,000. In 1872, with the cost of the war behind

---

[83] Guralnik, David B., Editor in Chief, Webster's New World Dictionary, Second College Edition, The World Publishing Company, 1978, p. 706
[84] Ibid, p. 210.

them, Congress repealed The Revenue Act of 1861 and the collection of income taxes ceased.

In 1894, Congress passed The Wilson-Gorman Tariff Act. The statute reduced the amount of tariffs charged on certain imported goods. However, it also established, for a period of five years, a 2% income tax on income in excess of $4,000…a fact that displeased a large number of citizens. While the people had tolerated the income tax charged to cover the cost of the Civil War, they were not so generous where this new levy on income was concerned. In *Pollock* v. *Farmers' Loan and Trust Company*, (1895), the U.S. Supreme Court ruled that Congress's attempt at establishing a federal income tax was unconstitutional, striking down that portion of The Wilson-Gorman Tariff Act.

The Court's decision concerning The Wilson-Gorman Tariff Act was grounded in the fact that the Constitution required direct taxes, such as income taxes, to be apportioned among the states. This meant that a state whose population constituted 10% of the citizenry must provide 10% of the tax revenue. However, it was essentially impossible to write an acceptable statute given the income disparity between states. For instant, if two states had equal populations, but the average income in one state was double the average income in the other state, those with lower incomes would be required to pay a much higher percentage of their income in taxes. As a result, an income tax such as that proposed in The Wilson-Gorman Tariff Act was deemed unconstitutional.

While the Court's decision was constitutionally based, it saw mixed reviews. Wealthier individuals and corporations praised the decision while farmers and common laborers saw it as a move to protect the assets of the wealthy. In its 1896 political platform, the Democrat Party included a provision calling for the establishment of an income tax. The provision also charged the Supreme Court with *judicial usurpation.*

In 1909, fifteen years after the Court's ruling in *Pollock* v. *Farmers' Loan and Trust Company*, Congress passed the Sixteenth Amendment, which authorized the implementation of a tax charged on income, and submitted it to the states for ratification. The tax was intended to apply to both personal income and corporate income. When the amendment was ratified in 1913, it effectively vacated the proportionality requirement established in Article I, Section 9, of the Constitution.

One truth of which many are unaware is the connection between the Sixteenth Amendment and the future Eighteenth Amendment. The organized temperance movement in the United States began in the early 1800's, although it could be argued that it had fledgling beginnings as early as the 1720's. However, the movement began gaining considerable support in the 1890's through the turn of the century. It was evident to many that the strength of that movement could well result in some kind of limit on the sale of alcohol in the United States. Given the fact that taxes on the sale of alcohol served as a significant source of federal revenue, those in Congress sought, through the introduction of an income tax, to protect the federal coffers.

In the earlier discussion of the Tenth Amendment, it was suggested that Chief Justice John Marshall's majority decision in *McCulloch v. Maryland*, (1819), contributed to the growth of the federal government in the nineteenth century. It could be said that the Sixteenth Amendment equally contributed to the federal government's dramatic growth in the twentieth century. The income tax soon became the single largest source of revenue for the federal government. Also, since tax rates are easily manipulated, tax revenues have grown exponentially. Tax rates are progressive, which means the higher the income, the higher the tax rate. The 1950's saw the highest federal tax rate, which was 92% on income over $400,000. Add to that the payment of state taxes, and an individual would have paid essentially 100% of income above $400,000 in income taxes.

During the 1950's, 1960's, and 1970's, the top federal tax rate did not drop below 70%. However, in 1981, during Ronald Reagan's Presidency, tax rates began to decline. The Economic Recovery Tax Act of 1981 reduced the top rate to 50%. Later, in The Tax Reform Act of 1986, the top rate dropped to 28.8%. The rates have bounced around since then with the current (2023) top rate standing at 37%.

The income tax has also been used in various ways to influence free will decisions of American taxpayers through adjustments to The Internal Revenue Code, which is the document that defines how taxes are calculated. For instance, by making charitable contributions and mortgage interest payments deductible from taxable income, Congress has encouraged people to donate to charitable organizations and to buy homes. This method has similarly been used to promote long-term investments and persuade individuals to save for retirement. There can be no doubt that strategic finessing of The Internal Revenue Code will continue to affect societal choices. In that vein, the impact of the Sixteenth Amendment has far surpassed the original purpose of raising money for the federal coffers.

Over the past few decades a discussion has swirled around the idea of a wealth tax in the United States with some of the more liberal members of Congress seemingly in favor. What is a wealth tax? This would constitute the federal government taxing a portion of the wealth an individual has accumulated beyond a certain amount. Some argue that wealth represents a person's assets *after paying taxes*. In that sense, such a move would be seen, not as a tax, but as *confiscation* of an individual's after tax savings. Others claim that the richest citizens of the United States have excesses that should be shared. It will be interesting if such a statute eventually passes Congress or is simply too politically toxic to garner the necessary support since those with considerable wealth tend to be the biggest political donors.

Chapter 11
Amendments 17-21

Seventeenth Amendment

The Senate of the United States shall be composed of two Senators from each State, elected by the people thereof, for six years; and each Senator shall have one vote. The electors in each State shall have the qualifications requisite for electors of the most numerous branch of the State legislatures.

When vacancies happen in the representation of any State in the Senate, the executive authority of such State shall issue writs of election to fill such vacancies: Provided, That the legislature of any State may empower the executive thereof to make temporary appointments until the people fill the vacancies by election as the legislature may direct.

This amendment shall not be so construed as to affect the election or term of any Senator chosen before it becomes valid as part of the Constitution.

The seven Articles of the U. S. Constitution were ratified by the requisite number of states in 1788. For roughly the next 120 years, Article I of the Constitution, which established the form of the legislative branch of the federal government and the process by which the people's representatives were selected, remained unaltered. Article I, Section 3, mapped out the method of selection for a state's representatives in Washington D.C. Members of the House of Representatives were selected by a popular vote of the people and Senators were chosen by the legislative body in each state.

The framers of the Constitution believed that having Representatives and Senators selected via two separate methods provided a better balance of power. The lower chamber, it was determined, would directly embody the *people's* interests while the upper chamber would focus on the *state's* interests. James Madison addressed this point in Federalist No. 62.

> Among the various modes which might have been devised for constituting this branch of the government, that which has been proposed by the convention is probably the most congenial with the public opinion. It is recommended by the double advantage of favoring a select appointment, and of giving to the State governments such an agency in the formation of the federal government as must secure the authority of the former, and may form a convenient link between the two systems[85]

While the case for state legislatures appointing Senators was seemingly well-reasoned, some saw it as an attempt to limit direct input by the citizens where federal representation was concerned. In the early 1800's some of the states voiced dissatisfaction with the appointment of Senators by state legislatures. It has been reported that as early as 1826, certain members of the House of Representatives presented resolutions to alter the method of selection of Senators to a direct vote of the people in each state. However, none of those resolutions were successful.

In the 1830's, the system the framers had designed with respect to the selection of Senators became a steady topic of debate for a couple of reasons. First, this method of selection became plagued with

---

[85] Madison, James, Federalist No. 62.

opportunities for backroom deals where the state's interests were not the highest priority. Wealthy power brokers, corrupt political organizations, and special interest groups were often accused of *purchasing* Senatorial seats.

Second, state legislatures often became stalemated when it came to choosing who would represent them in Washington. As a consequence, a Senate seat could remain vacant for a long stretch, leaving that state without equal representation. An example can be found in the state of Delaware where, in 1895, the legislature was deadlocked. It took 217 ballots over a period of 114 days to settle the matter, leaving the state with less than full representation in Washington.

In the post-Civil War era, the method of selection of Senators was again highly debated. In 1866 Congress passed a statute regulating the time and procedure for electing senators. This was evidently a response to disputed elections in Indiana and New Jersey. However, Congress did not take that opportunity to address the long-standing discussion over Senatorial selection.

Over the course of the next few decades, some states took it upon themselves to address the issue and still remain faithful to the Constitution. A very popular solution involved including the names of Senatorial candidates on the primary ballots. The legislature would then appoint the candidate who received the most votes. By the 1890's, many states had implemented some form of indirect popular vote in selecting their Senators. Some states went so far as to adopt a scheme known as the *Oregon System*. The name derived from the fact that it originated in that state. Under that method, candidates for the state legislature were required to acknowledge on the ballot whether or not they would accept the results of a non-binding direct election for U.S. Senator. By 1908, twenty-eight of the forty-five states employed some form of direct elections.

Many state legislatures were disappointed that Congress had not addressed an issue for which they believed there was an easy fix. By 1905, thirty-one state legislatures had passed resolutions calling on Congress to address the issue by either (1) passing an amendment changing the method of Senatorial selection to a direct vote of the citizens, (2) organizing a conference between the states to develop an amendment to that affect, or (3) holding a constitutional convention where a newly drawn Constitution could include direct elections of Senators.

Beginning in 1893, in response to the many requests, numerous amendments were proposed in Congress providing for the direct election of Senators. These amendments generally passed in the House of Representatives. However, for nearly two decades these amendments were stalled in the Senate by certain very influential Senators, perhaps out of concern that they would not be the people's choice in an open election. Finally, in June of 1911, the Seventeenth Amendment passed both the House of Representatives and the Senate and was ratified by the necessary number of states on April 8, 1913.

Article I, Section 3, provided for the replacement of Senators in case a vacancy occurred. When a Senate seat was vacated, either by resignation or some other event, it was the responsibility of the state legislature to appoint a replacement. If such vacancy occurred while the state legislature was not in session, it would be left to the governor of the state to name a temporary replacement, assuming the state legislature had agreed to extend that authority to the governor.

The Seventeenth Amendment reiterates the method described in Article I with slight modification since Senators would now be selected by a direct vote of the people. Starting in 1913, someone appointed to fill a Senate vacancy would serve until such time as the governor of that state could arrange for an election by direct vote of the people to name a replacement.

Issues have risen concerning what constitutes a temporary appointment. For instance, if a Senate seat has two years left in the term that the seat is vacated, can a temporary appointment be made to complete the term? The amendment states no specific timeline. However, for that length of time, it has been argued the state would be obligated to allow the people to select their replacement.

An event took place in Illinois that resulted in litigation concerning the Seventeenth Amendment. President Barack Obama served as a Senator from Illinois beginning on January 5, 2005. He vacated that seat in November 2008 when he was selected as President of the United States. With more than three years left for his term in the Senate, the state of Illinois needed to find a replacement.

The amendment reads that the Senate "shall be composed of Senators...elected by the people." In case of a vacancy in the Senate, the amendment calls for the governor to schedule an election so the people may choose a replacement. The statement, "the executive authority of such State shall issue writs of election to fill such vacancies" indicates that scheduling an election is not optional, but mandated by the amendment. Governor Rod Blagojevich had other plans. Using his power to appoint, he sought to auction off the balance of that term to the highest bidder. In 2012 he was convicted on seventeen of twenty counts of corruption and sentenced to fourteen years in prison. His sentence was commuted by President Trump in 2020.

Blagojevich's misconduct resulted in *Judge v. Backer*, (2010), with plaintiffs insisting that the governor was obligated to schedule an election. The trial judge determined that the governor was not obliged to schedule an election *quickly*, ruling that the length of a *temporary* assignment was a subjective matter. The Seventh Circuit Court of Appeals disagreed, delivering the following opinion.

> ...the second paragraph of the Seventeenth Amendment establishes a rule for all circumstances: it imposes a duty on state executives to make sure that an election fills each vacancy; it obliges state legislatures to promulgate rules for vacancy elections; and it allows for temporary appointments until an election occurs. This demarcation of constitutional powers and duties between state executives and state legislatures advances the Seventeenth Amendment's primary objective of guaranteeing that senators are selected by the people of the states in popular elections.[86]

---

[86] Epps, Garrett, *A Court Looks at the Real Problem With the 17th Amendment* - theatlantic.com, Accessed December 24, 2023.

Eighteenth Amendment
Section 1

After one year from the ratification of this article the manufacture, sale, or transportation of intoxicating liquors within, the importation thereof into, or the exportation thereof from the United States and all territory subject to the jurisdiction thereof for beverage purposes is hereby prohibited.

In the early 1500's the world experienced a religious transformation that has come to be known as the Reformation Movement. With the rise of men like Martin Luther, John Calvin, and other religious leaders of that time who struggled with certain teachings of the Roman Catholic Church, the world experienced the birth of Protestantism. The movement would eventually result in the establishment of various denominations over the next few centuries.

The seventeenth century saw a slight stagnation of Protestantism, which continued for roughly a century. This was due in large part to a European philosophical movement known as the Enlightenment, which stressed a world view focused on logic rather than belief or faith, thus de-emphasizing the importance of religious teachings. That movement heavily influenced the views of many English colonists in America. The church did not die out, but neither did it experience the growth it had seen earlier. However, this turned around in the eighteenth century with what is now known as the Great Awakening. From roughly 1720 to 1750, the English colonies in America experienced a religious revival and Protestantism saw phenomenal growth. It was during the Great Awakening of the eighteenth century that people began to take notice of the evil influence of alcohol on society. In religious circles, alcohol came to be seen as the enemy of God.

The dramatic church growth of the Great Awakening was interrupted slightly by the French and Indian War (1754-1763) and by America's struggles with England that immediately followed that war. For the next three decades (roughly 1765-1795) America was focused on (1) securing independence from what was seen as a tyrannical Great Britain and (2) establishing a new nation.

With the volatility of the Revolutionary War solidly in the past and the foundation of a new nation firmly established, beginning around 1795 a new religious revival, known as the Second Great Awakening, began to emerge. Key figures of that revival included men like Timothy Dwight and Lyman Beecher in the New England area, Charles Finney in western New York, and Alexander Campbell and Barton Stone in Kentucky and Tennessee. These names and locations demonstrate the breadth and influence of the movement. It was during this time, particularly in the 1820's and 1830's, that there was a renewed focus on the evils of alcohol and its negative impact on society. In essence, the religious community blamed much of the world's ills on the consumption of alcohol. This was the true beginning of the temperance movement in the United States.

The temperance movement saw its roots in religious groups. In the 1890's Carrie Nation, who was notorious for entering and demolishing barrooms with a hatchet, became somewhat of a figurehead for the movement. However, others outside the religious community also subscribed to the view that alcohol was detrimental to society. This included groups like the Order of Good Templars, which saw its beginning in Utica, New York, in 1851, and the Anti Saloon League that formed in Ohio in 1893. It is also true that similar groups of prohibitionists were contiguously forming overseas in places like Ireland, Great Britain, and several other European nations.

While many movements that tend to weaken over time, the voices calling for government action to limit the sale of alcohol in America only grew louder. By the early 1900's, the noise was deafening. The problem for Congress was the federal government's reliance on tax dollars received through the sale of alcoholic beverages. However, Congress was able to overcome that concern with the addition of the Sixteenth Amendment (1913) providing for an income tax on American citizens.

While the population in general seemed opposed to prohibition, the influence of the temperance movement was strong. In fact, some states invoked their own limits on alcohol. For instance, in 1838, Massachusetts passed a law forbidding the sale of spirits in quantities of less than 15 gallons. The Maine Law (1851) represented the first statewide prohibition of the sale of liquor. Over the next few years, at least a dozen other states followed suit. Had it not been for the disruption caused by World War I (1914-1918), the Eighteenth Amendment may well have been adopted a few years earlier.

While the Eighteenth Amendment restricted the production, transportation, and sale of liquor, it did not prohibit consumption of alcohol. Neither did it prohibit production of alcoholic beverages for personal use. It is not surprising, then, that the production of alcoholic beverages on private property became the norm during the years the Eighteenth Amendment was in effect.

It seemed unrealistic to have this amendment go into effect immediately upon ratification. After all, the sale of liquor was not a small thing in America. Saloon owners and others would need time to adjust to this prohibition. For this reason, the Eighteenth Amendment led with a clause providing for a one-year delay on implementation once ratified. The amendment passed both the House of Representatives and the Senate in December 1917. It was then ratified by the necessary three-fourths of the states in January 1919, and became effective one year later.

Adoption of the Eighteenth Amendment did not result in much litigation. One case, *Hawke v. Smith*, (1920), was more about the Constitution of the state of Ohio than it was about the Eighteenth Amendment. In the state of Ohio, the state's Constitution allowed the citizens of the state to challenge the legislature's ratification of an amendment via a petition signed by six percent of voters. After the Ohio legislature ratified the amendment, such a petition was presented.

The Supreme Court disallowed the petition, stating that the clause in the state's Constitution was itself unconstitutional. The Court ruled that the U. S. Constitution made no provision for the citizenry to override ratification of an amendment by the state's legislative body.

In the end, Ohio's ratification of the Eighteenth Amendment was upheld.

Section 2

The Congress and the several States shall have concurrent power to enforce this article by appropriate legislation.

The amendment called for Congress to pass legislation to enforce prohibition – a campaign steered by Andrew Volstead, who served as chairman of the House Judiciary Committee at the time. It was Volstead who guided The National Prohibition Act (better known as The Volstead Act) through Congress. The statute conferred upon the Treasury Department the authority to enforce the Eighteenth Amendment – an authority/responsibility, in this case, that was to be shared equally with the states. President Woodrow Wilson vetoed the bill, but to no avail as Congress overrode that veto. As principled as these efforts may have been, reality set in over the ensuing years as enforcement of the Eighteenth Amendment and the accompanying Volstead Act proved far more challenging than Congress had anticipated.

Section 3

This article shall be inoperative unless it shall have been ratified as an amendment to the Constitution by the legislatures of the several States, as provided in the Constitution, within seven years from the date of the submission hereof to the States by the Congress.

Experience is a fine teacher and Congress had learned a valuable lesson over the nearly one-hundred thirty years since the original twelve amendments were submitted to the states for ratification in 1789. The lesson was that unless the states were motivated to act, they might drag their feet when it came to addressing the ratification of a proposed amendment. For instance, the Twenty-seventh Amendment was submitted to the states in 1789 and, as of 1917, had not yet been ratified.

Amendments were generally ratified over a reasonable period of time (usually 2-4 years). While Congressional inspiration might not be necessary (the Eleventh Amendment was ratified in one month due to the states' self-interests), Congress believed the unpopularity of the Eighteenth Amendment might make it vulnerable to delays and that ratification may require a bit of coaxing. The solution was to include in the body of the amendment a time limit of seven years for ratification. Failure to attain ratification from the requisite three-fourths of the states by the end of that seven year period would result in nullification of the amendment.

Since this was the first amendment for which Congress had set a time limit for ratification, it is not surprising that the proposal faced legal scrutiny. In *Dillon v. Gloss*, (1921), the constitutionality of a seven year time limit for ratification was challenged. The Supreme Court ruled in favor of the limit set by Congress, writing:

> Whether a definite period for ratification shall be fixed, so that all may know what it is and speculation on what is a reasonable time may be avoided, is, in our opinion, a matter of detail which Congress may determine as an incident of its power to designate the mode of ratification. It is not questioned that seven years, the period fixed in this instance, was reasonable if power existed to fix a definite time;

nor could it well be questioned considering the periods within which prior amendments were ratified.[87]

Nineteenth Amendment

The right of citizens of the United States to vote shall not be denied or abridged by the United States or by any State on account of sex.

Congress shall have power to enforce this article by appropriate legislation.

The age-old contention that men sought to keep women out of the political arena in order to maintain their own power structure is not as cut and dried as many have proposed. In fact, history demonstrates that the primary reason men sought to separate women from government was to protect them from the brutality of politics. However, the view that women require protection where politics is concerned may have been overstated. History proves that women can be politically shrewd and have often shown themselves to be equal, if not superior to the venomous atmosphere that dominates the business of politics.

With few exceptions, prior to the twentieth century women stayed out of politics. A couple of exceptions were Cleopatra of Egypt in the first century BCE and Joan of Arc in fifteenth century France (although it may be argued that her involvement was at least as religious as it was political). Additionally, Europe and India saw a handful of female political leaders strewn throughout the nineteenth century. However, certain women became strong political figures in

---

[87] Justia US Supreme Court Center, *Dillon v. Gloss* :: 256 U.S. 368 (1921) :: https//supreme.justia.com, Accessed December 26, 2023.

the latter part of the twentieth century including Indira Ghandi (India), Golda Meir (Israel), Isabel Perón (Argentina), and Margaret Thatcher (United Kingdom)..

Given this peek into human history, it is easy to understand why opposition to women's suffrage was prevalent in the earliest days of the Union. No women were involved in the writing of the Declaration of Independence, The Articles of Confederation, or the U. S. Constitution. Neither could women vote or serve in elected positions in the government – state or federal. Still, a number of women certainly would have had input since most of the Founding Fathers were married men who tended to listen to their wives and to appreciate their point of view. Yet, women were not directly involved.

The Nineteenth Amendment, which awarded women the right to vote in America, was adopted in 1920. However, the struggle that led to its ratification has roots in the early days of the Union. Ancient history did not offer much promise for the women's suffrage movement. Still, in a newborn country like the United States of America, many saw an opportunity to advance the role of women in this new land.

From the years that saw the colonists' separation from England through the earliest days of the Union, women's suffrage was not even in the peripheral vision of the founders. In fact, it is safe to say that even the women of America did not want the founders to take their collective eye off the ball of independence. They were fully aware that they would never see progress for the suffrage movement if those men failed.

Not all women were barred from participation in those early days. For instance, in New Jersey, women who possessed more than $250 were allowed to vote as early as 1787. Later, in 1837, Kentucky allowed certain women to participate in school elections. At first that privilege affected only propertied widows with school-age children. However, the following year the right to vote was conferred on all propertied widows and unmarried women. Those, however, were clearly exceptions to the rules concerning participation of women at any level of politics.

The first convention in America that focused on women's rights took place in Seneca Falls, New York, in 1848, although the strategizing began several years earlier. Two women, Lucretia Mott of Philadelphia, Pennsylvania, and newlywed Elizabeth Cady Stanton of Albany, New York, accompanied their husbands as delegates to the World's Anti-Slavery Convention in London in 1840. These two, who initially met at the convention, were infuriated when those charged with establishing the convention protocols announced that women would not be allowed to participate in the main sessions. The female attendees were then dismissed from the main floor of the convention and consigned to a "women's section."

During what they saw as their *banishment*, the two women spent their time discussing the idea of holding a mass meeting where they could focus on women's rights. Lucretia Mott was a part of the Quaker tradition where she served as a minister. The Quakers held women in high esteem and women were vocal and influential in the church. In 1850, Lucretia penned *Discourse on Women* where she argued that women should possess political and legal rights equal to the rights of men. She also advocated, in that document, for substantive changes to property laws for married women who had, to that point, been sorely overlooked.

Elizabeth Cady Stanton was herself a woman of independent thinking. She had evidently demonstrated the substance of her convictions by eliminating the word "obey" from her wedding vows. Both women were fully committed to the abolition of slavery. Their unswerving commitment to equality for those imprisoned by slavery seemed to fuel their passion for equality among women who, they believed, faced their own form of servitude.

In 1848, Lucretia Mott and her sister, Martha Coffin Wright, met with Elizabeth Cady Stanton and some other interested friends to develop their plans for a convention focused on women's rights. The group decided on a satisfactory location, the Wesleyan Chapel in Seneca Falls and, on July 19-20, 1848, their vision became a reality as more than 300 men and women attended. The primary result of the convention was the penning of a document titled the *Declaration of Sentiments*.

The document detailed what the attendees saw as a pattern of suppression of American women. Examples of suppression included a number of issues from denial of land ownership to disparate educational opportunities and exclusion from politics and political office. One of the most compelling arguments was their claim that they were subjected to the laws of the land while being barred from offering input concerning those laws. This was some of the same reasoning advanced by the Founding Fathers against England when they penned the grievances in the Declaration of Independence.

Stanton met Susan B. Anthony in 1851 and the two became fast friends with a strong common interest. They worked together toward the advancement of women's rights and saw some early limited success. For instance, the state of Kansas entered the Union in 1861 and immediately gave propertied women the right to vote in school elections, although a ballot proposal for equal suffrage in Kansas in 1867 fell short of passage.

The two women worked together for the next few years when, in 1861, the Civil War broke out. Both women were strong advocates for the abolition of slavery. They followed up on Lincoln's Emancipation Proclamation with the formation of the Women's Loyal National League in 1863 – a platform they used to advocate for passage and ratification of the Thirteenth Amendment.

Having temporarily tabled their primary focus on women's rights during the war to advance the cause of the abolition of slavery, the two women took up the mantle again in the Reconstruction period following the war. The movement saw some success as, in Wyoming, women achieved the right to vote and hold public office in1869 and, although it was not yet a state, women received full suffrage rights in the Territory of Utah in 1870. The movement did experience a setback, however, when, in 1887, the United States Congress revoked the right of women to vote in Utah. That decision was based primarily in the objectionable practice of polygamy that was prominent in the territory. Knowing that Utah would eventually seek the status of statehood, that rejection was meant to send a clear message about the kind of values that would be expected from any territory joining the Union.

Through the 1890's, assorted locations acquiesced to the demands of suffrage to varying degrees including Colorado, Kentucky, Ohio, Utah (again), and Idaho. In the early years of the twentieth century the suffrage movement saw additional success in places like Arizona, California, Illinois, Oregon, and the state of Washington. Similar proposals were defeated in the states of Michigan and Wisconsin.

By 1878, the suffrage movement had made sufficient headway that a constitutional amendment was introduced in Congress that would have preserved women's suffrage rights as constitutional rights. Though the proposal failed to attain the necessary congressional support, advocates of the amendment were undeterred and the same amendment was proposed every year thereafter.

Theodore Roosevelt had served as Vice President (1900-1901) under President William McKinley and as President (1901-1908) after McKinley's death in 1901. In 1912, he returned as a third-party candidate for President, running for the office with women's suffrage as a plank on his political platform. He lost his bid for President, but his campaign had contributed much to public awareness where the suffrage movement was concerned.

Woodrow Wilson, who was elected President in 1912 and was sworn into office in March 1913, was at best a lukewarm supporter of an amendment in favor of women's suffrage. Still, he was not a full-fledged opponent as history demonstrates. Unfortunately for the movement, he and Congress were distracted by the onset of World War I in 1914. However, following the war, and on the heels of the unprecedented 1917 election of Jeanette Rankin, a Montana woman, to Congress, Wilson advocated in favor of suffrage and Congress approved the proposed amendment. The House of Representatives passed the amendment on May 21, 1919, and it passed the Senate two weeks later, on June 4, 1919. While certain states refused to ratify the amendment, in August 1920, Tennessee provided the final vote necessary to secure adoption.

With the passage and ratification of an amendment that had staunch opposition on many fronts, it is not surprising that the amendment met with legal challenges. On October 12, 1920, two women, Cecilia Streett Waters and Mary D. Randolph, both citizens of Maryland, registered to vote in Baltimore. Seeking to have their names removed from the list of voters, Oscar Leser and others brought this suit in *Leser v. Garnett*, (1922). Despite the passage of the Nineteenth Amendment, Leser maintained that the Constitution of Maryland still limited the suffrage to men. The case alleged that the Nineteenth Amendment infringed on the state's sovereignty and also challenged the legitimacy of ratification by certain states. The plaintiff insisted that:

> ...so great an addition to the electorate, if made without the state's consent, destroys its autonomy as a political body.[88]

The Court denied the claim in keeping with the precedent established earlier in *Hawke v. Smith* (see discussion on Eighteenth Amendment). In that case, the Court had ruled that the citizens of Ohio could not reverse the ratification of an amendment by its state legislature. In *Leser v. Garnett*, the Court similarly found that:

> ...the function of a state Legislature in ratifying a proposed amendment to the federal Constitution, like the function of Congress in proposing the amendment, is a federal function derived from the federal Constitution; and it transcends any limitations sought to be imposed by the people of a state.[89]

Twentieth Amendment
Section 1

The terms of the President and the Vice President shall end at noon on the 20th day of January, and the terms of Senators and Representatives at noon on the 3d day of January, of the years in which such terms would have ended if this article had not been ratified; and the terms of their successors shall then begin.

When compared to the divisive character of certain other amendments, the Twentieth Amendment is largely non-controversial. The Thirteenth Amendment, which abolished slavery, and the

---

[88] FindLaw Caselaw, *LESER v. GARNETT*, 258 U.S. 130 (1922) | https//caselaw.findlaw.com, Accessed December 27, 2023.
[89] ibid.

Nineteenth Amendment, which addressed women's suffrage, were both laden with political wrangling. However, the Twentieth Amendment can be viewed as a simple matter of governmental maintenance.

Because procedures were not well established, the first election in the United States was held over a period of weeks (December 15, 1788 to January 10, 1789). Nearly one month later, on February 4, 1789, the Electoral College convened and votes were submitted to Congress from the ten states that were represented. New York, North Carolina, and Rhode Island did not participate. New York failed to provide any Electors and North Carolina and Rhode Island could not participate as they had not yet ratified the Constitution.

That first election consisted of 69 Electors with each Elector casting two votes for president. Once a quorum was established, Congress counted and certified the electoral vote count on April 6, 1789. At that time, George Washington was elected as President, receiving 69 of the available 69 electoral votes. John Adams, who received the second highest count of electoral votes (34), was selected as Vice President.

Articles I and II of the Constitution did not specify dates or other details concerning the election of Congress and the president. In fact, decisions concerning those details were specifically and intentionally left in the hands of Congress. For that first election, Congress established April 30, 1789 as the date the chosen president and vice president would be sworn into office. On that date, at Federal Hall in

New York City, which was the first capital of the United States, George Washington took the oath of office for President of the United States.

The election of 1792 was held between November 2, 1792 and December 5, 1792, resulting in another win for George Washington with John Adams retaining his role as Vice President. This time the votes were counted in a joint session of Congress on February 13, 1793 and Washington took the oath of office on March 4, 1793, in the city of Philadelphia. In 1796, the election was held between the dates of November 4, 1796 and December 7, 1796, and John Adams was sworn in as President on March 4, 1797, upon the expiration of George Washington's second term in office. These terms were set in 1788 by Congress. As in 1789, these same dates applied to members of Congress who were elected in those years and this pattern continued for more than 140 years.

Some in Congress suggested that the time between the counting of the votes and the presidential inauguration was excessive. Also at issue was the fact that Article I, Section 4, called for Congress to assemble "at least once in every Year, and such Meeting shall be on the first Monday in December, unless they shall by Law appoint a different Day." This meant that from the time of the election in November, thirteen months could pass before a new Congress was required to meet. It also left a lame duck president and a lame duck Congress in office far too long.

One factor that persuaded Congress to act on this matter was Republican President Warren G. Harding's attempt, in 1922, to force a ship subsidy bill through the lame duck session of Congress. The bill was a key component of Harding's America First program. The legislation sought to expand the nation's merchant marine fleet by subsidizing the construction of cargo ships by private companies. It was opposed by labor and farm groups who considered it a power grab by commercial interests and the shipping industry. The unpopularity of the proposal caused it to fail even in the heavily Republican Congress.

On March 2, 1932, Senator George W. Norris of Nebraska, a progressive Republican, proposed what became known as the "Lame Duck Amendment." The purpose was to shorten the time between the election and the dates the newly elected officials would take office. The amendment called for both the returning and newly elected members of Congress to be seated on January 3rd following the election. It also established January 20th following the election as the date for the newly elected/returning president to take the oath of office and assume control of the executive branch of government.

Section 2

The Congress shall assemble at least once in every year, and such meeting shall begin at noon on the 3d day of January, unless they shall by law appoint a different day.

Article I, Section 4, required Congress to meet a minimum of once each year and that meeting should be held on the first Monday in December. Congressional assembly was not limited to that date, but it was set as a minimum requirement. Still, the excessive distance between the election and the date of required assembly left a hole in the process. It meant that a newly elected Congress could go for more than a year before their first meeting. Additionally, the second session of Congress was scheduled to take place one year later than the first, which would be after the election of a new Congress. That meant that Congress's second mandated session would consist of lame duck members. An unfortunate consequence was that a legislature might meet only once in a non-lame duck session.

The lengthy delay between elections and congressional and presidential transitions was a result of a seeming misstep by Congress. By setting the date of transition as March 4th, and with the first congressional session scheduled for December, a considerable gap developed. The possibility of leaving the halls of Congress vacant for a year was deemed unacceptable. Any number of disasters might remain unaddressed during such a long period. It also meant that, if no presidential candidate reached the required number of Electors and the decision concerning the Presidency was left to Congress, the choosing of the president would be in the hands of a lame duck House of Representatives. To alleviate this potential disaster, the "Lame Duck Amendment" called for the first meeting of Congress to take place on January 3rd following the election.

Why did Congress allow one hundred forty years to pass prior to addressing this evident flaw? It seems the idea of holding congressional office in a lame duck session was appealing since someone who would be leaving Congress could, over a four-month period, make political decisions without being held accountable to his/her constituents. This was especially true in the House of Representatives where turnover was much higher than in the Senate.

Between 1876 and 1924 more than seventy constitutional amendments were proposed to address the situation, but each amendment failed to find the necessary votes in Congress. In fact, the Twentieth Amendment was proposed five times between 1922 and 1932. However, it always failed to find support in the lower chamber. Members of the House apparently found the prospect of holding office during a lengthy lame duck session simply too powerful an attraction. However, the amendment finally passed in 1932 and had been ratified by all 48 states by the end of 1933.

Section 3

If, at the time fixed for the beginning of the term of the President, the President elect shall have died, the Vice President elect shall become President. If a President shall not have been chosen before the time fixed for the beginning of his term, or if the President elect shall have failed to qualify, then the Vice President elect shall act as President until a President shall have qualified; and the Congress may by law provide for the case wherein neither a President elect nor a Vice President elect shall have qualified, declaring who shall then act as President, or the manner in which one who is to act shall be selected, and such person shall act accordingly until a President or Vice President shall have qualified.

It is a morbid thought to suggest that a newly elected president might die prior to taking office. Nonetheless, death is a formidable adversary and Congress realized the challenges that would arise if such an event were to occur. Section 3, by establishing protocols for such an event, was designed to address such a possibility allowing for a smooth transition between administrations.

In the case of the death of a president elect, the amendment called for the vice president elect to assume the office of president. This was a common sense decision since one of the responsibilities of a vice president is to assume the role of president if, for any reason, the president cannot fulfill the duties of the office.

The amendment also recognized that a situation might arise where no one has qualified for the presidency. For instance, Congress could be faced with a scenario where no presidential candidate received the majority of electoral votes necessary to be declared the winner of the election. If the votes were split between more than two candidates, or if two candidates received an equal number of electoral votes, the inauguration process might be delayed. Therefore, it was necessary to develop a line of succession to address such a situation.

In modern politics, candidates for president and vice president run as a team and generally receive the same number of electoral votes. If no one receives sufficient votes to take the office of president, it also means no one has qualified as vice president. In that case, it is up to Congress to appoint an acting president until a winner has been determined. Under current law, it stands to reason that the Speaker of the House, as third in the line of succession (see Twenty-fifth Amendment), would serve as acting president until the process of presidential selection is completed in the House of Representatives in accordance with Article I, Section 1, Clause 3. However, the Speaker may have his/her hands full given the responsibility of the House to select a president. In such a case, Congress is free to select someone else to temporarily fill the office of president. Fortunately, the nation has never faced a situation that required the employment of Section 3.

Section 4

The Congress may by law provide for the case of the death of any of the persons from whom the House of Representatives may choose a President whenever the right of choice shall have devolved upon them, and for the case of the death of any of the persons from whom the Senate may choose a Vice President whenever the right of choice shall have devolved upon them.

This section sounds quite similar to the provisions of Section 3, but it is slightly different. Section 3 designs the procedures to be followed if a president elect were to die prior to taking office. Section 4 addresses the possibility that a candidate for president or vice president could die at a time when the decision concerning the outcome of the election has already been placed in the hands of Congress.

No specific procedures are laid out in Section 4. It was believe that it was sufficient to simply authorize Congress to deal with such a situation as the members see fit, allowing Congress to "by law provide for the case of the death of any of the persons from whom the House of Representatives may choose a president." In other words, the House would be left to vote for a president from among the remaining candidates. As with Section 3, the United States is fortunate in that, to date the nation has never faced a situation requiring the implementation of Section 4.

Section 5

Sections 1 and 2 shall take effect on the 15th day of October following the ratification of this article.

Most previous amendments became effective upon the certification of ratification by the states. The only amendment that included an effective date was the Eighteenth Amendment, which established the prohibition of the sale and transport of alcohol. In that case, the amendment took effect one year after ratification. This was done in an effort to allow for the sundry economic adjustments that the nation would need to make prior to its implementation.

Where the Twentieth Amendment was concerned, it was unknown how long it would take for the states to ratify the amendment. However, Congress chose to name an effective date of October 15th following ratification. Since elections are held in November, no matter when the amendment was ratified, the country could be sure that Sections 1 and 2 would apply to the first election following ratification.

Section 6

This article shall be inoperative unless it shall have been ratified as an amendment to the Constitution by the legislatures of three-fourths of the several States within seven years from the date of its submission.

Also beginning with the Eighteenth Amendment, it became a semi-common practice for Congress to establish a time limit for the ratification process for a proposed amendment. The time limit helped the nation to avoid the embarrassment and unpredictability of an unratified amendment being *in the wind* for decades, and even centuries.

Twenty-first Amendment
Section 1

The eighteenth article of amendment to the Constitution of the United States is hereby repealed.

Constitutional amendments can have unforeseen consequences, and this was especially true where the Eighteenth Amendment was concerned. While the goal of a sober-minded nation may have been idealistic, it was also unrealistic. Once the amendment was activated, it became clear that prohibition could not quench America's thirst for alcohol. That craving, combined with the sinister motives of greedy men, would never allow such idealism to triumph. Arguably the most impactful and enduring result of the era of prohibition was its contribution to the birth and growth of a previously unknown level of crime in the United States. While America was no stranger to crime, the Prohibition era has rightfully been credited with the introduction of the term *organized crime*.

The Eighteenth Amendment was ratified in January of 1919, but it would not go into effect for one year. In anticipation of implementation of the Eighteenth Amendment, plans for the subversive production, transport, and sale of alcohol began to develop. This involved the practices of bootlegging, speakeasies, and illegal distilling operations.

Bootlegging referred to the illegal transportation of alcohol. The term came into use in the late 1800's, referring to the practice of traders transporting alcohol by concealing flasks of liquor in boot tops when illegally trading with Native Americans or delivering alcohol in states where it had already been banned. During Prohibition, the term was commonly applied to any illegal manner of alcoholic transport.

Saloons/taverns were popular and well-attended prior to Prohibition but, in 1920, the public sale of alcohol became illegal. However, such locations remained popular. The difference during Prohibition was that they were no longer public. They became known as *speakeasies* and served as an underground operation for the sale and consumption of alcohol. The nickname *speakeasy* referred to the fact that a (whispered) password was generally required for a person to gain entrance.

Criminal gangs in the early 1900's were generally involved in things like prostitution, robbery, and drugs, but the illegality of alcohol served up an enticement. Complementing that illegality was the fact that the secretive nature of the business of alcohol required more resources and better organization than one-person distilling operations or individual owners of speakeasies could provide. As a result, the criminal element in places like Chicago saw an incredible business opportunity to use their resources to *syndicate* the processes of distilling, transporting, and selling the product. Thus the word *Syndicate* became synonymous with organized crime.

It was arguably the challenge of illegality that escalated the demand for alcohol. The popularity of intoxicating beverages during Prohibition provided an avenue of exponential growth for the Syndicate and men like Al Capone were at the center of that expansion, though others also profited. During the Prohibition years, Capone became the most famous and notorious bootlegger resulting in the unsavory designation of *most wanted criminal* in the United States. Al Capone said concerning Prohibition:

Prohibition is a business. All I do is supply a public demand.[90]

After years of a successful underground operation, the Syndicate became one of the most successful businesses in America and it was clear that Prohibition had proven to be an utter failure. At the same time, members of the Mafia (which originated in Italy and Sicily) had begun to spread their own form of crime in America. Prohibition was seen as a perfect fit for the Mafia, which became a major player in this illegal trade. With the onset of the Depression beginning in 1929, not only did demand for alcohol increase, but many people insisted that Prohibition was shrinking the economy, eliminating necessary jobs, and reducing badly needed federal revenues. It became commonly

---

[90] Encyclopedia.com, *Twenty-first Amendment | www.encyclopedia.com*, Accessed January 6, 2024

accepted that the Eighteenth Amendment was doing more societal harm than good.

Franklin D. Roosevelt ran for President in 1932 and incorporated the unpopularity of Prohibition into his campaign. A pledge to repeal the Eighteenth Amendment was an important plank of his platform. With the wind of the Depression in his sails, his pledge to end Prohibition undoubtedly aided in his victory. Roosevelt assumed the Presidency on January 20, 1933. One month later, on February 20, 1933, Congress proposed the Twenty-first Amendment. It was successfully passed by Congress and signed by the president. Ratification was completed on December 5, 1933.

Section 2

The transportation or importation into any State, Territory, or possession of the United States for delivery or use therein of intoxicating liquors, in violation of the laws thereof, is hereby prohibited.

What is to be made of this awkwardly worded amendment? After all, if, upon ratification, the Eighteenth Amendment would be repealed, why would the Twenty-first Amendment prohibit transportation or importation of intoxicating liquors across state lines? While the amendment legalized alcohol in the United States, Congress also wanted to respect the right of individual states in making their own laws concerning such substances.

Despite the amendment's passage and ratification, certain states chose to continue the practice of Prohibition. This included states like Utah, which was ironically the thirty-sixth state to ratify the Twenty-first Amendment providing the last requisite (three-fourths of the states) to accomplish adoption. North Carolina and South Carolina initially rejected the amendment. However, in short order these states repealed their own laws of prohibition. Five other states — Georgia, Louisiana, Nebraska, North Dakota, and South Dakota — did not immediately ratify the amendment, but joined in ratification within a couple years. Three other states — Kansas, Oklahoma, and Mississippi — held out for years. Kansas kept laws of Prohibition on the books until 1948. Oklahoma repealed its Prohibition laws in 1959 and Mississippi finally legalized alcohol in 1966.

Section 3

This article shall be inoperative unless it shall have been ratified as an amendment to the Constitution by conventions in the several States, as provided in the Constitution, within seven years from the date of the submission hereof to the States by the Congress.

As with previous amendments, Congress set a time limit for ratification of the Twenty-first Amendment. If within seven years the amendment failed to receive ratification by at least three-fourths of the states which, at the time, would have meant ratification by thirty-six states, the amendment would be deemed to have failed the ratification process and would become null and void.

The amendment was submitted to the states for ratification following congressional approval and Franklin D. Roosevelt's signature in early 1933. The amendment received sufficient support from the states and went into effect by the end of 1933.

Chapter 12
Amendments 22-27

Twenty-second Amendment
Section 1

No person shall be elected to the office of the President more than twice, and no person who has held the office of President, or acted as President, for more than two years of a term to which some other person was elected President shall be elected to the office of the President more than once. But this Article shall not apply to any person holding the office of President when this Article was proposed by the Congress, and shall not prevent any person who may be holding the office of President, or acting as President, during the term within which this Article becomes operative from holding the office of President or acting as President during the remainder of such term.

In 1796 George Washington, at age 64, chose to withdraw from the Presidency having served two terms in office. Nothing in the Constitution prevented him from serving again and he undoubtedly would have won an additional term in office, but he decided to end his Presidency after two four-year terms. His retirement did not legally limit a president to two terms, but it did set a precedent that many others chose to follow. That standard was respected by Thomas Jefferson who also stepped down in 1809 after his second term in office.

The Constitution did not place a limit on the number of terms a president could hold the office. Alexander Hamilton, writing in Federalist No. 69, stated:

> That magistrate is to be elected for four years; and is to be re-eligible as often as the people of the United States shall think him worthy of their confidence.[91]

On rare occasion certain men have sought a third presidential term. For instance, in 1880 Ulysses S. Grant ran for a third term, but failed to receive the Republican nomination. On another occasion, Theodore Roosevelt, who was serving as vice president, assumed the presidency when the President, William McKinley, was assassinated in 1901. Roosevelt served out the balance of McKinley's term, then ran and won the election for president in 1904. Having served nearly two full terms, Roosevelt chose not to run again in 1908. However, in 1912 he once again threw his hat into the presidential ring, seeking to serve a third term. Roosevelt lost that election to Woodrow Wilson.

Franklin D. Roosevelt is the only individual who served as president for more than two terms. He won elections for the office in 1932, 1936, 1940, and 1944. He served three full terms, but died after serving less than three months of his fourth term, passing away on April 12, 1945. The Vice President, Harry S. Truman, assumed the office at the time.

Truman created the Hoover Commission, led by former President Herbert Hoover, with the goal of recommending ways to reorganize

---

[91] Hamilton, Alexander, Federalist No. 69.

and reform the federal government by reducing the number of federal agencies and increasing government efficiency in the years following World War II and the Korean War. One of the commission's recommendations was that an individual should be allowed to serve as president for a maximum of two terms. The only exception would involve a vice president who assumed the office due to the death or incapacity of the president. If, under such circumstances, that individual served less than two years of the former president's term, a third term would be acceptable. The Twenty-second Amendment was one of many recommendations proposed by the Hoover Commission.

Those who favored the amendment held that allowing an individual to remain in the office of president for more than two terms would place too much political power in the hands of one person. On the opposite side, there were those who believed that, in a true republic, the people should be allowed to vote for their choice for president no matter how long that person may have served. In the end, those with the former view won the day.

Prior to submission to the states for ratification, a proposed constitutional amendment requires the signature of the president. That may lead some to wonder why a president would be willing to agree to an amendment limiting his time in office. However, the amendment did not limit the time Truman could remain in office. He was specifically excluded from the limitations listed in the amendment. The proposal specifically did "...not apply to any person holding the office of president when this Article was proposed by the Congress."

This meant that Truman was exempted from the limitation provided by the amendment.

Democrats had controlled the White House since Roosevelt was first elected in 1932, a fact that weighed heavily on Republicans. However, Republicans were able to take control of Congress in the election of 1946. The amendment was proposed in 1947 during Truman's first term in office following the death of President Roosevelt and was easily passed by a Republican-dominated Congress. Truman was re-elected in 1948 and the Twenty-second Amendment was ratified in 1951, roughly half way through Truman's second term.

Having been exempted from the provisions of the Twenty-second Amendment, Truman could have run for a third term in 1952, but decided to bow out. With no clear solution in the Korean War and his perceived softness where Communism was concerned, he saw his popularity wane and believed he would not win a third term.

There is one theoretical loophole where the Twenty-second Amendment is concerned. The amendment precludes someone who has served two terms as president from being *elected* to the office for a third term. However, if a future president should select as a vice presidential candidate (or appoint in the event of a vacancy in that office) someone who has served two terms as president, that vice president could legitimately assume the office should anything prevent the president from fulfilling the obligations of the office. While this loophole has been discussed, no solutions have been proposed and no such circumstance has arisen.

Some subsequent presidents and others have suggested repealing the Twenty-second Amendment believing it (1) artificially limits the people's right to vote for the candidate of their choice and (2) effectively turns a second-term president into a lame duck president, since he is prevented from running for a third term. However, to date no law suit has been brought to challenge the legitimacy or constitutionality of the amendment.

Section 2

This article shall be inoperative unless it shall have been ratified as an amendment to the Constitution by the legislatures of three-fourths of the several States within seven years from the date of its submission to the States by the Congress.

Congress again set a time frame for ratification of the Twenty-second Amendment. If within seven years the amendment failed to achieve ratification by at least three-fourths of the states, the opportunity for ratification would expire and the proposed amendment would become null and void. The Twenty-second Amendment was ratified by the requisite number of states on February 27, 1951.

Twenty-third Amendment
Section 1

The District constituting the seat of Government of the United States shall appoint in such manner as the Congress may direct:

A number of electors of President and Vice President equal to the whole number of Senators and Representatives in Congress to which the District would be entitled if it were a State, but in no event more than the least populous State; they shall be in addition to those appointed by the States, but they shall be considered, for the purposes of the election of President and Vice President, to be electors appointed by a State; and they shall meet in the District and perform such duties as provided by the twelfth article of amendment.

The Seat of Government Clause is found in Article I, Section 8, Clause 17, of the U. S. Constitution, This clause provided for the establishment of a distinct geographical location that could serve as the seat of the federal government. That clause grants Congress exclusive authority over the site, meaning it would not exist as an equal and independent state.

While the seat of government is recognized in the Federalist Papers, it is only mentioned tangentially in relation to the various states' access to the seat of government. No arguments were made in favor of such a location as its existence was understood to be reasonable and necessary. Its non-state status was meant to protect other states from competing against one particular state that, serving as the home of federal headquarters, might receive preferential treatment from Congress.

One problem that arose out of the District's non-state status was that its residents could not be recognized as citizens of any particular state in the Union. Residents of the District were required to pay federal taxes and were subject to federal laws including an equal obligation to military service. However, due to their lack of state citizenship, residents were not allowed to participate in federal elections, nor were they provided with representation in the halls of Congress. This complaint smacked of the refrain *taxation without representation*, which was a primary grievance raised by those who had so vigorously sought to separate themselves from England in the late 1700's.

A movement was afoot in the late 1800's to grant voting rights to the residents of the District of Columbia (D.C.). A writer for the Washington Evening Times by the name of Theodore Noyes published several articles calling for voting rights for D.C. residents. Noyes was a co-founder of *The Citizens' Joint Committee on National Representation for the District of Columbia*. This group lobbied for congressional passage of an amendment to extend voting rights to D.C. residents. In 1888, Senator Henry Blair of New Hampshire proposed an amendment to the Constitution granting the District of Columbia voting rights, but the proposal failed to receive necessary congressional support.

The Twenty-third Amendment sought to remedy the issue of voting rights by awarding electoral votes for the Presidency to the District of Columbia. The amendment did not grant statehood, but it did provide the residents with the opportunity to have a voice in the selection of the president. Electoral votes were granted in a number "to which the District would be entitled if it were a State, but in no event more than the least populous State."

The Twenty-third Amendment was proposed in 1960. One year prior two new states, Alaska and Hawaii, had been admitted to the

Union. Based on their populations, Alaska was awarded three electoral votes while Hawaii was awarded four electoral votes. Five other states (Delaware, North Dakota, South Dakota, Vermont, and Wyoming) also each held three electoral votes.

According to the 1960 Census, the population of the District of Columbia was 763,956 while eleven states had populations under 700,000. The District of Columbia was to be awarded electoral votes not "more than the least populous State." At the time, Alaska was the least populated state and had three electoral votes as did other less populated states. Therefore, upon ratification of the Twenty-third Amendment, Washington D.C.'s selection for president would be represented by three electoral votes.

The Twenty-third Amendment remedied the issue of presidential elections where the residents of the District of Columbia were concerned, but it did not address the District's lack of representation in Congress. This was partly addressed in 1970 when Congress voted to allow residents of the District the right to select a non-voting delegate to the House of Representatives.

Certain organizations continue to unsuccessfully vie for D.C. statehood. Some believed that dream might become a reality when, in 1978, Congress approved The District of Columbia Voting Rights Amendment. The amendment would have repealed the Twenty-third Amendment and afforded District residents full statehood rights. However, the amendment failed to receive ratification by the requisite number of states and was never adopted.

Section 2

The Congress shall have power to enforce this article by appropriate legislation.

Beginning with the Thirteenth Amendment, Congress began adding an Enforcement Clause to those amendments that might involve additional congressional action. The inclusion of such a clause here suggests that Congress believed additional laws may be required to fully implement the provisions of the amendment.

Twenty-fourth Amendment
Section 1

The right of citizens of the United States to vote in any primary or other election for President or Vice President, for electors for President or Vice President, or for Senator or Representative in Congress, shall not be denied or abridged by the United States or any State by reason of failure to pay any poll tax or other tax.

Through the history of the United States, the issue of voting rights has been addressed on various fronts. During the nation's founding, little consideration was given to the idea of voting eligibility. When the Constitution was ratified, it was generally accepted that only property-owning Caucasian males should be allowed to vote.

In the post-Civil War era, a person's right to vote was not addressed significantly at the federal level. Other than passage of the Fifteenth Amendment in 1870, which prohibited states from denying the vote to anyone based on race, the issue of voting rights was viewed generally as a matter for the states.

Certain southern states took advantage of the federal government's disinterest in the post-Reconstruction era by influencing the vote through underhanded methods. By the late 1880's most of those states who had been part of the Confederacy imposed a poll tax, charging citizens a small fee, purportedly intended to offset the cost of carrying out the election process. In reality, however, such a tax tended to serve the political class quite well. It was properly assumed that previous slaves and poor farmers might have difficulty paying even a small fee and, as a result, would opt out of the election process. For instance, Georgia law provided that a small poll tax:

> ...shall be levied and collected each year from every inhabitant of the state between the ages of 21 and 60 a poll tax of one dollar, but that the tax shall not be demanded from the blind or from females who do not register for voting. Georgia Code, 1933, § 92-108.[92]

The scheme of influencing/controlling the voting process through the use of a poll tax received early support from the Supreme Court. In *Breedlaw v. Suttles*, (1937), the Court determined, in keeping with historical precedent, that voting was a privilege awarded by the states and not by the federal government. The Court made several rulings in the case that addressed the voting rights of women and others with respect to poll taxes. However, the central decision by the Court stated that:

---

[92] Justia US Supreme Court Center, *Breedlove v. Suttles*: 302 U.S. 277 (1937), https//supreme.justia.com, Accessed January 15, 2024.

Voting is a privilege derived not from the United States, but from the State, which may impose such conditions as it deems appropriate, subject only to the limitations of the Fifteenth and Nineteenth Amendments and other provisions of the Federal Constitution.[93]

A poll tax was seen by the Court as a legitimate exercise of a state's taxing authority even if that tax was tied to something like a person's right to vote. This was in keeping with comparable findings such as the Court's ruling concerning the taxation of firearms when, in *United States v. Miller,* (1939), such taxation was not considered an infringement upon the Second Amendment right to bear arms, but simply an additional cost of exercising that right.

The primary claim in *Breedlaw v. Suttles* was that Georgia law had an adverse impact on a female citizen's ability to exercise her right to vote. The Court disagreed with that assessment. In fact, the Court was so vigorous in its support of the Georgia poll tax that it added the following comment.

It is fanciful to suggest that the Georgia law is a mere disguise under which to deny or abridge the right of men to vote on account of their sex.[94]

During the civil rights battles of the mid-twentieth century it became evident that poll taxes were being used primarily as a matter of restricting the voting process to certain classes of voters. They were the primary tool used by many states to control who would vote in elections. In 1962, Congress sought to deprive states of the opportunity to limit voting through poll taxes. After contentious debates, the

---

[93] ibid.
[94] ibid.

amendment received the requisite state votes to achieve ratification in 1964.

The state of Virginia attempted to circumvent that newly passed amendment by offering voters a choice between paying the tax or providing a notarized/witnessed residency certificate at least six months prior to each election. This was challenged in Court in *Harman v. Forssenius*, (1965), and the Virginia requirement was found to be at odds with the Twenty-fourth Amendment. Later, in *Harper v. Virginia State Board of Directors*, (1966), this tax was once again weighed against the Equal Protection Clause of the Fourteenth Amendment and found to be a matter of discrimination. In that case the Court found that:

> A State's conditioning of the right to vote on the payment of a fee or tax violates the Equal Protection Clause of the Fourteenth Amendment.[95]

Section 2

The Congress shall have power to enforce this article by appropriate legislation.

Congress again added an Enforcement Clause. In this case, there was reasonable concern that states would seek methods to circumvent and thwart the provisions of this amendment. This can be seen in the State of Virginia's attempt to charge a poll tax even after the ratification of the Twenty-fourth Amendment.

---

[95] Justia US Supreme Court Center, *Harper v. Virginia Bd. of Elections*: 383 U.S. 563 (1966). https//supreme.justia.com,, Accessed January 15, 2024.

Twenty-fifth Amendment
Section 1

In case of the removal of the President from office or of his death or resignation, the Vice President shall become President.

Article II, Section 1, Clause 6, of the U. S. Constitution provides instructions concerning the process that must be followed if, for any reason, the president is unable to fulfill the duties of the office. That clause states:

> In Case of the Removal of the President from Office, or of his Death, Resignation, or Inability to discharge the Powers and Duties of the said Office, the Same shall devolve on the Vice President, and the Congress may by law provide for the Case of Removal, Death, Resignation or Inability, both of the President and Vice President, declaring what Officer shall then act as President, and such Officer shall act accordingly, until the Disability be removed, or a President shall be elected.

The text seems rather straightforward. However, complications arose over the application of this clause when, on April 4, 1841, President William Henry Harrison passed away. The clause seemed clear enough. The powers and duties of the Presidency "Shall devolve on the Vice President." At the time, the Vice President was John Tyler and, in keeping with Article II, Section 1, Clause 6, he immediately assumed the duties of the office of President.

Issues quickly rose concerning John Tyler's position as President. Tyler was not popular among the members of William Henry Harrison's Cabinet. Some believed he was a difficult man who lacked the disposition required in the role of President. Tyler was at his home in Virginia when he learned of the President's death and immediately returned to Washington, presuming that he would be sworn in *as President*. However, upon his return, members of the Cabinet referred to him as Acting President. The situation gained Tyler the unflattering nickname of *His Accidency*.

As some of the Cabinet members read Article II, the argument was made that Tyler should not assume the Presidency, but should be considered Acting President until a replacement could be named by Congress or a new election could be held. In that vein, it was also argued that Tyler should not be allowed, as Acting President, to assume the *full* powers and duties of the office, but that his decisions should require Cabinet approval.

The seeming constitutional crisis ultimately begged the question: **What did the framers of the Constitution have in view with the words "the Same shall devolve on the Vice President?"** Was it merely the duties of the office that should (temporarily) devolve to the vice president, or did the framers have in view the presidency itself? Tyler assembled Harrison's Cabinet to discuss the matter. In that meeting, he gave the following speech.

> I beg your pardon, gentlemen. I am sure I am very glad to have in my cabinet such able statesmen as you have proved yourselves to be, and I shall be pleased to avail myself of your counsel and advice, but I can never consent to being dictated to as to what I shall or shall not do. I, as president, will be responsible for my administration. I hope to have your cooperation in carrying out its measures. So long as you

325

see fit to do this I shall be glad to have you with me. When you think otherwise, your resignations will be accepted.[96]

Tyler's stubbornness paid off. On April 6, 1841, he was sworn in as President of the United States. This series of events, which led to Tyler's assumption of the office of the President, came to be known as the *Tyler Precedent*. Moving forward from the time of Tyler's Presidency, it was accepted that the vice president, upon the president's death, would assume the office of the president and not merely the duties of that office.

This precedent was faithfully followed for more than one-hundred years following Tyler's proclamation. It was exercised upon the deaths of Zachary Taylor (1850), Abraham Lincoln (1865), James Garfield (1881), William McKinley (1901), Warren Harding (1923), Franklin D. Roosevelt (1945), and John F. Kennedy (1963). Tyler had, seemingly single-handedly, settled for the nation the question of the framers' intent where Article II, Section 1, Clause 6, was concerned.

While the question of succession to the Presidency had been settled by precedent, a number of questions remained unanswered. The Twenty-Fifth Amendment not only codifies the *Tyler Precedent*, but seeks to resolve certain other issues involving the office of the president. For instance: **What should happen upon the removal or resignation of the president?** Since a president's removal from office would result in a vacancy in the office, in keeping with the principle established in the *Tyler Precedent* as codified in the Twenty-fifth

---

[96] McNamara, Robert, John Tyler's Presidency and the Tyler Precedent (thoughtco.com), Accessed January 16, 2024

Amendment, the vice president would become President of the United States.

Section 2

Whenever there is a vacancy in the office of the Vice President, the President shall nominate a Vice President who shall take office upon confirmation by a majority vote of both Houses of Congress.

On occasion, the office of vice president has remained vacant for various lengths of time. In fact, seven vice presidents have died while in office and one other has resigned. Recognizing this potential dilemma, Congress determined that a method of response under such circumstances should be developed. It was decided that the best approach would be for the president to nominate an individual to fill the office. After all, the vice president is initially chosen by the president in the election process and it seemed wise that the existing president should have someone of his choosing.

It would be critical for the president to choose someone for the office of vice president with whom he would be comfortable – someone he could trust with the presidency itself. Yet, there would be an issue in that this chosen candidate would have by-passed the normal election process where the people could decide on the candidate.

It was determined that, like other nominees for offices in the executive branch, the Senate should approve any vice-presidential candidate under its constitutional responsibility of Advice and Consent (Article II, Section 2). However, given the uniqueness of the office and the fact that the situation necessarily by-passes the normal election

327

process, it was decided that filling the office of vice president in this fashion would require passage by a majority vote in both chambers of Congress.

Section 3

Whenever the President transmits to the President pro tempore of the Senate and the Speaker of the House of Representatives his written declaration that he is unable to discharge the powers and duties of his office, and until he transmits to them a written declaration to the contrary, such powers and duties shall be discharged by the Vice President as Acting President.

An unresolved question was whether the vice president would become president or acting president if the president, for any reason, could not (temporarily) carry out the duties of the office. Also unresolved was the issue of whether the president, upon regaining the ability to fulfill the duties, could be reinstated to the office of president. These questions have divided constitutional scholars over the years. Section 3 addresses these issues.

If the president is, for any reason, incapacitated or unable to carry out the duties of the office of president, it is his responsibility to inform the President pro tempore of the Senate and the Speaker of the House of Representatives of the situation. If the circumstance is temporary in nature, the vice president will assume the role of acting president for the time during which the president is unavailable. However, the president would return to the office of president, discharging the powers and duties thereof by again informing the President pro tempore of the Senate and the Speaker of the House of

Representatives that he was no longer incapacitated and was fully capable of resuming those duties.

Section 4

Whenever the Vice President and a majority of either the principal officers of the executive departments or of such other body as Congress may by law provide, transmit to the President pro tempore of the Senate and the Speaker of the House of Representatives their written declaration that the President is unable to discharge the powers and duties of his office, the Vice President shall immediately assume the powers and duties of the office as Acting President.

Thereafter, when the President transmits to the President pro tempore of the Senate and the Speaker of the House of Representatives his written declaration that no inability exists, he shall resume the powers and duties of his office unless the Vice President and a majority of either the principal officers of the executive department or of such other body as Congress may by law provide, transmit within four days to the President pro tempore of the Senate and the Speaker of the House of Representatives their written declaration that the President is unable to discharge the powers and duties of his office. Thereupon Congress shall decide the issue, assembling within forty-eight hours for that purpose if not in session. If the Congress, within twenty-one days after receipt of the latter written declaration, or, if Congress is not in session, within twenty-one days after Congress is required to assemble, determines by two-thirds vote of both Houses that the President is unable to discharge the powers and duties of his office, the Vice President shall continue to discharge the same as Acting President; otherwise, the President shall resume the powers and duties of his office.

There is a presumption in Section 3 that a president would be capable of informing the President pro tempore of the Senate and the Speaker of the House of an inability to perform the duties of the office of president. However, this may not always be the case. For example, James Garfield was in a coma for eighty days before dying from an assassin's bullet (1881) and Woodrow Wilson suffered a stroke and was an invalid for the last year-and-a-half of his term (1921). Who, then, should have the responsibility of making such a decision on the president's behalf?

When President John F. Kennedy was assassinated in 1963 his Vice President, Lyndon B. Johnson, was sworn in as President. However, many were concerned about Johnson's health as he had suffered a severe heart attack several years earlier. The occasion raised the question: **If the president was to become incapacitated and was unable to properly inform the President pro tempore of the Senate and the Speaker of the House of Representatives of an inability to carry on the duties of the office, who should make the call?** This concern resulted in the proposal of Section 4 of the Twenty-fifth Amendment.

It was important that any plan proposed in the amendment not be construed as a political maneuver to replace a president. Consequently, Congress determined that the members of the president's trusted Cabinet, designated in the amendment as "principal officers of the executive departments," would be in the best position to make such a call. Thus, it was decided that, should such a condition arise:

> ...a majority of either the principal officers of the executive departments or of such other body as Congress may by law provide, transmit to the President pro tempore of the Senate and the Speaker of the House of Representatives their written declaration that the President is unable to discharge the powers and duties of his office.

The amendment provides for the president's return to office if he "transmits to the President pro tempore of the Senate and the Speaker of the House of Representatives his written declaration that no inability exists." However, such return would be conditioned on agreement by the President's Cabinet that the circumstance that originally prevented his discharge of the duties of the office has, indeed, been remedied.

It is possible that the president may inform the proper authorities that he is once again capable of returning to the office, but the Cabinet and vice president disagree with that assessment. If the vice president and a majority of Cabinet members believe the president is still incapable of executing the duties of the office, it is their responsibility/duty to formally inform the appropriate congressional authorities. However, this declaration must occur within four days of the president's official statement that he is capable of returning to the role of president.

In the event that the vice president and a majority of Cabinet members inform Congress that they believe the president is still incapable of returning to office, the burden of the decision rests with the Senate and the House of Representatives. Within the time frames established in the amendment, it is incumbent on the two chambers of Congress to meet and vote concerning the president's return. If each chamber, by a two-thirds majority, determines that the president is incapable of returning to office, the president will remain out of office. However, should the two chambers either (1) fail to meet and vote according to the timelines established in the amendment or (2) fail to achieve a two-thirds majority to prevent the president's return, the president will resume his role as Chief Executive Officer of the United States.

Twenty-sixth Amendment
Section 1

The right of citizens of the United States, who are eighteen years of age or older, to vote shall not be denied or abridged by the United States or by any State on account of age.

For the first 79 years following the ratification of the U. S. Constitution, the rules concerning voting eligibility were set by the individual states. In many states, only male Caucasian property owners could participate. However, in the early to mid-nineteenth century, a few states began to allow women to vote on local issues and later in general elections. Certain other states allowed free Black men to vote. Ratification of the Fifteenth Amendment (1870), which recognized the right of people of other races to vote, was the first strategic move toward nationalizing rules concerning voter eligibility. This was followed, in 1920, by ratification of the Nineteenth Amendment, which awarded women the right to vote in America.

Other than the stipulations designated in those two amendments, voting eligibility was still generally determined by the individual states and, in most states, the minimum age requirement remained at age twenty-one. However, in the 1950's, President Dwight D.

Eisenhower voiced his support for lowering the voting age to eighteen. His reasoning was understandable given his history as a general in the U. S. army. He believed that, since eighteen-year-olds could be drafted into the armed services and forced to fight for the country, they ought to be allowed a voice in how the country was governed. In his 1954 State of the Union Address, he commented:

> For years our citizens between the ages of 18 and 21 have, in time of peril, been summoned to fight for America. They should participate in the political process that produces this fateful summons.

Congress passed, and President Lyndon B. Johnson signed, The Voting Rights Act of 1965 prohibiting racial discrimination with respect to voting eligibility. However, that statute did not address President Eisenhower's concern about lowering the voting age. In 1970 Congress passed, and President Richard M. Nixon signed into law, an extension of the Voting Rights Act, lowering the age of eligibility to eighteen in federal and state elections. Although, it is said that even President Nixon questioned the constitutionality of this extension.

When a law appears to conflict with the U. S. Constitution, it is often challenged in court and the case generally ends up at the Supreme Court. This statute was no exception. In fact, the statute appeared to conflict with the Fourteenth Amendment, Section 2, which protected the right to vote for the "male inhabitants of [each] state, being twenty-one years of age, and citizens of the United States."

The states of Oregon and Texas filed suit, insisting that the law violated the powers reserved to the states to set their own voting age limits. In *Oregon* v. *Mitchell*, (1970), the U. S. Supreme Court found the statute to be *partially* constitutional. The Court was strongly divided on the issue. In that ruling, it was determined that, while the federal government could rightfully establish a universal voting age for federal elections, setting the voting age for state and local elections was a privilege that must be reserved to the individual states. As a result, states were required to allow eighteen to twenty-year-olds to vote for federal offices (President, Vice-President, Senators, and members of the House of Representatives). However, it was clear from this ruling that establishing a universal minimum voting age could only be achieved through the amendment process.

Following that court battle, the Vietnam War raged on and young men were actively being drafted to fight that war. As a consequence, the voices of student activists on college campuses and their supporters grew louder. The cause was strengthened by the fact that more than half of the servicemen killed in that war were between the ages of eighteen and twenty.

In early 1971, Congress proposed this amendment lowering the voting age on a national basis. The amendment was passed by Congress on March 5, 1971 and was ratified by the states on July 1, 1971. That four-month stretch constitutes the second-shortest time period (see Eleventh Amendment) between congressional approval of an amendment and ratification by the states.

An issue that has arisen as a result of this amendment is the matter of residency. Between the ages of eighteen and twenty, it is not uncommon for those attending college to remain on the college campus during the year, although their permanent residence may be in another city or even another state. Courts have consistently held that a student who moves to a location solely to attend college and does not otherwise intend to make that place his/her home may not register to vote there. Instead, the student must register at his/her permanent residence (generally the home of parents or guardians).

Some courts have made enforcement of the residency requirement difficult for election officials. Many courts have held that the Equal Protection Clause of the Fourteenth Amendment prevents officials from singling out college students by requiring proof of residency from students living in dormitories or in off-campus housing. It is a battle that continues to be waged in the court system.

Section 2

The Congress shall have power to enforce this article by appropriate legislation.

Congress again added this provision, which was becoming a standard addition where amendments are concerned. Section 2 recognizes the possible need for further legislative action at the federal level to ensure universal implementation. The Section provides for the passing of future legislation in order to effect enforcement of this amendment.

Twenty-seventh Amendment

No law, varying the compensation for the services of the Senators and Representatives, shall take effect, until an election of Representatives shall have intervened.

The Congress of the United States determines its own pay via statute, which is an overt conflict of interest. This conflict was recognized even by the congressional members who proposed this amendment. It was their attempt to give the citizens of the United States some influence on how the legislature's pay should be decided. The proposal was intended to prevent legislators from giving a self-serving raise by delaying the effective date for any pay raise authorized by Congress. According to the amendment, no pay raise could take effect until after a new election had taken place.

The Twenty-seventh Amendment was originally referred to the state legislatures for ratification in 1789 along with those ten proposals that eventually came to be known as the Bill of Rights. It was the second of twelve amendments proposed at the time. Also known as The Congressional Compensation Act of 1789, it had long been assumed to be dead. It was originally ratified by only six states (of the eleven needed), having been rejected by five states in the 1790's. In protest to a controversial congressional pay raise, the Ohio legislature breathed temporary life into the amendment by ratifying it in 1873. However, other states failed to follow suit.

The provision remained dormant, and even forgotten, until the state of Wyoming ratified it in 1978, but with little fanfare. However, in 1982, an undergraduate research paper penned by Gregory Watson, a student at the University of Texas at Austin, argued the viability of the amendment despite the fact that it was nearly two hundred years old. An aide to a Texas legislator evidently picked up the argument and revived interest in the amendment, beginning a crusade in favor of ratification. In 1992, Michigan became the thirty-eighth state to ratify the amendment, thus meeting the requisite number of states necessary for adoption. Interestingly, according to Brittanica.com:

> Watson had received a "C" for the paper, his professor saying that the argument that the amendment was still pending was not convincing.[97]

The amendment's ratification must have given Mr. Watson a sense of satisfaction. After all, he had accomplished something with a college paper that was unprecedented – a change in the way Congress conducts business. However, perhaps equally satisfying is the fact that, according to legaldictionary.net:

> In early 2017, the University of Texas at Austin officially changed Watson's term paper grade from a "C" to an "A."[98]

The Twenty-seventh Amendment has been impactful. Prior to its ratification, Congress had a history of authorizing for itself what many considered to be generous raises, surpassing those in the private sector. Then, in 1989, prior to the amendment's ratification in 1992, Congress passed The Government Ethics Reform Act of 1989. This was seemingly in anticipation of the likely ratification of the Twenty-

[97] Britannica, *Twenty-seventh Amendment | Ratification, Congressional Pay, Limitations* | www.britannica.com , Accessed January 20, 2024.
[98] Legal Dictionary, *27th Amendment - Definition, Examples, Cases, Processes.* www.legaldictionary.net, Accessed January 20, 2024.

seventh Amendment. The statute provided for an automatic cost of living adjustment for members of Congress each year based on the annually reported employment cost index. The last year this formula was implemented was 2009 when congressional pay was raised by 2.8%. This resulted in an annual congressional salary of $174,000. Members of the congressional leadership, such as Speaker of the House and Senate Majority and Minority Leaders, receive more.

Beyond 2009, members of Congress have consistently voted not to accept the automatic adjustment delineated in The Government Ethics Reform Act of 1989. It is difficult to say if that decision is based on ethical or political concerns, and that probably varies among members. Still it has the same affect. It is evident, however, that the Twenty-seventh Amendment has given members of Congress a more measured approach where their own salary increases are concerned.

It is difficult to imagine anyone questioning the constitutionality of the Twenty-seventh Amendment, especially since it is difficult to envision any grounds for such a challenge. To date, no law suits have emerged. The only group that might gain advantage by overturning the amendment would be federal legislators, and to bring such a self-serving law suit would undoubtedly have a negative impact on a legislator's electability. Therefore, the Twenty-seventh amendment remains the latest in the list of amendments that have, over its more than two-hundred-year history, been added to the Constitution of the United States.

Reflections

Human history is replete with quality literature, both fiction and nonfiction. While exceptional works are plentiful, a strong argument can be made that the Declaration of Independence and the Constitution of the United States are two of the finest documents ever written. The Declaration of Independence, with its reasoned logic concerning the purpose and role of government, combined with its recognition of unalienable rights, offers a striking portrait of an idyllic relationship between a government and the governed.

It is said that a three-legged stool does not wobble. Indeed, three legs actually prevent the stool from wobbling because the feet of the three legs are always on the same plane. For this reason, a three-legged stool stands firm even when placed on an uneven floor. This was the idea behind the three-pronged approach to government established by the framers of the U. S. Constitution. The three legs of the U. S. government (legislative, executive, and judicial), are intended to keep each other in check so that no branch of government achieves too much power.

Equally important is the fact that, in the United States, the representatives in government are chosen by the people. The intent, in keeping with the ideals advanced in the Declaration of Independence, is that a government should only have power and authority that is approved by the citizens it represents. The purpose of government is not to lord over the people, but to provide for a peaceful coexistence for mankind.

Thomas Paine, in his insightful work titled *Common Sense*, made the observation that "government, even in its best state, is a necessary evil; in its worst state, an intolerable one."[99] What follows here is a qualified agreement with these comments. For instance, Thomas Paine is correct in that government is necessary, particularly where sizeable populations are expected to live together in harmony. In theory, it is the role of government to provide the citizenry with a social environment that will allow that harmony to flourish.

Paine's conclusion that government "is a necessary evil" is true in a sense, but the better case can be made that government is *unnecessarily evil*. Government might be considered an entity, but it is not, in itself, a living and breathing being. It is a human invention. It consists of, and draws its breath from, people. Government has no emotions or cunning. It has no more inherent evil intent than a table or a lamp, both of which are inventions of men.

The evil by which Paine characterized government can only be attributed to the fact that the offices of government are occupied by human beings. Consequently, a government tends to take on the characteristics of those inside that government whose motives are less than pure. Have men of flawed character and questionable intentions occupied the White House? Does Congress consist of many individuals whose self-interests outweigh their concerns for the well-

---

[99] Paine, Thomas, *Common Sense*, Fall River Press, 1995, p. 1.

being of their constituents? Have judges sat in courtrooms, and even behind the bench of the Supreme Court, who have little regard for the Constitution? The answer to each of these questions is a resounding *yes*! One need only weigh the words of the Constitution against the multitude of dubious rulings delivered by the courts to recognize these failures. Some of those decisions are documented in this book.

These observations do not apply universally. Some individuals do enter the world of politics out of a sense of patriotism and a sincere desire to make America a great place to live. Additionally, judgeships have, at times, been occupied by justices who fully embrace both the text and the spirit of the U. S. Constitution. Still, the old cliché is true in that *power corrupts and absolute power corrupts absolutely*. For this reason, it is critical that citizens hold to account those in positions of authority at all levels of government (local, state, and federal).

There is a fundamental misunderstanding where the Supreme Court is concerned that has led to bold disregard for the Constitution. Much of the citizenry and many justices seem to believe it is the role of the Supreme Court to *generate* the meaning of the Constitution. They believe the Constitution means what the Court says it means even if the result contradicts a plain reading of the text. This confusion is a result of the Court's inconsistent and sometimes flawed application of constitutional principles. Consequently, many people are less concerned with the words of the Constitution and more concerned with the words coming from the Supreme Court.

The founders never intended for the Court to give new meaning to a Constitution that is plainly written or to stretch that meaning beyond reasonable limits. In the Federalist Papers it is made clear that it is the role of the Court to *evaluate* the legitimacy of a statute (written by Congress) by viewing it through the lens of constitutional constraints. According to Alexander Hamilton, writing in Federalist No. 78, it is the Court's role to *ascertain* the meaning of the Constitution rather than to *create* that meaning.

> The interpretation of the laws is the proper and peculiar province of the courts. A constitution is, in fact, and must be regarded by the judges, as a fundamental law. It therefore belongs to them to ascertain its meaning, as well as the meaning of any particular act proceeding from the legislative body. If there should happen to be an irreconcilable variance between the two, that which has the superior obligation and validity ought, of course, to be preferred; or, in other words, the Constitution ought to be preferred to the statute, the intention of the people to the intention of their agents.[100]

Thomas Paine was right in that government is a *necessary evil*, but it is also true that government need not be evil if the people's representatives are honorable. Unfortunately, finding such people who are willing to serve in a representative republic is a challenge. The power that is naturally accessible to those in government tends to attract people who are attracted to power. Still, it is not unreasonable to believe that the design of the representative republic developed by the founders and delineated in the Articles of the U. S. Constitution may be the best history has to offer.

---

[100] Hamilton, Alexander, Federalist No. 78.

Bibliography

AMA Journal of Ethics, *The Constitutionality of the Affordable Care Act*: https://journalofethics.ama-assn.org

American Library Association, *Foundations of Free Expression: Historic Cases:Schenk v. United States*, https://www.ala.org/advocacy/intfreedom/censorship/courtcases,

Articles of Confederation

Blake, Aaron, citing Ruth Bader-Ginsburg, *What Ruth Bader Ginsburg really said about Roe v. Wade* - The Washington Post, https://www.washingtonpost.com, accessed

Britannica, *Presser-v-Illinois*, https://www.britannica.com/topic/

Britannica, *Tenth Amendment, United States Constitution*, www.britannica.com/topic/tenthamendment.

Britannica, *Twenty-seventh Amendment | Ratification, Congressional Pay, Limitations |* www.britannica.com.

Casetext, *Burdick v. United States*, https://casetext.com

Casetext, *Seven-Sky v. Holder*, https://casetext.com

Congressional Research Service, *The Disqualification Clause*, https://crsreports.congress.gov.

Constitution Annotated, *Article I, Section 8, Clause 1*, constitution.congress.gov,

Constitutional Law Reporter, *Amendment 14: Section 2,* https:// constitutionallaw reporter.com,

Cornell Law School Legal Information Institute, *Bribery*, https://www.law.cornell.edu/wex/bribery#:~:text=Overview%3A,a%20public%20or%20legal%20duty.

Cornell Law School Legal Information Institute, *Haupt v. United States*, https://www.law.cornell.edu/constitution-conan/article-3/section-3/clause-1/aid-and-comfort-to-the-enemy-as-treason.

Cummings, Kira, Legal Knowledge Base, *Has the 14th Amendment Section 3 ever been used?* www.legalknowledgebase.com

Encyclopedia.com, *Twenty-first Amendment* | www.encyclopedia.com

Epps, Garrett, *A Court Looks at the Real Problem With the 17th Amendment* – www.theatlantic.com,

FindLaw, *Treason Under the Constitution,* https://constitution.findlaw.com/article3/ annotation24.html

FindLaw Caselaw, *LESER v. GARNETT* :: 258 U.S. 130 (1922) :: https://caselaw.findlaw.com.

Founders Online, Adams, John, *From John Adams to Horatio Gates, 23 March 1776,* https://founders.archives.gov

Founders Online, Washington, George, *From George Washington to the United States Senate and House of Representatives,* https://founders. archives.gov/documents/Washington/ 05-04-02-0361

Guralnik, David B., Editor in Chief, Webster's New World Dictionary, Second College Edition, The World Publishing Company, 1978

Hamilton, Alexander, Federalist No. 8

Hamilton, Alexander, Federalist No. 19

Hamilton, Alexander, Federalist No. 22

Hamilton, Alexander, Federalist No. 23

Hamilton, Alexander, Federalist No. 25

Hamilton, Alexander, Federalist No. 41

Hamilton, Alexander, Federalist No. 62

Hamilton, Alexander, Federalist No. 65

Hamilton, Alexander, Federalist No. 69

Hamilton, Alexander, Federalist No. 76

Hamilton, Alexander, Federalist No. 78.

Hamilton, Alexander, Federalist No. 80

Hamilton, Alexander, Federalist No. 81

Howe, Amy, *The Supreme Court and the president's pardon power* - SCOTUSblog

Immigration History, *Nationality Act of 1790*, https://immigrationhistory.org /item/1790-nationality-act/

Jefferson, Thomas, Founders Online, *From Thomas Jefferson to Jared Sparks, 4 February 1824,*, https://founders.archives.gov/documents/Jefferson/98-01-02-4020

Jefferson, Thomas, *Summary View of the Rights of British America*, Avalon Project - Summary View of the Rights of British America, https:// avalon.law.yale.edu

Jefferson, Thomas, *Thomas Jefferson on Slavery* https://studyboss.com/essays/ thomas-jefferson-on-slavery.html

Jefferson, Thomas, *Why Thomas Jefferson's Anti-Slavery Passage Was Removed from the Declaration of Independence*, history.com

Justia Law, U.S. Code, Title 10, Section 246, Subtitle A – *Militia: Composition and Classes,*, https://law.justia.com

Justia U.S. Law, *Luther v. Borden*, https://law.justia.com/constitution/us/article-4/21-guarantee-of-republican-form-of-government.html

Justia U. S. Law, *Suits Against States*, https://law.justia.com

Justia US Supreme Court Center, *Breedlove v. Suttles* :: 302 U.S. 277 (1937) :: https://supreme.justia.com,

Justia US Supreme Court Center, *Chicago v. Morales* :: 527 U.S. 41 (1999) :: https://supreme.justia.com,

Justia US Supreme Court Center, *Dillon v. Gloss* :: 256 U.S. 368 (1921) :: https://supreme.justia.com,

Justia U.S. Supreme Court, *District of Columbia v. Heller*, 554 U.S. 570 (2008) https://supreme.justia.com.

Justia US Supreme Court Center, *Harper v. Virginia Bd. of Elections* :: 383 U.S. 663 (1966) :: https://supreme.justia.com,

Justia US Supreme Court Center, *Miller v. Alabama* :: 567 U.S. 460 (2012) :: https://supreme.justia.com,

Justia US Supreme Court Center, *Mullane v. Central Hanover Bank & Trust Co.* :: 339 U.S. 306 (1950) :: https://supreme.justia.com,

Legal Dictionary, *27th Amendment - Definition, Examples, Cases, Processes|* www.legaldictionary.net.

Legal Dictionary, *Terry v. Ohio - Case Summary and Case Brief,* www.legaldictionary.net.

Legal Information Institute, *National Federation of Independent Business v. Sebelius* | www.law.cornell.edu.

Madison, James, Federalist No. 14.

Madison, James, Federalist No. 38.

Madison, James, Federalist No. 42

Madison, James, Federalist No. 44

Madison, James, Federalist No. 51

Madison, James, Federalist No. 62.

McNamara, Robert, *John Tyler's Presidency and the Tyler Precedent* | www.thoughtco.com.

Mullen, Matt, Onion, Amanda, Sullivan, Missy, Zapatra, Christian, editors, *Writing of Declaration of Independence*, www.history.com, accessed Jun 23, 2022

National Archives, *Presidential Pardons and Congressional Amnesty to Former Confederate Citizens, 1865–1877*, https://www.archives.gov/files/research/naturalization/411-confederate-amnesty-records.pdf

National Constitution Center, *On This Day: The first bitter, contested presidential election takes place* | https://constitutioncenter.org

National Park Service, *The Supreme Court Decides in Chisholm v. Georgia*, https://nps.gov,

Oyez, *Stogner v. California*, www.oyez.org/cases/2002/01-1757

Oyez, *United States v. Reese*. https://www.oyes.org/cases/1850-1900/92us214.

Paine, Thomas, *Common Sense*, Fall River Press, 1995.

Paine, Thomas, *The Crisis*, https://www.ushistory.org/Paine/crisis/c-03.htm

Schuessler, Jennifer, citing Jessie Serfilippi, New York Times, *Alexander Hamilton, Enslaver? New Research Says Yes* | https://www.nytimes.com

The National Constitution Center, *Interpretation and Debate: The Eighth Amendment* | https://constitutioncenter.org,

The National Constitution Center, *The Slave Trade Clause*, https://constitutioncenter.org/the-constitution/articles/article-i/clauses/761

The Founders Constitution, *Joseph Story, Commentaries on the Constitution , 3:88 1192--93*, https://press-pubs.uchicago.edu/founders/documents/a1_8_14s3.html,

The Tenth Amendment – Definition and Famous Cases, infotracer.com

Thompson, Austin, *Can a Person Refuse a Presidential Pardon?* | Mental Floss

U.S. Code, Chapter 115, §2381, *Treason, Sedition, and Subversive Activity*, https://uscode.house.gov/view.xhtml

U. S. Government Publishing Office, *Armed Forces*, https://www.govinfo.gov/content/pkg/USCODE-2016-title10/pdf/USCODE-2016-title10-subtitleA-partI-chap13.pdf.

U. S. History, *The Gaspee Affair*, https://www.ushistory.org/declaration/related/gaspee.html,

University of Chicago Press, *Amendment VIII: Debate in Virginia Ratifying Convention*, https://press-pubs.uchicago.edu.com,

Printed in the USA
CPSIA information can be obtained
at www.ICGtesting.com
LVHW011939160324
774454LV00012B/442